Richard Henry Dana

The Seaman's Manual

Richard Henry Dana

The Seaman's Manual

ISBN/EAN: 9783954272716
Erscheinungsjahr: 2013
Erscheinungsort: Bremen, Deutschland

© maritimepress in Europäischer Hochschulverlag GmbH & Co. KG, Fahrenheitstr. 1, 28359 Bremen. Alle Rechte beim Verlag und bei den jeweiligen Lizenzgebern.

www.maritimepress.de | office@maritimepress.de

Bei diesem Titel handelt es sich um den Nachdruck eines historischen, lange vergriffenen Buches. Da elektronische Druckvorlagen für diese Titel nicht existieren, musste auf alte Vorlagen zurückgegriffen werden. Hieraus zwangsläufig resultierende Qualitätsverluste bitten wir zu entschuldigen.

THE
SEAMAN'S MANUAL;

CONTAINING

A TREATISE ON PRACTICAL SEAMANSHIP,

WITH PLATES;

A DICTIONARY OF SEA TERMS;

CUSTOMS AND USAGES OF THE MERCHANT SERVICE;

LAWS RELATING TO THE PRACTICAL DUTIES OF MASTER AND MARINERS.

BY R. H. DANA, Junʀ.,

AUTHOR OF
"TWO YEARS BEFORE THE MAST."

LONDON:
EDWARD MOXON, DOVER STREET.

MDCCCXLI.

DEDICATION.

To all sea-faring persons, and especially to those commencing the sea-life;—to owners and insurers of vessels;—to judges and practitioners in maritime law;—and to all persons interested in acquainting themselves with the laws, customs, and duties of seamen;—this work is respectfully dedicated by

THE AUTHOR.

PREFACE TO THE ENGLISH EDITION.

THIS work is published at the same time in England and in America. In the latter country it appears under the title of the " Seaman's Friend ;" while that of the " Seaman's Manual" is adopted in the British edition, as more significant of the nature of the book. Mr. Dana has here embodied in a small space and unpretending form a variety of information, which it is hoped may be extensively useful. Not that men who have been bred to the sea can be supposed to derive much instruction from the elementary hints of a book of this kind. Seamanship, like every other manual art, is thoroughly acquired by practice; and skill in its various branches can only be arrived at by actual experience. But young beginners will find useful helps in their study of the duties of sea-life, in the details and explanations here collected from the best available sources. Very few of the terms or the methods of management, in the Merchant Service of America, differ in any material respect from those which are used in English vessels. There is probably less difference in the sea-language common to both services than may be detected as peculiar in the different great sea-ports of the mother country; and in like manner, the received usages and modes of discipline have the close affinity which is the natural result arising from common origin, laws, and general customs. It may therefore be expected without presumption, that the abstract given in this little work of the rules established in American ships will be found applicable to the practice in our own; and even where they differ, may suggest useful comparisons. At any rate, it is desirable to know what system obtains and is successful among a body of seamen which, in numbers, and the extent of commerce carried on by them, are only second in importance to those of Great Britain.

The laws of the United States relative to shipping, are considered in Part III. of this work, in reference to the rights and duties of the officers and crews respectively. A gentleman of the legal profession has appended a few notes, with the view of showing points of difference where they exist in the British laws.

Finally, it is hoped that the various classes of society which are led by their callings, duty, or affection, to take an interest in sea-faring men, and who may wish to know something of their business and their language, will find this little Manual useful for occasional reference. It cannot be expected to have the same claims to public favour as the Author's former work. But even in these pages, which only aim at being useful, the reader will not fail to perceive indications of the same good sense and right spirit which were so conspicuous in that remarkable production.

THE EDITOR.

LONDON, *4th October,* 1841.

CONTENTS.

PART I.

A PLAIN TREATISE ON PRACTICAL SEAMANSHIP.

CHAPTER I.

GENERAL RULES AND OBSERVATIONS, PAGES 1—7.

Construction of Vessels, 1.—Tonnage and Carriage of Merchant Vessels, 2—Proportions of Spars, 2—Placing the Masts, 4.—Size of Anchors and Cables, 4.—Lead-lines, 5—Log-line, 5.—Ballast and Lading, 6.

CHAPTER II.

CUTTING AND FITTING STANDING RIGGING, PAGES 7—14.

Cutting Lower Rigging, 7.—Fitting Lower Rigging, 8.—Cutting and fitting Topmast Rigging, 9.—Jib, Topgallant, and Royal Rigging, 10.—Rattling, 11.—Standing Rigging of the Yards, 11.—Breast-backstays, 14.

CHAPTER III.

FITTING AND REEVING RUNNING RIGGING, PAGES 15—19.

To reeve a Brace, 15.—Fore, Main, and Cross-jack Braces, 15.—Fore and Main Topsail Braces, 15.—Mizen Topsail Braces, 16.—Fore, Main, and Mizen Topgallant and Royal Braces, 16.—Halyards, 16.—Spanker-brails, 17.—Tacks, Sheets, and Clewlines, 17.—Reef-tackles, Clew-garnets, Buntlines, Leachlines, Bowlines, and Slablines, 18.

CHAPTER IV.

TO RIG MASTS AND YARDS, PAGES 19—26.

Taking in Lower Masts and Bowsprit, 19.—To rig a Bowsprit, 20.—To get the Tops over the Mast-heads, 20.—To send up a Topmast, 21.—To get on a Topmast Cap, 22.—To rig out a Jib-boom, 22.—To cross a Lower Yard, 22.—To cross a

Topsail Yard, 23.—To send up a Topgallant Mast, 23.—Long, Short, and Stump Topgallant Masts, 23.—To rig out a Flying Jib-boom, 24.—To cross a Topgallant Yard, 25.—To cross a Royal Yard, 25.—Skysail Yards, 25.

CHAPTER V.

TO SEND DOWN MASTS AND YARDS, PAGES 26—28.

To send down a Royal Yard, 26.—To send down a Topgallant Yard, 27.—To send down a Topgallant Mast, 27.—To house a Topgallant Mast, 27.—To send down a Topmast, 28.—To rig in a Jib-boom, 28.

CHAPTER VI.

BENDING AND UNBENDING SAILS, PAGES 28—33.

To bend a Course, 28.—To bend a Topsail by the Halyards, 29; by the Buntlines, 30.—To bend Topgallant Sails and Royals, 30.—To bend a Jib, 31.—To bend a Spanker, 31.—To bend a Spencer, 31.—To unbend a Course, 32.—To unbend a Topsail, 32.—To unbend a Topgallant Sail or Royal, 32.—To unbend a Jib, 32.—To send down a Topsail or Course in a Gale of Wind, 32.—To bend a Topsail in a Gale of Wind, 32.—To bend one Topsail or Course, and send down the other at the same time, 32.

CHAPTER VII.

WORK UPON RIGGING.—ROPE, KNOTS, SPLICES, BENDS, HITCHES, PAGES 33—44.

Yarns, Strands, 33.—Kinds of Rope: Cable-laid, Hawser-laid, 34.—Spunyarn, 34.—Worming, Parcelling, and Service, 34.—Short Splice, 35.—Long Splice, 35.—Eye Splice, 36.—Flemish Eye, 36.—Artificial Eye, 36.—Cut Splice, 36.—Grommet, 37.—Single and Double Walls, 37.—Matthew Walker, 37.—Single and Double Diamonds, 37.—Spritsail Sheet-knot, 38.—Stopper Knot, 38.—Shroud and French Shroud Knots, 38.—Buoy-rope Knot, 39.—Turk's Head, 39.—Two Half-hitches, Clove-hitch, Overhand Knot, and Figure-of-eight, 39.—Standing and Running Bowlines, and Bowline upon a Bight, 40.—Square Knot, 40.—Timber Hitch, Rolling Hitch, and Blackwall Hitch, 40.—Cat's Paw, 41.—Sheet Bend, Fisherman's Bend, Carrick Bend, and Bowline Bend, 41.—Sheep-shank, 42.—Selvagee, 42.—Marlinspike Hitch, 42.—To pass a Round Seizing, 42.—Throat Seizing, 42.—Stopping and Nippering, 43.—Pointing, 43.—Snaking and Grafting, 43.—Foxes, Spanish Foxes, Sennit, French Sennit, Gaskets, 43.—To bend a Buoy-rope, 44.—To pass a Shear-lashing, 44.

CHAPTER VIII.

BLOCKS AND PURCHASES, PAGES 44—46.

Parts of a Block, Made and Morticed Blocks, 44.—Bull's-eye, Dead-eye, Sister-block, 45.—Snatch-block, Tail-blocks, Tackles, Whip, Gun-tackle, Luff-tackle, Luff-upon-Luff, Runner-tackle, Watch-tackle, Tail-tackle, and Burtons, 45.

CHAPTER IX.

MAKING AND TAKING IN SAIL, PAGES 46—60.

To loose a Sail, 46.—To set a Course, 47.—To set a Topsail, 47.—To set a Topgallant Sail or Royal, 48.—To set a Skysail, 48.—To set a Jib, Flying Jib, or Fore Topmast Staysail, 48.—To set a Spanker, 48.—To set a Spencer, 48.—To take in a Course, 48.—To take in a Topsail, 49.—To take in a Topgallant Sail or Royal, 50.—To take in a Skysail, 50.—To take in a Jib, 50.—To take in a Spanker, 50.—To furl a Royal, 50.—To furl a Topgallant Sail, 52.—To furl a Topsail or Course, 52.—To furl a Jib, 52.—To stow a Jib in Cloth, 53.—To reef a Topsail, 53.—To reef a Course, 55.—To turn out Reefs, 55.—To set a Topgallant Studdingsail, 56.—To take in a Topgallant Studdingsail, 57.—To set a Topmast Studdingsail, 57.—To take in a Topmast Studdingsail, 59.—To set a Lower Studdingsail, 59.—To take in a Lower Studdingsail, 60.

CHAPTER X.

GENERAL PRINCIPLES OF WORKING A SHIP, PAGES 61—64.

Action of the Water upon the Rudder, Headway, Sternway, 61.—Action of the Wind upon the Sails, Head Sails, After Sails, 62.—Centre of Gravity or Rotation, 63.—Turning a Ship to or from the Wind, 64.

CHAPTER XI.

TACKING, WEARING, BOXING, &c., PAGES 65—72.

To tack a Ship, 65.—To tack without fore-reaching, 66.—Tacking against a heavy head Sea, 67.—Tacking by hauling of all, 67.—To trim the yards when close-hauled, 67.—Missing Stays, 67.—Wearing, 68.—To wear under Courses, under a Mainsail, under bare poles, 68.—Box-hauling, 69.—Short-round, 70.—Club-hauling, 70.—Drifting in a Tide-way, 71.—Backing and filling in a Tide-way, 71.—Clubbing in a Tide-way, 71.

CHAPTER XII.

GALES OF WIND, LYING-TO, GETTING ABACK, BY THE LEE, &c., PAGES 72—75.

Lying-to, 72.—Scudding, 73.—To heave-to after Scudding, 73.—Taken aback, 74.—Chapelling, 74.—Broaching-to, 75.—Brought by the Lee, 75.

CHAPTER XIII.

ACCIDENTS, PAGES 75—79.

On Beam-ends, 75.—Losing a Rudder, 76.—A Squall, 77.—A Man Overboard, 78.—Collision, 78.

CHAPTER XIV.

HEAVING-TO BY COUNTER-BRACING, SPEAKING, SOUNDING, HEAVING THE LOG, PAGES 79—82.

Counter Bracing, 79.—Speaking, 79.—Sounding, 80.—Heaving the Log, 81.

CHAPTER XV.

COMING TO ANCHOR, PAGES 82—86.

Getting ready for Port, 82.—Mooring, 83.—A Flying Moor, 84.—Clearing Hawse, 84.—To anchor with a Slip-rope, 85.—To slip a Cable, 85.—Coming-to at a slipped Cable, 85.

CHAPTER XVI.

GETTING UNDER WAY, PAGES 86—90.

Unmoor, 86.—To get under Way from a single Anchor, 86.—To cut and fish an Anchor, 87.—To get under Way with a Wind blowing directly out, and riding head to it, 88.—To get under Way, riding head to the Wind, with a Rock or Shoal close astern, 88.—To get under Way, riding head to Wind and Tide, and to stand out close-hauled, 89.—To get under Way wind-rode, with a Weather-tide, 89.—To get under Way tide-rode, casting to Windward, 89.—To get under Way, tide-rode, wearing round, 90.

A DICTIONARY OF SEA TERMS, 91—135.

PART II.

CUSTOMS AND USAGES OF THE MERCHANT SERVICE.

CHAPTER I.

THE MASTER, PAGES 136—146.

Beginning of the Voyage, 136.—Shipping the Crew, 137.—Outfit, Provisions, 138.—Watches, 139.—Navigation, 140.—Log-book, Observations, 140.—Working Ship, 141.—Day's Work, 143.—Discipline, 145.

CHAPTER II.

THE CHIEF MATE, PAGES 146—154.

Care of Rigging and Ship's Furniture, 146.—Day's Work, 146.—Working Ship, 147.—Getting under Way, 147.—Coming to Anchor, 148.—Reefing and Furling, 148.—Duties in Port, Account of Cargo, Stowage, 148.—Station, Watch, and All-hands Duties, 149.—Log-book, Navigation, 153.

CHAPTER III.

SECOND AND THIRD MATES, PAGES 154—162.

Second Mate: Navigation, 154.—Station, Watch Duties, 155.—Day's Work, 155, 158.—Working Ship, 159.—Reefing, Furling, and Duties Aloft, 157.—Care of Ship's Furniture, 160.—Stores, 160.—Duties in Port, 161.—Third Mate, 161.

CHAPTER IV.

CARPENTER, COOK, STEWARD, &c., PAGES 162—167.

Carpenter: Working Ship, 163.—Seaman's Work, Helm, Duty aloft, Station, 163.—Work at his Trade, 164.—Berth and Mess, 164.—Standing Watch, 164.—Sailmaker, 164.—Steward: Duty in Passenger-ships, 165; in other Vessels, 166,—Relation to Master and Mate, Duty aloft and about decks, Working Ship, 166.—Cook: Berth, Watch, and All-hands Duty, care of Galley, Duty Aloft, 166.—Idlers, 167.

CHAPTER V.

ABLE SEAMEN, PAGES 168—173.

Grades, 168.—Rating 169.—Requisites of an Able Seaman, 170.—Hand, Reef, and Steer, 170.—Work upon Rigging, 170.—Sailmaking, 171.—Day's Work, 171.—Working Ship, Reefing, Furling, 171.—Watch Duty, 172.—Coasters and Small Vessels, 173.

CHAPTER VI.

ORDINARY SEAMEN, PAGES 174—176.

Requisites, 174.—Hand, Reef, and Steer; Loose, Furl, and Set Sails; Reeve Rigging, 174.—Work upon Rigging, 175.—Watc Duty, 175.

CHAPTER VII.

BOYS, PAGES 176—178.

Requisites, Wages, 176.—Day's Work, Working Ship, Duties Aloft, and about Decks, 176.

CHAPTER VIII.

MISCELLANEOUS, PAGES 178—186.

Watches, 178.—Calling the Watch, 179.—Bells, 180.—Helm, 180.—Answering, 182 (at Helm, 182).—Discipline, 183.—Stations, 184.—Food, Sleep, &c., 185.

PART III.

LAWS RELATING TO THE PRACTICAL DUTIES OF MASTER AND MARINERS.

CHAPTER I.

THE VESSEL, PAGES 187—196.

Title, 187.—Registry, Enrolment, and Licence, 188.—Certificate of Registry or Enrolment, 193.—Passport, 193.—Sea Letter, List of Crew, Bill of Health, Clearance, Manifest, Invoice, Bill of Lading, Charter-Party, Log-Book, List of Passengers and Crew, List of Sea-stores, 193.—Medicine Chest, 193.—National Character of Crew, 194.—Provisions, 195.—Passengers, 195.

CONTENTS.

CHAPTER II.

MASTER'S RELATION TO VESSEL AND CARGO, PAGES 197—212.

Revenue Duties and Obligations, 197.—List of Crew, 198.—Certified Copy, 199.—Certified Copy of Shippinging Articles, 202.—Sea Letter, Passport, List of Passengers, Manifest, Sea-stores, 202, 203.—Unloading, 202, 204.—Post-office, 204.—Forfeitures, 203, 204, 205.—Report, 204.—Coasting License, 204 —Power to Sell and Pledge, 205.—Keeping and Delivering Cargo, 208.—Deviation, 209.—Collision, 210.—Pilot, 211.—Wages and Advances, 212.

CHAPTER III.

MASTER'S RELATION TO PASSENGERS AND OFFICERS, PAGES 212—214.

Treatment of Passengers, 212.—Removal of Officers, 213.

CHAPTER IV.

MASTER'S RELATION TO THE CREW, PAGES 214—224.

Shipment, 214.—Shipping Articles, 215.—Discharge, 217.—Imprisonment, 219.—Punishment, 220.—Power of Consuls as to Punishment, 220—224.

CHAPTER V.

PASSENGERS, PAGES 224—226.

Provisions, 224.—Treatment, 225.—Passage Money, 225.—Deportment, 225.—Services, 225.

CHAPTER VI.

MATES AND SUBORDINATES, PAGES 236—231.

Mates included in Crew, 226.—Removal, 226.—Succession, 227.—Log-book, Wages, Sickness, 227-8.—Punishment, 228.—Subordinates, 230.—Pilots, 230.

CHAPTER VII.

SEAMEN; SHIPPING CONTRACT, PAGES 231—235.

Shipping Contract, 231.—Erasures and Interlineations, 233.—Unusual Stipulations, 234.—Violation of Contract, 234.

CHAPTER VIII.

SEAMEN, CONTINUED, PAGES 235—238.

Rendering on Board, 235.—Refusal to Proceed, 236.—Desertion or Absence during the Voyage, 237.—Discharge, 238.

CHAPTER IX.

SEAMEN, CONTINUED, PAGES 239—243.

Provisions, 239.—Sickness, Medicine Chest, 240.—Hospital Money, 241.—Relief in Foreign Ports, 242.—Protection, 243.

CHAPTER X.

SEAMEN, CONTINUED, PAGES 243—248.

Punishment, 243.—Revolt and Mutiny, 245.—Embezzlement, 247.—Piracy, 247.

CHAPTER XI.

SEAMEN'S WAGES, PAGES 248—259.

Wages affected by Desertion or Absence, 248.—By Misconduct, 253.—By Imprisonment, 254.—By Capture, 255.—By Loss of Vessel or Interruption of Voyage, 256.—Wages on an Illegal Voyage, 258.—Wages affected by Death or Disability, 258.

CHAPTER XII.

SEAMEN, CONCLUDED, PAGES 259—264.

Recovery of Wages, 259.—Remedies, 259.—Time for commencing Suits, 261.—Interest on Wages, 262.—Salvage, 262.

Plate I
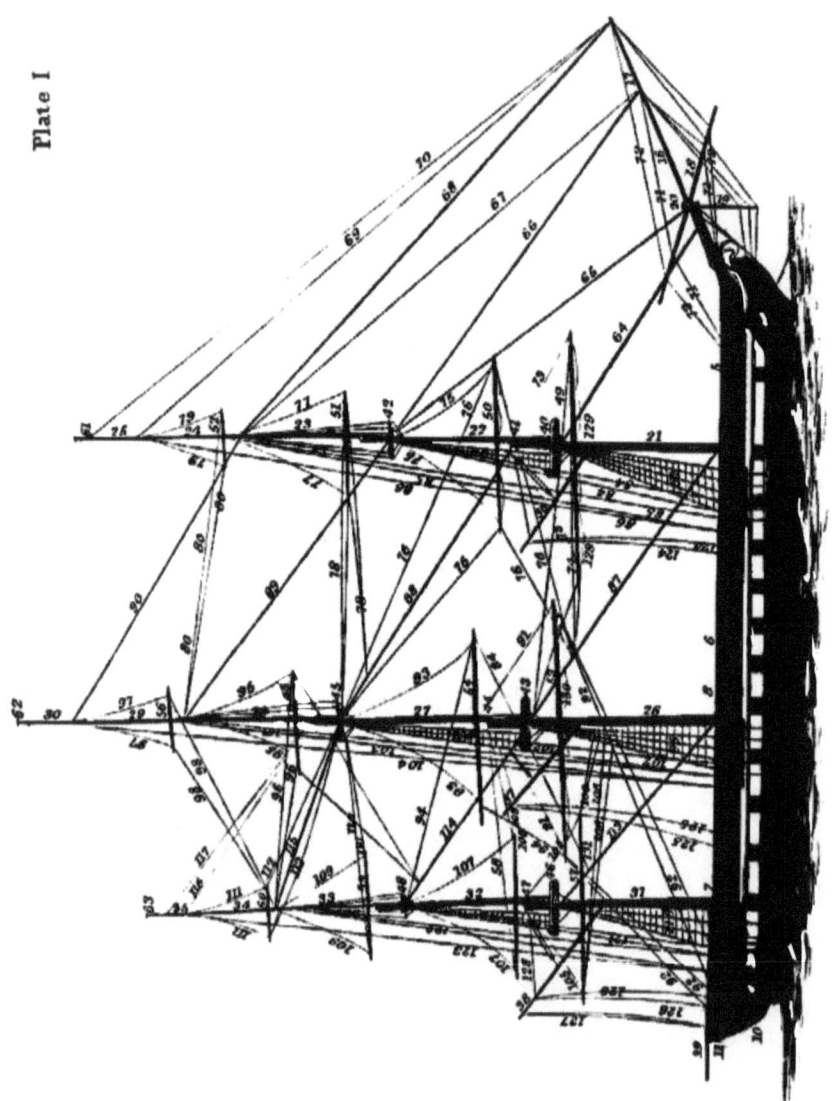

PLATE I.

THE SPARS AND RIGGING OF A SHIP.

INDEX OF REFERENCES.

1 Head.
2 Head-boards.
3 Stem.
4 Bows.
5 Forecastle.
6 Waist.
7 Quarter-deck.
8 Gangway.
9 Counter.
10 Stern.
11 Tafferel.
12 Fore chains.
13 Main chains.
14 Mizen chains.
15 Bowsprit.
16 Jib-boom.
17 Flying jib-boom.
18 Spritsail yard.
19 Martingale.
20 Bowsprit cap.
21 Foremast.
22 Fore topmast.
23 Fore topgall. mast.
24 Fore royal mast.
25 Fore skysail mast.
26 Main mast.
27 Main topmast.
28 Main topgall. mast.
29 Main royal mast.
30 Main skysail mast.
31 Mizen mast.
32 Mizen topmast.
33 Mizen topgall. mast.
34 Mizen royal mast.
35 Mizen skysail mast.
36 Fore spencer gaff.
37 Main spencer gaff.
38 Spanker gaff.
39 Spanker boom.
40 Fore top.
41 Foremast cap.
42 Fore topm. cross-tr.
43 Main top.
44 Mainmast cap
45 Main topm. cross-tr.
46 Mizen top.
47 Mizenmast cap.
48 Mizen topmast crosstrees.
49 Fore yard.
50 Fore topsail yard.
51 Fore topgallant yard.
52 Fore royal yard.
53 Main yard.
54 Main topsail yard.
55 Main topgallant yard.
56 Main royal yard.
57 Cross jack yard.
58 Mizen topsail yard.
59 Mizen topgall. yard.
60 Mizen royal yard.
61 Fore truck.
62 Main truck.
63 Mizen truck.
64 Fore stay.
65 Fore topmast stay.
66 Jib stay.
69 Fore topgallant stay.
70 Fore skysail stay.
71 Jib guys.
72 Flying-jib guys.
73 Fore lifts.
74 Fore braces.
75 Fore topsail lifts.
76 Fore topsail braces.
77 Fore topgallant lifts.
78 Fore topgall. braces.
79 Fore royal lifts.
80 Fore royal braces.
81 Fore rigging.
82 Fore topmast rigging.
83 Fore topgall. shrouds.
84 Fore topmast backstays.
85 Fore topgallant backstays.
86 Fore royal backstays.
87 Main stay.
88 Main topmast stay.
89 Main topgallant stay.
90 Main royal stay.
91 Main lifts.
92 Main braces.
93 Main topsail lifts.
94 Main topsail braces.
95 Main topgallant lifts.
96 Main topgalt. braces.
97 Main royal lifts.
98 Main royal braces.
99 Main rigging.
100 Main topmst. rigging.
101 Main topgallant rigging.
102 Main topmast backstays.
103 Main topgallt. backstays.
104 Main royal backstays.
105 Cross-jack lifts.
106 Cross-jack braces.
107 Mizen topsail lifts.
108 Mizen topsail braces.
109 Mizen topgallt. lifts.
110 Mizen topgal. braces.
111 Mizen royal lifts.
112 Mizen royal braces.
113 Mizen stay.
114 Mizen topmast stay.
115 Mizen topgallt. stay.
116 Mizen royal stay.
117 Mizen skysail stay.
118 Mizen rigging.
119 Mizen topmast rigg.
120 Mizen topgall. shrds.
121 Mizen topmast backstays.
122 Mizen topgallant backstays.
123 Mizen royal backst.
124 Fore spencer vangs.
125 Main spencer vangs.
126 Spanker vangs.
127 Ensign halyards.
128 Spanker peak halyds,
129 Foot-rope to fore yd.
130 Foot-rope to main yd.
131 Foot rope to crossjack yard.

PLATE II.

A SHIP'S SAILS.

INDEX OF REFERENCES.

1 Fore topmast staysail.
2 Jib.
3 Flying jib.
4 Fore spencer.
5 Main spencer.
6 Spanker.
7 Foresail.
8 Fore topsail.
9 Fore topgallant sail.
10 Fore royal.
11 Fore skysail.
12 Mainsail.
13 Main topsail.
14 Main topgallant sail.
15 Main royal.
16 Main skysail.
17 Mizen topsail.
18 Mizen topgallant sail.
19 Mizen royal.
20 Mizen skysail.
21 Lower studdingsail.
21[a] Lee ditto.
22 Fore topmast studdingsail.
22[a] Lee ditto.
23 Fore topgallant studdingsail.
23[a] Lee ditto.
24 Fore royal studdingsail.
24[a] Lee ditto.
25 Main topmast studdingsail.
25[a] Lee ditto.
26 Main topgallant studdingsail.
26[a] Lee ditto.
27 Main royal studdingsail.
27[a] Lee ditto.

Plate II

I. Dower, Sc.

Plate III.

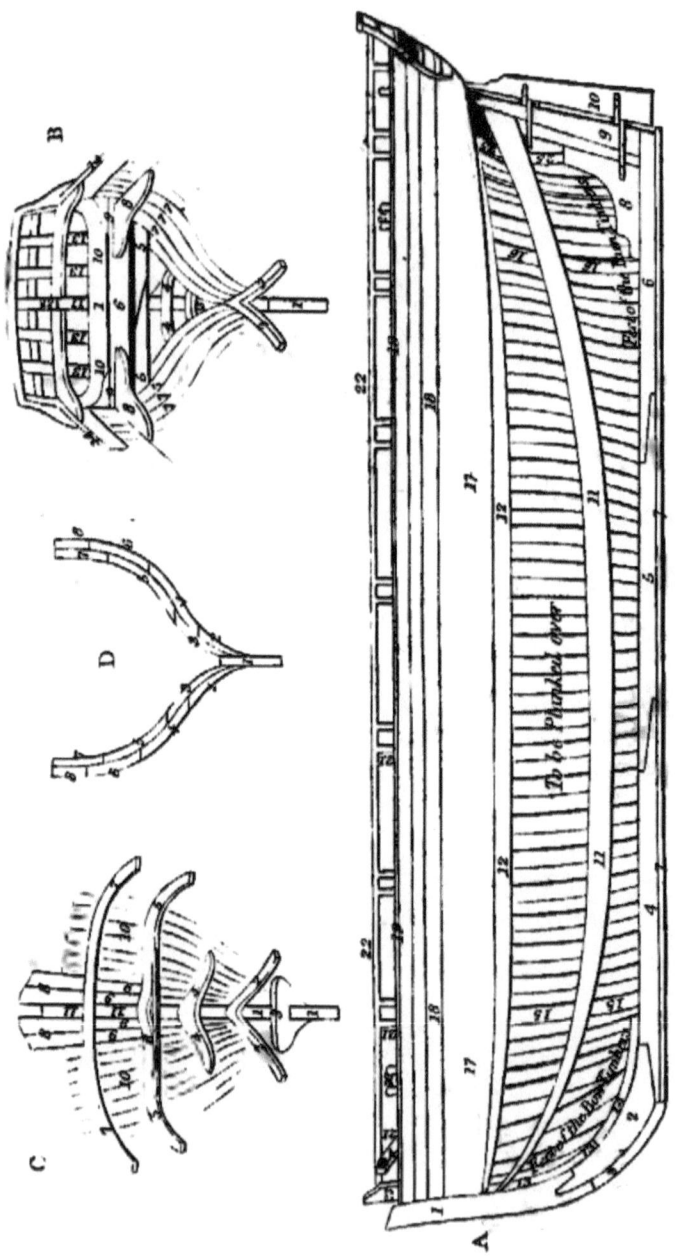

PLATE III.

THE FRAME OF A SHIP.

INDEX OF REFERENCES.

A. THE OUTSIDE.

1 Upper stem-piece.
2 Lower stem-piece.
3 Gripe.
4 Forward keel-piece.
5 Middle keel-piece.
6 After keel-piece.
7 False keel.
8 Stern knee.
9 Stern post.
10 Rudder.
11 Bilge streaks.
12 First streak under the wales.
13 Apron.
14 Lower apron.
15 Fore frame.
16 After frame.
17 Wales.
18 Waist.
19 Plank-shear.
20 Timber-heads.
21 Stanchions.
22 Rail.
23 Knight-heads.
24 Cathead.
25 Fashion timbers.
26 Transoms.
27 Quarter pieces.

B. THE INSIDE OF THE STERN.

1 Keelson.
2 Pointers.
3 Chock.
4 Transoms.
5 Half transoms.
6 Main transom.
7 Quarter timbers.
8 Transom knees.
9 Horn timbers.
10 Counter-timber knee.
11 Stern-post.
12 Rudder-head.
13 Counter timbers.
14 Upper-deck clamp.

C. THE INSIDE OF THE BOWS.

1 Keelson.
2 Pointers.
3 Step for the mast.
4 Breast-hook.
5 Lower-deck breast-hook.
6 Forward beam.
7 Upper-deck clamp.
8 Knight-heads.
9 Hawse-timbers.
10 Bow timbers.
11 Apron of the stem.

D. THE TIMBERS.

1 Keelson.
2 Floor timbers.
3 Naval timbers or ground futtocks.
4 Lower futtocks.
5 Middle futtocks.
6 Upper futtocks.
7 Top timbers.
8 Half timbers, or half top-timbers.

PLATE IV.

EXPLANATIONS.

SHIP.—A ship is square-rigged throughout; that is, she has tops, and carries square sails on all three of her masts.

BARK.—A bark is square-rigged at her fore and main masts, and differs from a ship in having no top, and carrying only fore-and-aft sails at her mizen mast.

BRIG.—A full-rigged brig is square-rigged at both her masts.

HERMAPHRODITE BRIG.—An hermaphrodite brig is square-rigged at her foremast; but has no top, and only fore-and-aft sails at her main mast.

TOPSAIL SCHOONER.—A topsail schooner has no tops at her foremast, and is fore-and-aft rigged at her mainmast. She differs from an hermaphrodite brig in that she is not properly square-rigged at her foremast, having no top, and carrying a fore-and-aft foresail, instead of a square foresail and a spencer.

FORE-AND-AFT SCHOONER.—A fore-and-aft schooner is fore-and-aft rigged throughout, differing from a topsail schooner in that the latter carries small square sails aloft at the fore.

SLOOP.—A sloop has one mast, fore-and-aft rigged.

HERMAPHRODITE BRIGS sometimes carry small square sails aloft at the main; in which case they are called BRIGANTINES, and differ from a FULL-RIGGED BRIG in that they have no top at the mainmast, and carry a fore-and-aft mainsail instead of a square mainsail and trysail. Some TOPSAIL SCHOONERS carry small square sails aloft at the main as well as the fore; being in other respects fore-and-aft rigged. They are then called MAIN TOPSAIL SCHOONERS.

THE SEAMAN'S FRIEND.

PART I.

CHAPTER I.

GENERAL RULES AND OBSERVATIONS.

Construction of vessels. Tonnage and carriage of merchant vessels. Proportions of the spars. Placing the masts. Size of anchors and cables. Lead-lines. Log-line. Ballast and lading.

CONSTRUCTION OF VESSELS.—As merchant vessels of the larger class are now built in the United States, the extreme length of deck, from the after part of the stern-post to the fore part of the stem, is from four and a half to four and three-fourths that of the beam, at its widest part. The Damascus, of 700 tons' measurement, built at Boston in 1839, and considered a fair specimen of our best freighting vessels, had 150 feet from stem to stern-post, and 32 feet 6 inches extreme breadth. The Rajah, of 530 tons, built at Boston in 1837, had 140 feet length, and 30 feet beam;—being each in length about four and six-tenths their beam.

A great contrast to this proportion is exhibited in the most recent statistics (1841) of vessels of the same tonnage in the English navy; as the following table will show:

		Tons.	Deck.	Beam.	Proportion.
English Navy.	Dido	734	120 ft.	37ft. 6 in.	3.20
	Pilot	492	105	33 6	3.13
	Alert	358	95	30 4	3.16
American Merchantmen.	Damascus	694	150	32 6	4.60
	Rajah	531	140	30 0	4.66

These may, perhaps, be considered the extremes of ship-building; and between these there is every grade of difference.

TONNAGE AND CARRIAGE OF MERCHANT VESSELS.—The amount a vessel will carry in proportion to her tonnage depends upon whether, and to what extent, she is full or sharp-built. A sharp-built vessel of 300 tons' measurement, will carry just about her tonnage of measurement goods. A sharp-built vessel of 200 tons or under would probably carry less than her measurement; if over 400 tons, she would increase gradually to fifty per cent. above her measurement. A sharp-built vessel of 600 tons is generally rated at 900 tons carriage. A full-built vessel of 300 tons, after the latest model of American freighting vessels, will carry 525 tons, or seventy-five per cent. above her measurement; and one of 500 tons would carry full double her measurement.

The following table may give a pretty fair average.

TONS OF MEASUREMENT GOODS.

Tonnage.	Full-built.	Sharp-built.
300	(.75) 525	(.00) 300
400	(.80) 725	(.40) 560
500	(1.00) 1000	(.50) 750
600	(1.33) 1400	(.50) 900

PROPORTIONS OF SPARS.—There is no particular rule for sparring merchant vessels; some being light and others heavy sparred; and some having long topmasts and short lower masts, and others the reverse. The prevailing custom now is, to spar them lightly, the main yard being a little less than double the beam; and the others proportioned by the main. Most merchant vessels now have the yards at the fore and main of the same size, for convenience in shifting sails; so that the same topsail may be bent on either yard.

The following table, taken from the "Seamen's Manual," will show the average proportions of the spars of merchant vessels of the largest class, as formerly built.

Main-mast, two and a half times the ship's beam.
Fore-mast, eight-ninths of the main-mast.
Mizen-mast, five-sixths of the main-mast.
Bowsprit, two-thirds of the main-mast.
Top-masts, three-fifths of the lower masts.
Topgallant-masts, one-half the length of their top-masts.
Jib-boom, the length of the bowsprit.
Main-yard, twice the beam.
Fore-yard, seven-eighths of the main-yard.
Maintopsail-yard, two-thirds of the main-yard.
Foretopsail-yard, two-thirds of the fore-yard.
Crossjack-yard, the length of the maintopsail-yard.
Topgallant-yards, two-thirds of the topsail-yards.
Mizentopsail-yard, the length of the maintopgallant-yard.
Royal-yards, two-thirds of the topgallant-yards.
Spritsail-yard, five-sixths of the foretopsail-yard.
Spanker-boom, the length of the maintopsail-yard.
Spanker-gaff, two-thirds of the boom.

For the thickness of the spars, the same book allows for the lower masts one inch and a quarter diameter at the partners, for every three feet of length; and nine-tenths in the middle, and two-thirds under the hounds, for every inch at the partners. For the yards, one inch at the slings, and half an inch at the yard-arms, within the squares, for every four feet of the length. For the breadth of the maintop, one half of the beam, and of the foretop, eight-ninths of the maintop.

The following are the proportions of the spars of the ship Damascus, before mentioned, built in 1839:

```
Main-mast         .   . 74 ft.  Head 11 ft. 6 in.  Size 26 in.
Fore-mast     .   .   . 70 ft.   „   11 ft. 6 in.   „   25 in.
Mizen-mast        .   . 68 ft.   „    8 ft. 6 in.   „   18 in.
Main and fore top-masts 41 ft.   „    6 ft. 6 in.   „   14½ in.
Mizen top-mast    .   . 32 ft.   „    5 ft.         „    9½ in.
Main topgallant-mast  . 23 ft. (15 ft. with 2 ft. head.)  9½ in.
Fore topgallant-mast  . 21 ft. 14 ft.  „  2 ft.  „  „    9½ in.
Mizen topgallant-mast   17 ft. 11 ft.  „ 18 in.  „
Main and fore-yards .  . 60 ft. yard-arms 2 ft. 6 in.
Main and fore topsail-yards 48 ft.  „   „  3 ft. 6 in.
Main topgallant-yard  . 37 ft.  „   „  2 ft.
```

Fore topgallant yard	.	. 34 ft.	yard-arms	2 ft.
Main royal	,,	. 27 ft. ,,	,,	1 ft. 6 in.
Fore royal	,,	. 24 ft. ,,	,,	1 ft. 6 in.
Main skysail	,,	. 17 ft.		
Fore skysail	,,	. 15 ft.		
Cross-jack	,,	. 44 ft. ,,	,,	2 ft.
Mizen topsail	,,	. 35 ft. ,,	,,	2 ft. 9 in.
Mizen topgallant	,,	. 25 ft. ,,	,,	1 ft. 6 in.
Mizen royal	,,	. 16 ft.		
Mizen skysail	,,	. 10 ft.		
Bowsprit, out-board	27 ft.		Size	26 in.
Jib-boom	.	. 42 ft.	Head 3 ft. ,,	14½ in.
Flying jib-boom		. 40 ft.	,, 3 ft. 6 in.	
Main pole	. .	. 12 ft., 10 above royal-mast, 5 in. in cap.		
Fore pole	.	. 11 ft., 9 ,, ,, ,, 4½ in. ,,		
Mizen pole	. .	9 ft., 7 ,, ,, ,,		
Spanker-boom		. 40 ft.		
Spanker-gaff	.	. 30		
Swinging-booms		. 40		

Topmast studdingsail-booms 34 ft.
Topgallant studdingsail-booms 27 ft., yards for do. 17 ft.

PLACING THE MASTS.—For a full-built ship, take the ship's extreme length and divide it into sevenths. Place the foremast one-seventh of its length from the stem; the mainmast three-sevenths from the foremast, and the mizenmast two-sevenths from the mainmast. If a vessel is sharp-built, and her stem and stern-post rake, her foremast should be further aft, and her mizenmast further forward, than the rule of sevenths would give. A common rule for placing the foremast, is to deduct three-fifths of a ship's beam from her length, for the curvature of the keel forward, which is called the keel-stroke, and place the mast next abaft the keel-stroke.

SIZE OF ANCHORS AND CABLES.—Various rules have been adopted for the weight of a ship's anchors. A vessel of 100 tons will generally have a best bower of 6 cwt. and a small bower of 5 cwt.; the weight of both being eleven pounds to a ton of the vessel. As a vessel increases in size, the proportion diminishes. A vessel of 700 tons will usually carry a best bower of 27 cwt. and a small bower of 24 cwt.; the weight of both being seven and a half pounds to a ton of the vessel. The *stream* should be a little more than one-third the weight of the best bower. The anchor-stock should be the length of the shank; its diameter should be half that of the ring, and its thickness one inch at the middle and half an inch at each end for every foot in length. Chain cables are usually ninety fathoms in length, for large-sized vessels, and sixty for small vessels, as schooners and sloops. The regulation of the United States Navy for chain cables, is one inch and a half for a sloop of war, and one and a quarter for brigs and schooners. In the merchant service, a ship of 400 tons would probably have a best bower cable of one and five-sixths, and a working bower of one and a quarter inches. A ship of 700 tons would have a best bower of one and five-eighths, and a working bower of one and a half inches. Chain cables have a shackle at every fifteen fathoms, and one swivel at the first shackle. Some have two swivels; and formerly they were made with a swivel between each shackle.

LEAD-LINES.—The *hand-lead* weighs usually seven pounds, and the hand-line is from twenty to thirty fathoms in length. The *deep-sea-lead* (pronounced dipsey) weighs from fourteen to eighteen or twenty pounds; and the deep-sea-line is from ninety to one hundred and ten fathoms. The proper way to mark a hand-line is, black leather at 2 and 3 fathoms; white rag at 5; red rag at 7; wide strip of leather, with a hole in it, at 10; and 13, 15 and 17 marked like 3, 5 and 7; two knots at 20; 3 at 30; and 4 at 40; with single pieces of cord at 25 and 35.

The deep-sea-line has one knot at 20 fathoms, and an additional knot at every 10 fathoms, with single knots at each intermediate 5 fathoms. It sometimes has a strip of leather at 10 fathoms, and from 3 to 10 is marked like the hand-line.

LOG-LINE.—The rate of a ship's sailing is measured by a log-line and a half-minute glass. The line is marked with a knot for each mile; the real distance between each knot being, however, $\frac{1}{120}$ of a mile, since a half-minute is $\frac{1}{120}$ of an hour. A knot being thus the same portion of a mile that a half-minute is of an hour, the number of knots carried off while the glass is running out will show the number of miles the vessel goes in an hour. Many glasses, however, are made for twenty-eight seconds, which, of course, reduces the number of feet for a knot to forty-seven and six-tenths. But as the line is liable to stretch and the glass to be affected by the weather, in order to avoid all danger of a vessel's overrunning her reckoning, and to be on the safe side, it is recommended to mark forty-five feet to a knot for a twenty-eight second glass. About ten fathoms is left unmarked next the log-ship, called *stray-line*. The object of this is that the log-ship may get out of the eddy under the stern, before the measuring begins. The end of the stray-line is marked by a white rag, and the first knot is forty-five or forty-seven feet from the rag. A single piece of cord or twine is put into the line for the first knot, one knot for the second, two for the fourth, three for the sixth, and so on, a single piece of cord being put in at the intermediate knots.

BALLAST AND LADING.—A ship's behaviour, as the phrase is, depends as much upon the manner in which she is loaded and ballasted, as upon her model. It is said that a vessel may be prevented from rolling heavily, if, when the ballast is iron, it is stowed up to the floor-heads; because this will bring the ship back, after she has inclined, with less violence, and will act upon a point but little distant from the centre of gravity, and not interfere with her stiff carrying of sail. The cargo should be stowed with the weightier materials as near as possible to the centre of gravity, and high or low, according to the build of the vessel. If the vessel is full and low built, the heavy articles should be stowed high up, that the centre of gravity may be raised and the vessel kept from rolling too much, and from being too laboursome. But a narrow, high-built vessel should have the heavy articles stowed low and near the keelson, which will tend to keep her from being crank, and enable her to carry sail to more advantage.

CHAPTER II.
CUTTING AND FITTING STANDING RIGGING.

Measuring and cutting lower rigging and lower fore-and-aft stays. Fitting the same. Measuring, cutting, and fitting topmast rigging, stays, and backstays. Jib, topgallant, and royal stays. Rattling down rigging. Cutting and fitting lifts, foot-ropes, brace-block straps, and pennants. Breast-backstays.

CUTTING LOWER RIGGING.—Draw a line from the side of the partners abreast of the mast, on the deck, parallel to the channels, and to extend as far aft as they do. On this line mark the places of each dead-eye, corresponding to their places against the channels. Send a line up to the mast-head, and fasten it to the mast by a nail above the bibbs, in a range with the centre of the mast, and opposite to the side the channel line is drawn upon. Then take the bight of the line around the forward part of the mast, and fasten it to the mast by a nail, opposite the first nail, so that the part between the nails will be half the circumference of the mast-head; then take the line down to the mark on the channel line for the forward dead-eye, and mark it as before; and so on, until you have got the distance between the mast and each mark on the channel line. Now cast off the line from the mast-head, and the distance between the end of the line, and each mark will give you the length of each shroud from the lower part of the mast-head. And, to make an allowance for one pair of shrouds overlaying another, you may increase the length of the pair put on second, that is, the larboard forward ones, by twice the diameter of the rigging; the third pair by four times; and so on.

The size of the lower rigging should be as much as eight and a half inches for vessels of seven or eight hundred tons, and from seven and a half to eight for smaller vessels, over three hundred tons.

For the length of the fore, main, and mizen stays and spring-stays, take the distance from the after part of the mast-head to their hearts, or to the place where they are set up, adding once the length of the mast-head for the collar.

The standing stays should be once and half the circumference of the shrouds.

FITTING LOWER RIGGING.—Get it on a stretch, and divide each pair of shrouds into thirds, and mark the centre of the middle thirds. Tar, worm, parcel, and serve the middle third. Parcel *with* the lay of the rope, working toward the centre; and serve *against* the lay, beginning where you left off, parcelling. Serve as taut as possible. In some vessels the outer thirds of the swifters are served; but matting and battens are neater and more generally used.

Formerly the middle third was parcelled over the service, below the wake of the futtock staff. Mark an eye at the centre of the middle third, by seizing the parts together with a round seizing. The eye of the pair of shrouds that goes on first should be once and a quarter the circumference of the mast-head; and make each of the others in succession the breadth of a seizing larger than the one below it. Parcel the score of the deadeye, and *heave* the shroud taut round it, turning in *with* the sun, if right-hand-laid rope, and *against* the sun, if hawser-laid; then pass the throat, seizing with nine or ten turns, the outer turns being slacker than the middle ones. Pass the quarter seizings half way to the end, and then the end seizings, and cap the shroud, well tarred under the cap. Make a Matthew Walker knot in one end of the lanyard, reeve the other end *out* through the dead-eye of the shroud, beginning at the side of the dead-eye upon which the end of the shroud comes, and *in* through the dead-eye in the channels, so that the hauling part of the lanyard may come in-board and on the same side with the standing part of the shroud. If the shroud is right-hand-laid rope, the standing part of the shroud will be aft on the starboard, and forward on the larboard side; and the reverse, if hawser-laid.

The neatest way of setting up the lower fore-and-aft stays, is by reeving them *down* through a bull's eye, with tarred parcelling upon the thimble, and setting them up on their ends, with three or four seizings. The collar of the stay is the length of the mast-head, and is leathered over the service. The service should go beyond the wake of the foot of the topsail, and the main-stay should be served in the wake of the foremast. The main and spring stays usually pass on different sides of the foremast, and set up at the hawse-pieces.

The bolsters under the eyes of the rigging should always be covered with tarred parcelling, marled on.

The starboard forward shroud goes on first; then the larboard; and so on. The fore stay and spring stay go over the shrouds; and the head stays always go over the backstays.

CUTTING AND FITTING TOPMAST RIGGING.—For the forward shroud, measure from the hounds of the topmast down to the after part of the lower trestle-trees, and add to that length half the circumference of the mast-head at the hounds. The eye is once and a quarter the circumference of the mast-head. The topmast rigging in size should be three fifths of the lower rigging. For the topmast backstays, measure the distance from the hounds of the mast down to the centre of the deck, abreast of their dead-eyes in the channels, and add to this length one half the circumference of the mast-head. Add to the length of the larboard pair, which goes on last, twice the diameter of the rope. The size of the fore and main topmast backstays is generally one quarter less than that of the lower rigging; and that of the mizen topmast backstays the same as that of the main topmast rigging.

The size of the topmast stays should be once and a quarter that of the rigging. The topmast rigging is fitted in the same manner as the lower. The backstays should be leathered in the wake of the tops and lower yards. The breast-backstays are turned in upon blocks instead of dead-eyes, and set up with a luff purchase. The fore topmast stay sets up on the starboard, and the spring stay on the larboard side of the bowsprit.

All the fore-and-aft stays are now set up on their ends, and should be leathered in their nips, as well as in their eyes.

The main topmast stay goes through a heart or thimble at the foremast-head, or through a hole in the cap, and sets up on deck or in the top; and the mizen topmast stay sets up at the mainmast-head, above the rigging.

JIB, TOPGALLANT, AND ROYAL RIGGING.—The jib stay sets up on its end on the larboard side of the head, and is served ten feet from the boom, and its collar is leathered like that of the topmast stay. The gaub lines or back ropes go from the martingale in-board. The guys are fitted in pairs, rove through straps or snatches on the spritsail yard, and set up to eye-bolts inside of or abaft the cat-heads. The foot-ropes are three quarters the length of the whole boom, and go over the boom-end with a cut splice. Overhand knots or Turks-heads should be taken in them at equal distances, to prevent the men from slipping, when laying out upon them.

The most usual method of fitting topgallant rigging in merchantmen, is to reeve it through holes in the horns of the crosstrees, then pass it between the topmast shrouds over the futtock staff, and set it up at an iron band round the topmast, just below the sheave-hole; or else down into the top and set it up there. To get the length of the starboard forward shroud, measure from the topgallant mast-head to the heel of the topmast, and add one half the circumference of the topgallant mast-head. Its size should be about five-sevenths of the topmast rigging. Each pair of shrouds should be served below the futtock staves. They are fitted like the topmast shrouds. The fore and aft stays of long topgallant masts go with eyes, and are served and leathered in the wake of the foot of the sails. The fore topgallant stay leads in on the starboard side of the bowsprit, and sets up to a bolt at the hawse-piece; the main leads through a chock on the after part of the fore topmast cross-trees, and sets up in the top; and the mizen usually through a thimble on the main cap, and sets up on its end.

The topgallant backstays set up on their end, or with lanyards in the channels; and for their length, measure from the mast-head to the centre of the deck, abreast the bolt in the channels.

The royal shrouds, backstays, and fore-and-aft stays, are fitted like those of the topgallant masts, and bear the same proportion to them that the topgallant bear to the topmast. The fore royal stay reeves through the outer sheave-hole of the flying jib-boom, and comes in on the larboard side; the main through a thimble at the fore jack-cross-trees; and the mizen through a thimble at the main topmast cap. The flying jib-stay goes in on the starboard side, and sets up like the jib-stay. The gear of the flying jib-boom is fitted like that of the jib-boom.

RATLING.—Swift the rigging well in, and lash handspikes or boat's oars outside at convenient distances, parallel with the shear-pole. Splice a small eye in the end of the rattlin, and seize it with yarns to the after shroud on the starboard side and to the forward on the larboard, so that the hitches may go with the sun. Take a clove hitch round each shroud, hauling well taut, and seize the eye of the other end to the shroud. The ratlins of the lower rigging should be thirteen, and of the topmast rigging eleven inches apart, and all square with the shear-pole.

STANDING RIGGING OF THE YARDS.—The first thing to go upon the lower yard-arm, next the shoulder, is the head-earing strap; the next, the foot-ropes; next, the brace-block; and lastly, the lift. The foot-ropes go with an eye over the yard-arm, are rove through thimbles in the end of the stirrups, (sometimes with Turks-heads, to prevent their slipping,) and are lashed to bolts or thimbles, but now usually to the iron trusses. The stirrups fit to staples in the yard with an eye-splice. The lifts should be single, and fitted with an eye over the yard-arm, and lead through a single block at the mast-head, and set up by a gun or luff tackle purchase, with the double block hooked to a thimble or turned in at the end, and the lower block to an eyebolt in the deck. Instead of brace-blocks on the fore and main yards, brace pennants fitted over the yard-arm with an eye are neater. The latest and neatest style of rigging lower yards is to have a strong iron band with rings and thimbles round each yard-arm, close to the shoulder; and then fit the lift, foot-rope, and brace-pennant, each to one of these rings, with an eye-splice round the thimble or with a hook. The lower lifts now, for the most part, cross each other over a saddle upon the cap, instead of going through blocks.

The inner ends of the foot-ropes to the topsail, topgallant and royal yards, cross each other at the slings; and on the topsail yard there are Flemish horses, spliced round thimbles on the boom-iron, and the other end seized to the yard, crossing the foot-rope. A neater mode is to hook the outer end of the Flemish-horse, so that it may be unhooked and furled in with the sails when in port. Next to the foot-ropes go on the brace-blocks, and lastly, the lifts. The rigging to the topgallant and royal yards is fitted similarly to that upon the topsail, except that there is nothing over the yard-arms but foot-rope, brace, and lift. The brace to the royal yard fits with an eye. The reef-tackle, studding-sail halyard, and other temporary blocks, are seized to the lower and topsail yard-arms, by open straps, so that they may be removed without taking off the lift. The topgallant studding-sail halyard block is often hooked to the boom-iron, under the yard.

The foot-ropes to the spanker-boom should be half the length of the boom, going over the end with a splice, covered with canvas, and coming in one-third of the way to the jaws, and seized to the boom by a rose-seizing through an eye-splice. The next to go over the boom-end are the guys, which are fitted with a cut-splice covered with canvas, and have a single block turned in at their other ends. To these single blocks are luff or gun-tackle purchases, going to the main brace-bumpkin. Their length should be two-fifths that of the boom. The topping-lifts are usually hooked into a band or spliced into bolts about one quarter the distance from the outer end of the boom, and reeved through single blocks under the top, with a double or single block at their lower ends.

All the splices and seizings of the standing rigging should be covered with canvas, if possible, except in the channels and about the head, where they are too much exposed to the washing of water. A vessel looks much neater for having the ends of the rigging, where eyes are spliced, or where they are set up on their ends aloft or on deck, covered with canvas, and painted white or black, according to the place where they are. The lanyards and dead-eyes of the smaller rigging which sets up in the top may also be covered with canvas. The lanyards, dead-eyes, and turnings-in of the rigging in the channels, should always be protected by Scotchmen when at sea, and the forward shroud should be matted or battened all the way up to the futtock staves.

In some smaller merchantmen the lower rigging is not unfrequently set up upon its end to bolts in the rail. This is very inconvenient on many accounts, especially as all the seizings have to be come up with, and the nip of the shroud altered, whenever it is at all necessary to set them taut. This soon defaces and wears out the ends; while with dead-eyes, only the lanyards have to be come up with. Some vessels set up their lower rigging with dead-eyes upon the rail. This is convenient in setting them up in bad weather, but does not give so much spread as when set up in the channels, and presents a more complicated surface to the eye. If the rigging is fitted in this way, you must deduct the height of the rail above the deck from the measure before given for cutting it.

BREAST-BACKSTAYS.—It is not usual, now, for merchant vessels to carry topmast breast-backstays. If they are carried, they are spread by the out-riggers from the top. Topgallant and royal breast backstays are used, and are of great assistance in sailing on the wind. There are various ways of rigging them out, of which the following is suggested as a neat and convenient one. Have a spar fitted for an out-rigger, about the size of one of the horns of the cross-trees, with three holes bored in it, two near to one end, and the third a little the other side of the middle. Place it upon the after horn of the cross-tree with the last-mentioned hole over the hole in the end of the horn of the cross-tree, and let the after topgallant shroud reeve through it. Reeve the topgallant and royal breast-backstays through the outer holes, and set them up by a gun-tackle purchase in the channels. The inner end of the out-rigger should fit to a cleat, and be lashed to the cross-tree by a lanyard. When the breast-backstays are to be rigged in, cast off the lanyard, and let the out-rigger slue round the topgallant shroud for a pivot, the inner end going aft, and the outer end, with the backstays, resting against the forward shroud. One of these out-riggers should be fitted on each side, and all trouble of shifting over, and rigging out by purchase, will be avoided.

CHAPTER III.

FITTING AND REEVING RUNNING RIGGING.

Fore braces. Main braces. Cross-jack braces. Fore, main, and mizen topsail braces. Fore, main, and mizen topgallant and royal braces. Trusses. Topsail tyes and halyards. Topgallant and royal halyards. Peak and throat halyards. Spanker brails. Fore and main tacks and sheets. Topsail, topgallant and royal sheets and clewlines. Reef tackles. Clew-garnets. Fore and main buntlines, leachlines, and slablines. Topsail clewlines and buntlines. Bowlines.

To REEVE A BRACE, begin on deck, and reeve to where the standing part is made fast. The *fore braces* reeve *up* through a block on the mainmast just below the rigging, *down* or *in* through the brace-block on the yard or at the end of the pennant, and the standing part is brought through the cheeks of the mast with a knot inside. The neatest way for reeving the *main brace* is *out* through a single block on the brace-bumpkin, *out* through the brace-pennant-block, *in* through an outer block on the bumpkin, and seized to the strap of the pennant. Another way is *out* through the bumpkin block, *out* or *down* through the pennant block, and secure the end to the bumpkin or to the fashion-piece below.

The *cross-jack braces* reeve *up* through the blocks on the after shroud of the main rigging, *up* through blocks on the yard, one-third of the way in from the yard-arm, and are seized to a bolt in the main-mast, or to the after shroud again.

The *fore topsail braces* reeve *up* through the blocks secured to the bibbs at the mainmast-head, *in* through the span-block at the collar of the main stay, *up* through the block on the yard, and are seized to the main topmast-head; or else *up* through a block at the topmast-head, down through the braceblock on the yard, and are seized to the collar on the main stay. The last way is the best. The *main topsail braces* are rove through span-blocks at the mizen-mast, below the top, *up* through the blocks on the yard, and are seized to the mizen topmast-head; or else *up* through a block at the mizen mast-head, *down* through a block on the yard, and secured to the mizen-mast. The first way is the best. The *mizen topsail braces* reeve *up* through the leading blocks or fair-leaders on the main rigging, *up* through blocks at the mainmast-head, or at the after part of the top, *up* through the yard blocks, and are seized to the cap.

The *fore* and *main topgallant braces* are rove *up* through blocks under the topmast cross-trees, *in* through span-blocks on the topmast stays, just below their collars, *up* through the blocks on the yards, and the main are usually seized to the head of the mizen topgallant mast, and the fore to the topmast stay, by the span-block. The *mizen topgallant braces* generally go single through a block at the after part of the main topmast cross-trees. The *royal braces* go single: the *fore*, through a block at the main topgallant mast-head; the *main*, through one at the mizen top-gallant mast-head; and the *mizen*, through a block at the after-part of the main topmast cross-trees.

HALYARDS.—The *lower yards* are now hung by patent iron trusses, which allow the yard to be moved in any direction; topped up or braced. The *topsail yards* have chain tyes, which are hooked to the slings of the yard, and rove through the sheave-hole, at the mast-head. The other end of the tye hooks to a block. Through this block a chain-runner leads, with its standing part hooked to an eye-bolt in the trestle-tree, and with the upper halyard block hooked to its other end. The halyards should be a luff purchase, the fly-block being the double block, and the single block being hooked in the channels. Sometimes they are a gun-tackle purchase, with two large single blocks. The lower block of the mizen topsail halyards is usually in the mizen tops, the fall coming down on deck.

The *fore* and *mizen topsail halyards* come down to port, and the main to the starboard. The *topgallant halyards* come down on opposite sides from the topsail halyards; though the fore and main usually come down by the side of the masts. The fore and main topgallant halyards sometimes hoist with a gun-tackle purchase, but the mizen and all the royal halyards are single.

The *throat and peak halyards* of the spanker are fitted in the following manner. The outer peak halyard block is put on the gaff, one-third of its length from the outer end, or a very little, if any, within the leach of the sail; and the inner one two-thirds in. The blocks are fitted round the gaff with grommet straps, and are kept in their places by cleats. The double block of the peak halyards is strapped to the bolt in the after part of the mizen cap, and the halyards are rove *up* through this, *in* through the blocks on the gaff, the inner one first, the standing part made fast to the double block, and the fall coming on deck. The upper block of the throat halyards is secured under the cap, and the lower block is hooked to an eye-bolt on the jaws of the gaff. This is a two-fold tackle.

THE SPANKER BRAILS.—The *peak brails* reeve though single blocks on the gaff, two on each side, generally span-blocks, and then through the throat brail blocks, as leaders, to the decks. The *throat brails* reeve through two triple blocks, strapped to eye-bolts under the jaws of the gaff, one on each side, through the two other sheaves of which the peak brails lead. Each brail is a single rope, middled at the leach of the sail.

TACKS, SHEETS, CLEWLINES, &c.—It is much more convenient to have the tack and sheet blocks of the courses fastened to the clews of the courses by hooks. Then they can be unhooked when the sail is furled, and, in light weather, a single rope with a hook, called a *lazy sheet*, can be used, instead of the heavy tacks and sheets with their blocks. This is also much more convenient in clewing up. The *main tack* is rove *aft* through the block in the waterways, *forward* through the block on the sail, and the standing part hooks to the block on deck. The *fore tack* goes through a block on the bumpkin. The *sheets* of the courses have the after block hooked to an eye-bolt in the side, abaft the channels, and the forward one hooked to the clew of the sail, the running part reeving through a sheave-hole in the rail. The sheets of all the square sails but the courses run from the clew of the sail, through sheave-holes in the yard-arms, through the quarter blocks, down on deck. The *topsail sheets* are chain, are clasped to the clews of the sail, and are fitted with a gun-tackle purchase at the foot of the mast. The *topgallant* and *royal sheets* are single. The *topsail* and *topgallant clew-lines* reeve through the quarter-blocks. The *royal clew-lines* are single, and the topsail and topgallant are a gun-tackle purchase.

The *reef-tackles* of the topsails reeve *up* through blocks on the lower rigging, or futtock shrouds, *down* through the block on the yard, down the leach of the sail and through the block on the leach, and are made fast to the yard on their own parts, with a clinch, outside of everything.

The *clew-garnets* reeve *out* through blocks, under the quarters of the yards, then *up* through blocks at the clew, and the standing part is made fast to the yard, to the block, or to a strap. The *buntlines* of the courses reeve through double or triple blocks under the forward part of the top, down forward of the sail, sometimes through thimbles in the first reef-band, and are clinched to the foot of the sail. The *leachlines* reeve through single blocks, on the yard, and are clinched to the leach of the sail. The *slabline* is a small rope rove through a block under the slings of the yard, and clinched to the foot of the sail. This is not much used in merchant vessels. The *topsail clewlines* lead like the clew-garnets of the courses. The *topsail buntlines* reeve forward through single blocks at the topmast-head, down through the thimbles of a lizard seized to the tye, just above the yard, and are clinched to the foot of the sail. The handiest way of reeving the *main bowline* is to have a single rope with the standing part hooked near the foremast, and reeve it *out* through a heart in the bridle. This will answer for both sides. The *fore bowline* may be rove through a single block at the heel of the jib-boom and hooked to the bridle. The bowlines to the other sails are toggled to the bridles and lead forward. Many vessels now dispense with all the bowlines except to the courses. This saves trouble, makes a ship look neater, and if the sails are well cut, they will set taut enough in the leach, without bowlines.

CHAPTER IV.

TO RIG MASTS AND YARDS.

Rigging the shears. Taking in lower masts and bowsprit. To rig a bowsprit. Getting the tops over the mast-heads. To send up a top-mast. To get on a top-mast cap. To rig a jib-boom. To cross a lower yard. To cross a topgallant yard. To send up a topgallant mast. Long, short, and stump topgallant masts. To rig out a flying jib-boom. To cross topgallant and royal yards. Skysail yards.

TAKING IN LOWER MASTS AND BOWSPRIT.—Shore up the beams upon which the heels of the shears will rest, if necessary, from the keelson. Parbuckle the shears aboard, with their heads aft. Raise their heads upon the taffrail, cross them, and pass the shear-lashing. Lash the upper block of a three-fold tackle under the cross, and secure the lower block to the breast-hooks, or to a toggle in the hawse-hole. You may also reeve and secure, in the same manner, a smaller purchase, which shall work clear of the first. Have two forward and two after guys clove-hitched to the shear-head, with cleats to prevent their slipping. Get a girt-line on one shear-head and a small tackle on the other, to slue and cant the mast. Let the fall of the main tackle come through the middle sheave, to prevent the blocks sluing in its strap. Reeve large heel tackles to rouse the shears aft with. Put long oak plank shoes under the heels;

and, if it be necessary, clap a thwart-ship tackle upon the two heels, or reeve a lashing, and put a stout plank between them, and bowse taut; which will prevent too great a strain coming upon the water-ways. Take the main tackle fall to the capstan; heave round, haul on the forward guy and after heel tackles, and raise the shear to an angle of about eighty degrees with the deck, and so that the main purchase will hang plumb with the partners of the mizen-mast. Lash a garland to the forward part of the mast, above the centre, and toggle the purchase to it. Heave the mast in over the bulwarks; fit the trestle-trees and after chock; reeve girt-lines by which men may be hoisted when the mast is in; point the mast in, and lower away. Always take in the mizen-mast first. Get in the main and then the fore-mast in the same manner, rousing the shears forward, with their shoes, by means of the heel tackles. Having stepped and secured the fore mast, carry the forward guys aft and rake the shears over the bows; toggle the lower block of the main tackle to a garland lashed to the upper part of the bowsprit inside of the centre. Put on the cap, and carry tackles or guys from the bowsprit-head to each cat-head, and clap on a heel tackle or guy. Heave the bowsprit, and direct it by the small tackles and guys.

To Rig a Bowsprit.—Lash collars for the fore stay, bobstays, and bowsprit shrouds, then for the spring stay, and put on the bees for the topmast stays; fit the man-ropes, pass the gammoning, and set up bobstays and shrouds.

To get the Tops over the Mast-heads.—Place the top on deck abaft the mast; get a girt-line on each side of the mast-head, and pass the end of each under the top, through the holes in the after part; clinch them to their own parts, and stop them to the fore part of the top with slip-stops. Have a guy to the fore and another to the after part of the top. Make the ends of a span fast to the after corners of the top, and bend a girt-line from the mast-head to the bight of the span, and stop it to the forward part of the top. Sway away on the girt-lines. When the fore part of the top is above the trestle-trees, cut the span-stops, and when the after part is above them, cast off the slip-stops. When the lubber-hole is high enough to clear the mast-head, haul on the forward guy, and let the top hang horizontally by the girt-lines. Lower away, place, and bolt it.

The fore and main tops are sent up from abaft, and the mizen from forward. The tops may be got over without the span and girt-line, by stopping the two girt-lines first rove to the middle as well as to the fore part of the top, and cutting the upper stops first.

To send up a Topmast.—Get the topmast alongside, with its head forward. Lash a top-block to the head of the lower-mast; reeve a mast-rope through it, from aft forward, and bring the end down and reeve it through the sheave-hole of the top-mast, hitching it to its own part a little below the topmast-head, and stopping both parts to the mast, at intervals. Snatch the rope and sway away. As soon as the head is through the lower cap, cast off the end of the mast-rope, letting the mast hang by the stops, and hitch it to the staple in the other end of the cap. Cast off the stops and sway away. Point the head of the mast between the trestle-trees and through the hole in the lower cap, the round hole of which must be put over the square hole of the trestle-trees. Lash the cap to the mast, hoist away, and when high enough, lower a little and secure the cap to the lower mast-head. (This is when it cannot be put on by hand.) If the cross-trees are heavy, they may be placed in the following manner. Sway away until the top-mast-head is a few feet above the lower cap. Send up the cross-trees by girt-lines, and let the after part rest on the lower cap and the forward part against the top-mast. Lower away the topmast until the cross-trees fall into their place, and then hoist until they rest on the shoulders. Lash on the bolsters, get girt-lines on the cross-trees to send up the rigging, and then put it over the mast-head, first the shrouds, then the backstays, and lastly the head-stays. Sway the topmast on end, fid it, and set up the rigging.

To GET ON A TOPMAST-CAP.—In vessels of the largest class, it may be necessary to send up the cap in the following manner, but it can usually be got up by hand. Or it may be fitted and the rigging put on over it. Send the cap up to the cross-trees by girt-lines, and place the round hole of the cap over the forward hole of the cross-trees; send aloft a topgallant studdingsail boom, and point its upper end through the holes in the cross-trees and cap, and lash the cap to it. Hook a tackle or girt-line to a strap on the lower end of the spar, and sway away until the cap is over the mast-head. Slue the spar so that the cap may come fair, lower away, and place the cap upon the mast-head. Unlash the spar and send it down.

To RIG OUT A JIB-BOOM.—Point the outer end through the collars of the stays. Reeve the heel-rope through a block at the bowsprit cap, through the sheave-hole at the heel of the boom, and secure the end to an eye-bolt in the cap on the opposite side. Rig the boom out until the inner sheave-hole is clear of the cap. Tar the boom-end, put on the foot-ropes and guys, and reeve the jib stay. Hoist up the martingale and rig it, and reeve the martingale stay and gaub-line. Rig the boom out to its place, and set up the jib and martingale stays.

To CROSS A LOWER YARD.—If the yard is alongside, reeve the yard rope through the jear block at the mast-head, make it fast to the slings of the yard, and stop it out to the yard-arm. Sway away, and cast off the stops as the yard comes over the side, and get the yard across the bulwarks. Lower yards are rigged now with iron trusses and quarter-blocks, which would be fitted before rigging the yard. Seize on the clew-garnet block, and put the rigging over the yard-arm; first the straps for the head-earings, then the foot-ropes, then the brace blocks or pennants, and last the eye of the lift. (The lifts, brace pennants, and foot-ropes are now spliced or hooked into rings with thimbles on an iron band, round the yard-arm, next the shoulders. In this way, there is no rope of any kind round the yard-arm.) Reeve the lifts and braces, get two large tackles from the mast-head to the quarters of the yard, and sway away on them and on the lifts, bearing off and sluing the yard by means of guys. Secure the yard by the iron trusses, and haul taut lifts and braces.

To cross a Topsail Yard.—As topsail yards now have chain tyes, there are no tye-blocks to seize on. The quarter-blocks are first seized on, and the parral secured at one end, ready to be passed. A single parral has an eye in each end, and one end is passed under the yard and over, and the eye seized to the standing part, close to the yard. After the yard is crossed, the other end is passed round the mast, then round the yard, and seized in the same manner. To pass a double parral, proceed in the same manner, except that the seizings are passed so as to leave the eyes clear and above the standing part, and then take a short rope with an eye in each end, pass it round the mast, and seize the eyes to the eyes of the first long rope. The parral is wormed, served and leathered. The parral being seized at one end, put on the head-earing straps, the foot-ropes, Flemish horses, and brace blocks. Bend the yard-rope to the slings, stop it out to the yard-arm, and sway away until the yard is up and down; then put on the upper lift in the top and the lower lift on deck, and reeve the braces. Sway away, cast off the stops, and take in upon the lower lift as the yard rises, till the yard is square; then haul taut lifts and braces and pass the parral.

To send up a Topgallant Mast.—Most merchantmen carry *long topgallant masts*. In these, the topgallant, royal, and skysail masts are all one stick. *A short topgallant mast* is one which has cross-trees, and above which a fidded royal-mast may be rigged. *A stump top-*

gallant mast has no cross-trees, or means for setting a mast above it, and is carried only in bad weather. Some short topgallant masts are rigged with a *withe* on the after part of the mast-head, through which a sliding-gunter-royal-mast is run up, with its heel resting in a step on the topmast cap.

To send up a long topgallant mast, put the jack over the topmast cap, with a grommet upon its funnel for the eyes of the rigging to rest upon; send up the rigging by girtlines, and put the eyes over the jack, first the topgallant shrouds, backstays and stays, then the royal rigging in the same order, with a grommet, then the skysail stay and backstay, and lastly the truck. Reeve a top-rope forward through a block at the topmast-head, through the hole in the cross-trees; through the sheave-hole at the foot of the top-gallant mast; carry it up the other side, and make it fast to its own part at the mast-head; stop it along the mast, and bend a guy to the heel. Sway away, and point through the jack; put on the truck, and the skysail, royal and topgallant rigging in their order; slue the mast so as to bring the sheaves of the tyes fore-and-aft; cast off the end of the top-rope, the mast hanging by the stops; make it fast to an eye-bolt on the starboard side of the cap, and sway away. When high enough, fid the mast and set up the rigging.

A short topgallant mast is sent up like a topmast, the cross-trees got over in the same manner; and the fidded royal-mast is sent up like a long topgallant mast.

To RIG OUT A FLYING JIB-BOOM.—Ship the withe on the jib-boom end, reeve a heel-rope through a block at the jib-boom end, and bend it to the heel of the flying jib-boom, and stop it along, out to the end. Haul out on the heel-rope, point through the withe, put on the rigging, in the same order with that of the jib-boom; reeve the guys, martingale, flying jib, royal and skysail stays; rig out, and set up the rigging. The heel of the boom rests against the bowsprit cap, and is lashed to the jib-boom.

The flying jib-boom should be rigged fully out before the fore topgallant mast is swayed on end.

To cross a Topgallant Yard.—Seize on the parral and quarter-blocks; reeve the yard-rope through the sheave-hole of the topgallant mast, make it fast to the slings of the yard, and stop it out to the upper end. Sway away, and when the upper yard-arm has reached the topmast-head, put on the upper lift and brace, sway away again, put on the lower lift and brace, cast off all the stops, settle the yard down square by lifts and braces, and pass the parral lashing.

To cross Royal Yards.—The royal yards are crossed in the same manner as the topgallant yards, except that in most merchantmen they would be sent up by the halyards instead of a yard-rope. If there is not a standing skysail, the quarter-blocks on the royal yard will be single.

Skysail Yards.—If the skysail is a standing sail, the yard is rigged like the royal yard, with lifts and braces, and the sail is fitted with sheets and clewlines; but if it is a flying skysail, the yard has neither lifts nor braces, and the clews of the sail are seized out to the royal yard-arms. There are various ways of rigging a flying skysail, of which the following is believed to be as convenient as any. Let the royal stay go round the mast-head, with a traveller, above the yard, so that the stay may travel up and down the skysail mast. Seize a thimble into the stay, close against the forward part of the grommet; lead the skysail halyards through the thimble, and make them fast to the centre of the yard, which will need no parrals underneath the royal stay. Make fast the ends of two small ropes for downhauls, to the skysail yard, about half way out on each yard-arm, and reeve them through small cleats on the after part of the royal yard, the same distance out on each yard-arm. These may be spliced into a single rope below the yard, which will go through a fair-leader in the cross-trees to the deck. By this means the skysail may be taken in or set without the necessity of sending a man aloft. Let go the halyards and haul on the downhaul, and the yard will be brought close down to the royal yard. To hoist it, let go the downhaul and royal stay, and haul on the halyards. When the royal is taken in, haul the skysail yard down with the royal yard, and furl the sail in with the royal.

CHAPTER V.

TO SEND DOWN MASTS AND YARDS.

To send down a royal yard—a topgallant yard—a topgallant mast. To house a topgallant mast. To send down a topmast. To rig in a jib-boom.

TO SEND DOWN A ROYAL YARD.—If the sail is bent to the yard, furl it, making the gaskets fast to the tye. Cast off the sheets and clewlines, and make them fast to the jack. Be careful to unreeve the clewlines through the quarter-blocks. Cast off the parral-lashing. Overhaul the tye a little, and stop it to the yard just outside of the quarter-block. If stopped too far out, the yard will not hoist high enough to get the lower lift off. Sway away on the halyards, which will cant the yard and hoist it. When high enough, cast off the lower lift and brace, (being careful not to let the brace go,) and make them fast to the jack. Lower away, and as the upper yard-arm comes abreast of the jack, clap a stop round the yard and tye, near the yard-arm, and cast off the lift and brace, making them fast to the jack. Lower away to the deck.

If the halyards are not single, the yard must be sent down by a yard-rope, like the topgallant yard. In some vessels, instead of making the sheets and clewlines fast to the jack, over-hand knots are taken in their ends, and they are let go. The sheets will run out to the topgallant yard-arms, and the clewlines will run to the fair-leaders in the cross-trees. In port, the main royal yard is sent down on the starboard side, and the fore and mizen on the larboard; but at sea, the tye is stopped out on the lee side, and the yard sent down in any way that is the most convenient.

To send down a Topgallant Yard.—Cast off the sheets, bowlines, buntlines, and clewlines, and make them fast to the cross-trees. Reeve a yard-rope through a jack-block at the mast-head, unhook the tye, cast off the parral-lashing, bend the yard-rope to the slings of the yard by a fisherman's bend, and stop it to the quarters of the yard. Sway away, and take off the lifts and braces, as with the royal yard.

To send down a Topgallant Mast.—Hook the top-block to the eye-bolt at the larboard side of the topmast cap; reeve the mast-rope through it, then through the sheave-hole in the foot of the topgallant mast, and hitch its end to the eye-bolt on the starboard side of the cap. Come up the rigging, stays and backstays, and guy the mast-head by them. Hoist a little on the mast-rope, and take out the fid. (The fid should always be fastened to the cross-trees or trestle-trees, by a lanyard.) Lower away until the mast is a little short of being through the cap. Then seize or rack together both parts of the mast-rope just above the sheave-hole; cast off the end of the mast-rope, letting the mast hang by the stops, and hitch it round the mast-head to its own part below the cap. Then lower away to the deck. If the rigging is to come on deck, round up the mast-rope for a girtline; if it is to remain aloft, lash it to the topmast cap, render the shrouds through the cross-trees, and stop them up and down the topgallant rigging. Sheep-shank the stays and backstays, and set them hand-taut. If the topmast is also to be sent down, take off the topmast cap and send it on deck.

To house a Topgallant Mast.—Proceed in the same manner, except that when the mast is low enough, belay the mast-rope, pass a heel-lashing through the fid-hole, and round the topmast.

To send down a Topmast.—Hook the top-block, reeve the mast-rope through it and through the sheave-hole in the foot of the mast, and hitch it to the staple at the other side of the cap. Lead the fall through a snatch-block to the capstan. Sling the lower yard, if it is to remain aloft, and unshackle the trusses, if they are of iron. Come up the rigging, stays and backstays, weigh the mast, take out the fid, and lower away. If the rigging is to remain aloft, lash the cross-trees to the lower cap. The rigging should be stowed away snugly in the top, and the backstays be snaked up and down the lower rigging.

To rig in a Jib-boom.—Reeve the heel-rope (if necessary), come up the stay, martingale stay and guys; unreeve the jib-stay, station hands at each guy, clear away the heel-lashing, haul in upon the guys, and light the boom on board. In most cases the boom will come in without a heel-rope. Make fast the eyes of the rigging to the bowsprit cap, and haul all taut.

CHAPTER VI.

BENDING AND UNBENDING SAILS.

To bend a course. To send up a topsail by the halyards—by the buntlines. To bend a topgallant sail—a royal—a jib—a spanker—a spencer. To unbend a course—a topsail—a topgallant sail or royal—a jib. To send down a topsail or course in a gale of wind. To bend a topsail in a gale of wind. To bend one topsail or course, and send down the other at the same time.

To bend a Course.—Stretch the sail across the deck, forward of the mast and under the yard; being careful to have the after part of the sail aft. Seize the clew-garnet blocks to the clews; also the tack and sheet blocks, unless they go with hooks or clasps. Reeve the buntlines through the thimbles of the first reef-band forward, if they are made to go so, and toggle their ends to the foot of the sail, or carry them through the eyelet-holes and clinch them to their own parts. Reeve the clewgarnets and leachlines; carry the bights of the buntlines under the sail, and rack them to their own parts; stop the head of the sail to the buntlines below the rackings; put robands to each eyelet-hole in the head of the sail; fasten the head and reef earings to their cringles, reeving the end of the reef-earings through the head cringle, and taking a bowline with them to their standing parts, and hitching the head-earings to the buntlines. Sway away on the buntlines, leachlines, and clewgarnets; when the sail is up, pass the head-earings, reeving *aft* through the straps on the yard, and *forward* through the head cringle. Haul out on the earings, making the sail square by the glut, and pass the earings round the yard, over and under, through the head-cringle at each turn, and make the end fast around the first turns. If the sail is new, ride down the head rope on the yard, and freshen the earings. Make fast the head of the sail to the jackstay by robands, and cast the stops off the buntlines.

To BEND A TOPSAIL.—Make fast the head and reef-earings to their cringles, passing the end of each reef-earing through the cringle above its own, and making it fast by a bowline to its own part. Put robands to each eyelet-hole in the head. If the sail is to be sent up by the topsail halyards, lay it on deck abaft the foot of the mast, make it up with its head and foot together, having the head and first reef cringles together and out, and also the bowline cringle and the clews out. Bight the sail in three parts on a pair of slings, having the end of the sail that belongs on the opposite yard-arm on top. Have the fly-block of the topsail halyards above the top, and rack the runner to the topmast backstay or after shroud. Hook the lower block to the slings around the sail, hoist the sail up into the top, cast off the slings, unhook the halyards, and pass the upper end of the sail round forward of the mast, ready for bending. (If the vessel is rolling or pitching, with a stiff breeze, the sail may be guyed and steadied as it goes up, by hooking a snatch-block, moused, to the slings around the sail, passing the hauling part of the halyards through it, and through another snatch-block on deck.) Get the clewlines, buntlines, sheets, bowlines, and reef-tackles ready for bending, the clove hooks of the sheets being stopped to the topmast rigging. Hook or clasp the sheets to the clews, reeve the clewlines and reef-tackles, toggle the bowlines, clinch or toggle the buntlines to the foot of the sail, and stop the head to the buntlines. Hoist on the buntlines and haul out on the reef-tackles, bringing the sail to the yard, and then pass the head-earings and make fast the robands as for a course. If the sail is to be sent up by the buntlines, lay the sail on the deck and forward of the mast, overhaul the buntlines down forward of the yard, on each side of the topmast stay and on the same side of the lower stay. Clinch the ends to the foot of the sail, bight them around under the sail and rack the bights to their standing parts, and stop the head of the sail to the standing parts below the rackings. Bend one bowline to the centre of the sail to guy it in going aloft. Have the earings bent and secured as before described, and the bights of the head-earings hitched to the buntlines. Sway it up to the top, and haul the ends in on each side of the mast; reeve the clewlines and reef-tackles, make fast the bowlines and sheets, the ends of which, if chain, should be racked to the topmast rigging, ready to be made fast to the clews. The gear being bent, hoist on the buntlines, haul out on the reef-tackles, pass the head-earings, cut the stops of the buntlines, and make fast the robands. Middle the sail on the yard by the glut, or by the centre cringle.

TO BEND TOPGALLANT SAILS AND ROYALS.—These are generally bent to their yards on deck; the royals always. After being bent to the yard, they are furled, with their clews out, ready for sending aloft. If the topgallant sail is to be bent aloft, send it up to the topmast cross-trees by the clewlines, or by the royal halyards; and there bend on the sheets, clewlines, buntlines and bowlines, and bring the sail to the yard as with a topsail.

To BEND A JIB.—Bend the jib halyards round the body of the sail, and the downhaul to the tack. Haul out on the downhaul, hoisting and lowering on the halyards. Seize the tack to the boom, the hanks to the luff of the sail, and the halyards to its head. Reeve the downhaul up through the hanks and make it fast to the head of the sail. Seize the middle of the sheet-pennant to the clew.

In some vessels the hanks are first seized to the sail, and the jib-stay unrove, brought in-board, and passed down through the hanks, as the sail is sent out, rove in its place and set up. This is more troublesome, and wears out the jib-stay.

To BEND A SPANKER.—Lower the gaff, and reeve the throat-rope through the hole in the gaff under the jaws, and secure it. Sometimes the head of the luff fits with a hook. Then haul out the head of the sail by the peak-earing, which is passed like the head-earing of a topsail. When the head-rope is taut, pass the lacings through the eyelet-holes, and round the jack-stay. Seize the bights of the throat and peak brails to the leach, at distances from the peak which will admit of the sail's being brailed up taut along the gaff, and reeve them through their blocks on the gaff, and at the jaws, on each side of the sail. The foot brail is seized to the leach just above the clew. Seize the luff of the sail to the hoops or hanks around the spanker mast, beginning with the upper hoop and hoisting the gaff as they are secured. The tack is hooked or seized to the boom or to the mast. Hook on the outhaul tackle. This is usually fitted with an eye round the boom, rove through a single block at the clew, and then through a sheave-hole in the boom.

Some spankers are bent with a peak outhaul; the head traversing on the jackstay of the gaff.

THE FORE AND MAIN SPENCERS are bent like the

spanker, except that they have no boom, the clew being hauled aft by a sheet, which is generally a gun-tackle purchase, hooked to an eye-bolt in the deck.

To UNBEND A COURSE.—Haul it up, cast off the robands, and make the buntlines fast round the sail. Ease the earings off together, and lower away by the buntlines and clew-garnets. At sea, the lee earing is cast off first, rousing in the lee body of the sail, and securing it by the earing to the buntlines.

To UNBEND A TOPSAIL.—Clew it up, cast off the robands, secure the buntlines round the sail, unhook the sheets, and unreeve the clewlines and reef-tackles; ease off the earings, and lower by the buntlines.

A *topgallantsail* is unbent in the same manner, and sent down by the buntlines. A *royal* is usually sent down with the yard.

To UNBEND A JIB.— Haul it down, cast off the hank seizings, and the tack-lashing, cast off and unreeve the downhaul and make it fast round the sail, and cast off the sheet-pennant lashings. Haul aboard by the downhaul, hoisting clear by the halyards.

The rules above given are for a vessel in port, with squared yards. If you are at sea and it is blowing fresh, and the topsail or course is reefed, to send it down, you must cast off a few robands and reef-points, and pass good stops around the sail; then secure the buntlines also around it, and cast off all the robands, reef-points, and reef-earings. Bend a line to the lee head-earing and let it go, haul the sail well up to windward, and make fast the lee earing to the buntlines. Get a hauling line to the deck, forward; ease off the weather earing, and lower away.

To bend a new topsail in a gale of wind, it has been found convenient to make the sail up with the reef-bands together, the points all being out fair, to pass several good stops round the sail, and send up as before. This will present less surface to the wind. One course may be sent up as the other goes down, by unbending the

PLATE V.

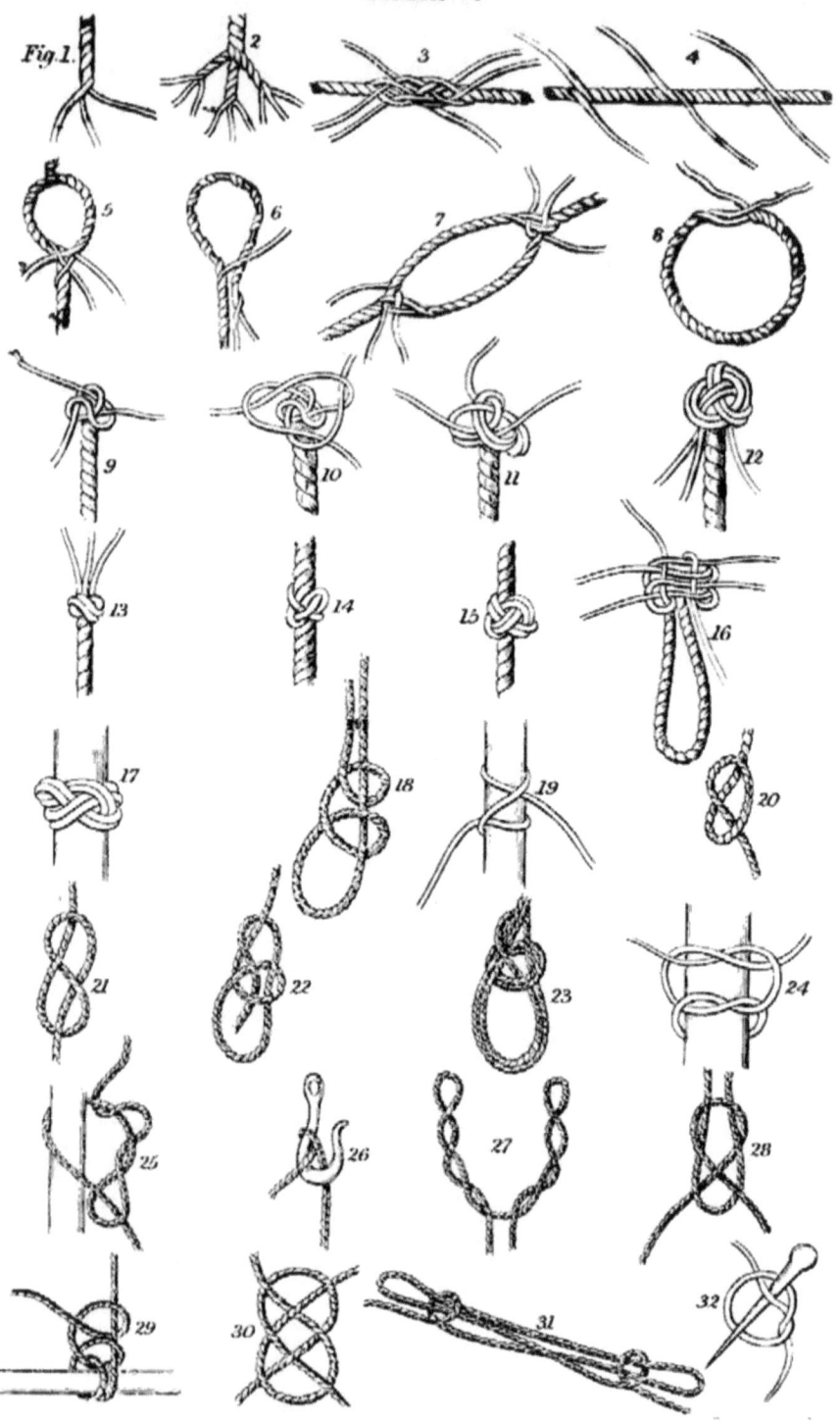

buntlines from the foot of the old sail, passing them down between the head of the sail and the yard, bending them to the foot of the new sail, and making the new sail up to be sent aloft by them, as before directed. Run the new sail up to the yard abaft the old one, and send the old one down by the leachlines and the head-earings, bent to the topmast studdingsail halyards, or some other convenient rope.

One topsail may be sent up by the topsail halyards, got ready for bending, and brought to the yard, while the old one is sent down by the buntlines.

CHAPTER VII.

WORK UPON RIGGING.—ROPE, KNOTS, SPLICES, BENDS AND HITCHES.

Kinds of rope. Spunyarn. Worming. Parcelling. Service. Short splice. Long splice. Eye splice. Flemish eye. Spindle eye. Cut splice. Grommet. Single and double wall. Matthew Walker. Single and double diamond. Spritsail sheet knot. Stopper knot. Shroud knot. French shroud knot. Buoy-rope knot. Half-hitches. Clove hitch. Overhand knot. Figure-of-eight. Bowline. Running bowline. Bowline-upon-a-bight. Square knot. Timber hitch. Rolling hitch. Blackwall hitch. Cat's paw. Sheet bend. Fisherman's bend. Carrick bend. Bowline bend. Sheep-shank. Selvagee. Marlinspike hitch. Round seizing. Throat seizing. Stopping. Nippering. Racking. Pointing. Snaking. Grafting. Foxes. Spanish foxes. Gaskets. Sennit. To bend a buoy-rope. To pass a shear-lashing.

THOSE ropes in a ship which are stationary are called *standing rigging*, as shrouds, stays, backstays, &c. Those which reeve through blocks or sheave-holes, and are hauled and let go, are called the *running rigging*, as braces, halyards, buntlines, clewlines, &c.

A rope is composed of threads of hemp, or other stuff. These threads are called *yarns*. A number of these yarns twisted together form a *strand*, and three or more strands twisted together form the rope.

The ropes in ordinary use on board a vessel are composed of three strands, laid RIGHT HANDED, (1.) or, as it is called, *with the sun.* Occasionally a piece of large rope will be found laid up in four strands, also *with* the sun. This is generally used for standing rigging, tacks, sheets, &c., and is sometimes called *shroud-laid.*

A CABLE-LAID ROPE (2.) is composed of nine strands, and is made by first laying them into three ropes of three strands each, *with* the sun, and then laying the three ropes up together into one, left-handed, or *against* the sun. Thus, cable-laid rope is like three small common ropes laid up into one large one. Formerly, the ordinary three-stranded right-hand rope was called *hawser-laid*, and the latter *cable-laid*, and they will be found so distinguished in the books; but among sea-faring men now, the terms *hawser-laid* and *cable-laid* are applied indiscriminately to nine-strand rope, and the three stranded, being the usual and ordinary kind of rope, has no particular name, or is called right-hand rope.

Right-hand rope must be coiled *with* the sun, and cable-laid rope *against* the sun.

SPUNYARN is made by twisting together two or more yarns taken from old standing rigging, and is called two-yarn or three-yarn spunyarn, according to the number of yarns of which it is composed. Junk, or old rigging, is first unlaid into strands, and then into yarns, and the best of these yarns made up into spunyarn, which is used for worming, serving, seizing, &c. Every merchant vessel carries a spunyarn-winch, for the manufacturing of this stuff, and in making it, the wheel is turned *against* the sun, which lays the stuff up with the sun.

WORMING a rope, is filling up the divisions between the strands, by passing spunyarn along them, to render the surface smooth for parcelling and serving.

PARCELLING a rope is wrapping narrow strips of canvas about it, well tarred, in order to secure it from being injured by rain-water lodging between the parts of the service when worn. The parcelling is put on *with* the lay of the rope.

SERVICE is the laying on of spunyarn, or other small stuff, in turns round the rope, close together, and hove taut by the use of a serving-board for small rope, and serving-mallet for large rope. Small ropes are sometimes served without being wormed, as the crevices between the strands are not large enough to make the surface very uneven; but a large rope is always wormed and parcelled before being served. The service is put on *against* the lay of the rope.

SPLICING, is putting the ends of ropes together by opening the strands and placing them into one another, or by putting the strands of the ends of a rope between those of the bight.

A SHORT SPLICE. (3.) Unlay the strands for a convenient length; then take an end in each hand, place them one within the other, and draw them close. Hold the end of one rope and the three strands which come from the opposite rope fast in the left hand, or, if the rope be large, stop them down to it with a rope-yarn. Take the middle strand, which is free, pass it *over* the strand which is first next to it, and through *under* the second, and out between the second and third from it, and haul it taut. Pass each of the six strands in the same manner; first those on one side, and then those on the other. The same operation may be repeated with each strand, passing each *over* the third from it, and *under* the fourth, and through; or, as is more usual, after the ends have been stuck once, untwist each strand, divide the yarns, pass one half as above described, and cut off the other half. This tapers the splice.

A LONG SPLICE. (4.) Unlay the ends of two ropes to a distance three or four times greater than for a short splice, and place them within one another as for a short splice. Unlay one strand for a considerable distance, and fill up the interval which it leaves with the opposite strand from the other rope, and twist the ends of these two together. Then do the same with two more strands. The two remaining strands are twisted together in the place where they were first crossed. Open the two last named strands, divide in two, take an overhand knot with the opposite halves, and lead the ends over the next strand and through the second, as the whole strands were passed for the short splice. Cut off the other two halves. Do the same with the others that are placed together, dividing, knotting, and passing them in the same manner. Before cutting off any of the half-strands, the rope should be got well upon a stretch. Sometimes the whole strands are knotted, then divided, and the half-strands passed as above described.

AN EYE SPLICE. (5.) Unlay the end of a rope for a short distance, and lay the three strands upon the standing part, so as to form an eye. Put one end through the strand next to it. Put the next end over that strand and through the second; and put the remaining end through the third strand, on the other side of the rope. Taper them, as in the short splice, by dividing the strands and sticking them again.

A FLEMISH EYE. (6.) Take the end of a rope and unlay one strand. Form an eye by placing the two remaining ends against the standing part. Pass the strand which has been unlaid over the end and in the intervals round the eye, until it returns down the standing part, and lies under the eye with the strands. The ends are then scraped down, tapered, marled, and served over with spunyarn.

AN ARTIFICIAL OR SPINDLE EYE.—Unlay the end of a rope and open the strands, separating each ropeyarn. Take a piece of wood, the size of the intended eye, and hitch the yarns round it. Scrape them down, marl, parcel, and serve them. This is now usually called a FLEMISH EYE.

A CUT SPLICE. (7.) Cut a rope in two, unlay each end as for a short splice, and place the ends of each rope against the standing part of the other, forming an oblong eye, of the size you wish. Then pass the ends through the strands of the standing parts, as for a short splice.

A Grommet. (8.) Take a strand just unlaid from a rope, with all its turns in it, and form a ring of the size you wish, by putting the end over the standing part. Then take the long end and carry it twice round the ring, in the crevices, following the lay, until the ring is complete. Then take an overhand knot with the two ends, divide the yarns, and stick them as in a long splice.

A single Wall Knot. (9.) Unlay the end of a rope. Form a bight with one strand, holding its end down to the standing part in your left hand. Pass the end of the next strand round this strand. Pass the remaining strand round the end of the second strand, and up through the bight which was made by the first strand. Haul the ends taut carefully, one by one.

A single Wall, crowned. (10.) Make the single wall as before, and lay one end over the top of the knot. Lay the second end over the first, and the third over the second and through the bight of the first.

A double Wall. (11.) Make the single wall slack, and crown it, as above. Then take one end, bring it underneath the part of the first walling next to it, and push it up through the same bight. Do the same with the other strands, pushing them up through two bights. Thus made, it has a double wall and a single crown.

A double Wall, double crowned. (12.) Make the double wall, single crowned, as above. Then lay the strands by the sides of those in the single crown, pushing them through the same bight in the single crown, and down through the double walling. This is sometimes called a Tack Knot, or a Topsail Sheet Knot.

A Matthew Walker Knot. (13.) Unlay the end of a rope. Take one strand round the rope and through its own bight; then the next strand underneath, through the bight of the first, and through its own bight; and the third strand underneath, through both the other bights, and through its own bight.

A Single Diamond Knot (14.) Unlay the end of a rope for a considerable distance, and with the strands form three bights down the side of the rope, holding them fast with the left hand. Take the end of one strand, and pass it with the lay of the rope over the strand next to it, and up through the bight of the third. Take the end of the second strand over the third and up through the bight of the first. Take the end of the third strand over the first and up through the bight of the second. Haul taut, and lay the ends up together.

A DOUBLE DIAMOND KNOT. (15.) Make a single diamond, as above, without laying the ends up. Follow the lead of the single knot through two single bights, the ends coming out at the top of the knot. Lead the last strand through two double bights. Haul taut, and lay the ends up.

A SPRITSAIL SHEET KNOT. (16.) Unlay two ends of a rope, and place the two parts together. Make a bight with one strand. Wall the six strands together, like a single walling made with three strands; putting the second over the first, and the third over the second, and so on, the sixth being passed over the fifth and through the bight of the first. Then haul taut. It may be *crowned* by taking two strands, and laying them over the top of the knot, and passing the other strands alternately over and under those two, hauling them taut. It may be *double walled* by next passing the strands under the walling on the left of them, and through the small bights, when the ends will come up for the second crowning; which is done by following the lead of the single crowning, and pushing the ends through the single walling, as with three strands, before described. This is often used for a *stopper knot*.

A STOPPER KNOT.—Single wall and double wall, without crowning, and stop the ends together.

A SHROUD KNOT.—Unlay the ends of two ropes, and place the strands in one another, as for a short splice. Single wall the strands of one rope round the standing part of the other, against the lay. Open the ends, taper, marl, and serve them.

A French Shroud Knot.—Place the ends of two ropes as before. Lay the ends of one rope back upon their own part, and single wall the other three strands round the bights of the first three and the standing part. Taper the ends, as before.

A Buoy-rope Knot.—Unlay the strands of a cable-laid rope, and also the small strands of each large strand. Lay the large ones again as before, leaving the small ones out. Single and double wall the small strands (as for a stopper knot) round the rope, worm them along the divisions, and stop their ends with spunyarn.

A Turks-head. (17.) This is worked upon a rope with a piece of small line. Take a clove-hitch slack with the line round the rope. Then take one of the bights formed by the clove-hitch and put it over the other. Pass the end under, and up through the bight which is underneath. Then cross the bights again, and put the end round again, under, and up through the bight which is underneath. After this, follow the lead, and it will make a turban, of three parts to each cross.

Two Half-hitches. (18.) Pass the end of a rope round the standing part and bring it up through the bight. This is a half-hitch. Take it round again in the same manner for two half-hitches.

A Clove-hitch (19.) is made by passing the end of a rope round a spar, over, and bringing it under and round behind its standing part, over the spar again, and up through its own part. It may then, if necessary, be stopped or hitched to its own part: the only difference between two half-hitches and a clove-hitch being that one is hitched round its own standing part, and the other is hitched round a spar or another rope.

An Overhand Knot. (20.) Pass the end of a rope over the standing part, and through the bight.

A Figure-of-eight. (21.) Pass the end of a rope over and round the standing part, up over its own part, and down through the bight.

A BOWLINE KNOT. (22.) Take the end of a rope in your right hand, and the standing part in your left. Lay the end over the standing part, and with the left hand make a bight of the standing part over it. Take the end under the lower standing part, up over the cross, and down through the bight.

A RUNNING BOWLINE.—Take the end round the standing part, and make a bowline upon its own part.

A BOWLINE UPON A BIGHT. (23.) Middle a rope, taking the two ends in your left hand, and the bight in your right. Lay the bight over the ends, and proceed as in making a bowline, making a small bight with your left hand of the ends, which are kept together, over the bight which you hold in your right hand. Pass the bight in your right hand round under the ends and up over the cross. So far, it is like a common bowline, only made with double rope instead of single. Then open the bight in your right hand and carry it over the large bights, letting them go through it, and bring it up to the cross and haul taut.

A SQUARE KNOT. (24.) Take an overhand knot round a spar. Take an end in each hand and cross them on the same side of the standing part upon which they came up. Pass one end round the other, and bring it up through the bight. This is sometimes called a REEF-KNOT. If the ends are crossed the wrong way, sailors call it a GRANNY-KNOT.

A TIMBER HITCH. (25.) Take the end of a rope round a spar, lead it under and over the standing part, and pass two or more round-turns round its own part.

A ROLLING HITCH.—Pass the end of a rope round a spar. Take it round a second time, nearer to the standing part. Then carry it across the standing part, over and round the spar, and up through the bight. A strap or a tail-block is fastened to a rope by this hitch.

A bend, sometimes called a *rolling hitch*, is made by two round-turns round a spar and two half-hitches round the standing part; but the name is commonly applied to the former hitch.

A BLACKWALL HITCH. (26.) Form a bight by putting the end of a rope across and under the standing part. Put the bight over the hook of a tackle, letting the hook go through it, the centre of the bight resting against the back of the hook, and the end jammed in the bight of the hook, by the standing part of the rope.

A CAT'S PAW. (27.) Make a large bight in a rope, and spread it open, putting one hand at one part of the bight and the other at the other, and letting the standing part and end come together. Turn the bight over from you, three times, and a small bight will be formed in each hand. Bring the two small bights together, and put the hook of a tackle through them both.

A SHEET BEND. (28.) Pass the end of a rope up through the bight of another, round both parts of the other, and under its own part.

A FISHERMAN'S BEND. (29.) Used for bending studdingsail halyards to the yard. Take two turns round the yard with the end. Hitch it round the standing part and both the turns. Then hitch it round the standing part alone.

A CARRICK BEND. (30.) Form a bight by putting the end of a rope over its standing part. Take the end of a second rope and pass it *under* the standing part of the first, *over* the end, and *up* through the bight, *over* its own standing part, and *down* through the bight again.

A BOWLINE BEND.—This is the most usual mode of bending warps, and other long ropes or cables, together. Take a bowline in the end of one rope, pass the end of the other through the bight, and take a bowline with it upon its own standing part. Long lines are sometimes bent together with half-hitches on their own standing parts, instead of bowlines, and the end seized strongly down.

A Sheep-shank. (31.) Make two long bights in a rope, which shall overlay one another. Take a half-hitch over the end of each bight with the standing part which is next to it.

A Selvagee.—Lay rope yarns round and round in a bight, and marl them down with spunyarn. These are used for neat block-straps, and as straps to go round a spar for a tackle to hook into, for hoisting.

A Marlinspike Hitch.—Lay the marlinspike upon the seizing-stuff, and bring the end over the standing parts so as to form a bight. Lay this bight back over the standing part, putting the marlinspike down through the bight, under the standing part, and up through the bight again.

To pass a Round Seizing.—Splice a small eye in the end of the stuff, take the other end round both parts of the rope, and reeve it through the eye. Pass a couple of turns, then take a marlinspike-hitch, and heave them taut. Pass six, eight, or ten turns in the same manner, and heave them taut. Put the end through under these turns and bring it out between the two last turns, or through the eye, and pass five, seven, or nine turns (one less than the lower ones) directly over these, as riders. The riders are not hove so taut. Pass the end up through the seizings, and take two cross turns round the whole seizing between the two, passing the end through the last turn, and heaving taut. If the seizing is small cordage, take a wall-knot in the end; if spunyarn, an overhand knot. The cross turns are given up now in nearly all vessels. After the riding turns are passed, the end is carried under the turns, brought out at the other end, and made fast snugly to the standing part of the rigging.

A Throat Seizing, where rigging is turned in, is passed and made fast like the preceding, there being no cross turns. A neat way to pass a throat seizing is to pass the turns rather slack, put a strap upon the end of the rigging, take a handspike or heaver to it and bear it down, driving home the seizing with a mallet and small fid.

Stopping, is fastening two parts of a rope together as for a round seizing, without a crossing.

Nippering, is fastening them by taking turns crosswise between the parts, to jam them; and sometimes with a round turn before each cross. These are called *racking turns*. Pass *riders* over these and fasten the end.

Pointing.—Unlay the end of a rope and stop it. Take out as many yarns as are necessary, and split each yarn in two, and take two parts of different yarns and twist them up taut into *nettles*. The rest of the yarns are combed down with a knife. Lay half the nettles down upon the scraped part, the rest back upon the rope, and pass three turns of twine taut round the part where the nettles separate, and hitch the twine, which is called the *warp*. Lay the nettles backwards and forwards as before, passing the warp, each time. The ends may be whipped and snaked with twine, or the nettles hitched over the warp and hauled taut. The upper seizing must be snaked. If the upper part is too weak for pointing, put in a piece of stick.

Snaking a seizing, is done by taking the end under and over the outer turns of the seizing alternately, passing over the whole. There should be a marline-hitch at each turn.

Grafting.—Unlay the ends of two ropes and put them together as for a short splice. Make nettles of the strands as before. Pass the warp and nettles belonging to the lower strands along the rope, as in pointing; then the nettles of the upper strands in the same manner. Snake the seizing at each end.

Foxes are made by twisting together three or more rope-yarns by hand, and rubbing them hard with tarred canvas. *Spanish foxes* are made of one rope-yarn, by unlaying it and laying it up the other way.

Gaskets.—Take three or four foxes, middle them, and plait them together into *sennit*. This is done by bringing the two outside foxes alternately over to the middle. The outside ones are laid with the right hand, and the remainder are held and steadied with the left. Having plaited enough for an eye, bring all the parts together, and work them all into one piece, in the same manner. Take out foxes at proper intervals. When finished, one end must be laid up, the other plaited, and the first hauled through. The name *sennit* is generally given to rope-yarns plaited in the same manner with these foxes. Sennit made in this way must have an odd number of parts. FRENCH SENNIT is made with an even number, taken over and under every other time.

TO BEND A BUOY-ROPE. Reeve the end through the eye in the other end, put it over one arm of the anchor, and haul taut. Take a hitch over the other arm. Or, take a clove-hitch over the crown, stopping the end to its own part, or to the shank.

TO PASS A SHEAR-LASHING.—Middle the lashing and take a good turn round both legs, at the cross. Pass one end up and the other down, around and over the cross, until half of the lashing is expanded. Then ride both ends back again on their own parts and knot them in the middle. Frap the first and riding turns together on each side with sennit.

CHAPTER VIII.

BLOCKS AND PURCHASES.

Parts of a block. Made and morticed blocks. Bull's-eye. Dead-eye. Sister-block. Snatch-block. Tail-block. Whip. Gun-tackle. Luff-tackle. Whip-upon-whip. Luff-upon-luff. Watch or tail-tackle. Runner-tackle.

BLOCKS are of two kinds, *made* and *morticed*. A *made block* consists of four parts,—the *shell*, or outside; the *sheave*, or wheel on which the rope turns; the *pin*, or axle on which the wheel turns; and the *strap*, either of rope or iron, which encircles the whole, and keeps it in its place. The sheave is generally strengthened by letting in a piece of iron or brass at the centre, called a *bush*.

A MORTICED BLOCK is made of a single block of wood, morticed out to receive a sheave.

All blocks are single, double, or three-fold, according to the number of sheaves in them.

There are some blocks that have no sheaves; as follows : a *bull's-eye*, which is a wooden thimble without a sheave, having a hole through the centre and a groove round it ; and a *dead-eye*, which is a solid block of wood made in a circular form, with a groove round it, and three holes bored through it, for the lanyards to reeve through.

A SISTER-BLOCK is formed of one solid piece of wood, with two sheaves, one above the other, and between the sheaves a score for the middle seizing. These are oftener without sheaves than with.

SNATCH-BLOCKS are single blocks, with a notch cut in one cheek, just below the sheave, so as to receive the bight of a fall, without the trouble of reeving and unreeving the whole. They are generally iron-bound, and have a hook at one end.

A TAIL-BLOCK is a single block, strapped with an eye-splice, and having a long end left, by which to make the block fast temporarily to the rigging. This tail is usually selvageed, or else the strands are opened and laid up into sennet, as for a gasket.

A TACKLE is a purchase formed by reeving a rope through two or more blocks, for the purpose of hoisting.

A WHIP is the smallest purchase, and is made by a rope rove through one single block.

A GUN-TACKLE PURCHASE is a rope rove through two single blocks and made fast to the strap of the upper block. The parts of all tackles between the fasts and a sheave, are called the *standing parts ;* the parts between sheaves are called *running parts ;* and the part upon which you take hold in hoisting is called the *fall*.

A WHIP-UPON-WHIP is where the block of one whip is made fast to the fall of another.

A LUFF-TACKLE PURCHASE is a single and a double block; the end of the rope being fast to the upper part of the single block, and the fall coming from the double block. A luff-tackle upon the fall of another luff-tackle is called *luff-upon-luff*.

A WATCH-TACKLE or TAIL-TACKLE is a luff-tackle purchase, with a hook in the end of the single block, and a tail to the upper end of the double block. One of these purchases, with a short fall, is kept on deck, at hand, in merchant vessels, and is used to clap upon standing and running rigging, and to get a strain upon ropes.

A RUNNER-TACKLE is a luff applied to a runner, which is a single rope rove through a single block, hooked to a thimble in the eye of a pennant.

A SINGLE BURTON is composed of two single blocks, with a hook in the bight of the running part. Reeve the end of your rope through the upper block, and make it fast to the strap of the fly-block. Then make fast your hook to the bight of the rope, and reeve the other end through the fly-block for a fall. The hook is made fast by passing the bight of the rope through the eye of the hook and over the whole.

CHAPTER IX.

MAKING AND TAKING IN SAIL.

To loose a sail. To set a course—Topsail—Topgallant sail—Royal—Skysail—Jib—Spanker—Spencer. To take in a course—Topsail—Topgallant sail or royal—Skysail—Jib—Spanker. To furl a royal—Topgallant sail—Topsail—Course—Jib. To stow a jib in cloth. To reef a topsail—Course. To turn out reefs. To set a topgallant studdingsail. To take in the same. To set a topmast studdingsail. To take in the same To set a lower studdingsail. To take in the same.

TO LOOSE A SAIL.—Lay out to the yard-arms and cast off the gaskets, beginning at the outermost and coming in. When the gaskets are cast off from both yard-arms, then let go the bunt gasket, (and jigger if there be one,) and overhaul the buntlines and leachlines. In loosing a topsail in a gale of wind, it is better to cast off the quarter-gaskets, (except the one which confines the clew,) before those at the yard-arms. Royals and top-gallant sails generally have one long gasket to each yard-arm; in which case it is not necessary to go out upon the yard, but the gaskets, after being cast off, should be fastened to the tye by a bowline.

To set a Course.—Loose the sail and overhaul the buntlines and leachlines. Let go the clew-garnets and overhaul them, and haul down on the sheets and tacks. If the ship is close-hauled, ease off the lee brace, slack the weather lift and clew-garnet, and get the tack well down to the water-ways. If it is blowing fresh and the ship light-handed, take it to the windlass. When the tack is well down, sharpen the yard up again by the brace, top it well up by the lift, reeve and haul out the bowline, and haul the sheet aft.

If the wind is quartering, the mainsail is carried with the weather clew hauled up and the sheet taken aft. With yards squared, the mainsail is never carried, but the foresail may be to advantage, especially if the swinging booms are out; in which case the heavy tack and sheet-blocks may be unhooked, and the *lazy sheets* hooked on and rove through a single tail block, made fast out on the boom. This serves to extend the clews, and is called a *pazaree* to the foresail.

To set a Topsail. Loose the sail, and keep one hand in the top to overhaul the rigging. Overhaul well the buntlines, clewlines, and reef-tackles, let go the topgallant sheets and topsail braces, and haul home on the sheets. Merchant vessels usually hoist a little on the halyards, so as to clear the sail from the top, then belay them and get the lee-sheet chock home; then haul home the weather sheet, shivering the sail by the braces, to help it home, and hoist on the halyards until the leaches are well taut, taking a turn with the braces, if the wind is fresh, and slacking them as the yard goes up.

After the sail is set, it is sometimes necessary to get the sheets closer home. Slack the halyards, lee brace, and weather bowline, clap the watch tackle upon the lee sheet first, and then the weather one, shivering the sail by the braces if necessary. Overhaul the clewlines and reef-tackles, slack the topgallant sheets, and hoist the sail up, taut leach, by the halyards.

To set a Topgallant Sail or Royal.—Haul home the lee sheet, having one hand aloft to overhaul the clew-lines, then the weather sheet, and hoist up, taut leech, by the halyards. While hauling the sheets home, if on the wind, brace up a little to shake the sail, take a turn with the weather brace, and let go the lee one; if before the wind, let go both braces; and if the wind is quartering, the lee one.

To set a Flying Skysail.—If bent in the manner described in this book, let go the brails and royal stay, and hoist on the halyards.

To set a Jib, Flying-Jib, or Fore Topmast Stay-sail.—Cast off the gasket, hoist on the halyards, and trim down the sheet.

To set a Spanker.—Hoist on the topping lifts, make fast the weather one, and overhaul the lee one. Let go the brails, and haul out on the outhaul. Be careful not to let the throat brail go before the head and foot. Trim the boom by the sheets and guys, and the gaff by the vangs.

To set a Spencer.—Take the sheet to the deck on the lee side of the stay, let go the brails, haul on the sheet, and trim the gaff by the vangs.

To take in a Course.—If the wind is light and there are hands enough, let go the tack, sheet, and bow-line, and haul up on the clew-garnets, buntlines, and leachlines, being careful not to haul the buntlines taut until the clews are well up. If light-handed, or the wind fresh, let go the bowline and ease off the tack, (being careful to let the bowline go before the tack,) and haul up the weather clew. Then ease off the sheet and haul up on the lee clew-garnet, and the buntlines and leachlines.

TO TAKE IN A TOPSAIL.—The usual mode of taking in a topsail when coming to anchor in light winds, is to lower away on the halyards and haul down on the clewlines and reef-tackles, (if the latter, run in the way described in this book,) until the yard is down by the lifts, rounding in on the weather brace, and hauling taut to leeward, when the yard is square. Then let go the sheets and haul up on the clewlines and buntlines. A better way is to start the sheets, clew about one-third up, then let go the halyards and take the slack in.

If the wind is fresh, and the yard braced up, lower away handsomely on the halyards, get the yard down by the clewlines and reef-tackles, rounding in on the weather brace, and steadying the yard by both braces. Then let go the weather sheet and haul up to windward first. The weather clew being up, let go the lee sheet and haul up by the clewline and buntlines, keeping the clew in advance of the body of the sail.

Sometimes, if the weather brace cannot be well rounded in, as if a ship is weak-handed, the sail may be clewed up to leeward a little, first. In which case, ease off the lee sheet, and haul up on the clewline; ease off the lee brace and round the yard in; and when the lee clew is about half up, ease off the weather sheet and haul the weather clew chock up. Haul the buntlines up after the weather clew, and steady the yard by the braces. There is danger in clewing up to leeward first that the sail may be shaken and jerked so as to split, before the weather clew is up; whereas, if clewed up to windward first, the lee clew will keep full, until the lee sheet is started.

When coming to anchor, it is the best plan to haul the clews about half up before the halyards are let go.

In taking in a close-reefed topsail in a gale of wind, the most general practice is to clew up to windward, keeping the sail full; then lower away the halyards, and ease off the lee sheet; clew the yard down, and haul up briskly on the lee clewline and the buntlines, bracing aback the moment the lee sheet is started.

To take in a Topgallant Sail or Royal.—If the wind is light, and from aft or quartering, let go the halyards and clew down, squaring the yard by the braces. Then start the sheets and clew up, and haul up the buntlines. If the yard is braced up, the old style was to let go the halyards, clew down and round in on the weather brace; clewing up to windward first, then start the lee clew, and haul up the lee clewline and the buntlines. But the practice now is to clew up to leeward first, which prevents the slack of the sail getting too much over to leeward, or foul of the clewline block under the yard, as it is apt to, if the weather clew is hauled up first.

If the wind is very fresh, and the vessel close-hauled, a good practice is to let go the lee sheet and halyards, and clew down, rounding in at the same time on the weather brace. Then start the weather sheet, and haul the weather clew chock up. Haul up the buntlines, and steady the yard by the braces.

To take in a Skysail.—If bent in the way described in this book, which is believed to be the most convenient, let go the halyards, haul down on the brails, and haul taut the royal stay.

To take in a Jib.—Let go the halyards, haul on the downhaul, easing off the sheet as the halyards are let go.

To take in a Spanker.—Ease off the outhaul, and haul well up on the lee brails, taking in the slack of the weather ones. Mind particularly the lee throat-brail. Haul the boom amid-ships, and steady it by the guys, lower the topping lifts, and square the gaff by the vangs.

To furl a Royal.—This sail is usually furled by one person, and is that upon which green hands are practised. For the benefit of beginners, I will give particular directions. When you have got aloft to the topgallant mast-head, see, in the first place, that the yard is well down by the lifts, and steadied by the braces; then see that both clews are hauled chock up to the blocks, and if they are not, call out to the officer of the deck, and have it done. Then see your yard-arm gaskets clear. The best way is to cast them off from the tye, and lay them across between the tye and the mast. This done, stretch out on the weather yard-arm, get hold of the weather leach, and bring it in to the slings taut along the yard. Hold the clew up with one hand, and with the other haul all the sail through the clew, letting it fall in the bunt. Bring the weather clew a little over abaft the yard, and put your knee upon it. Then stretch out to leeward, and bring in the lee leach in the same manner, hauling all the sail through the clew, and putting the clew upon the yard in the same way, and holding it there by your other knee. Then prepare to make up your bunt. First get hold of the foot-rope, and lay it on the yard and abaft; then take up the body of the sail, and lay it on the yard, seeing that it is all fairly through the clews. Having got all the sail upon the yard, make a *skin* of the upper part of the body of the sail, large enough to come well down abaft and cover the whole bunt when the sail is furled. Lift the skin up, and put into the bunt the slack of the clews (not too taut), the leach and foot-rope, and the body of the sail; being careful not to let it get forward under the yard, or hang down abaft. Then haul your bunt well upon the yard, smoothing the skin, and bringing it down well abaft, and make fast the bunt-gasket round the mast, and the jigger, if there be one, to the tye. The glut will always come in the middle of the bunt, if it is properly made up. Now take your weather yard-arm gasket and pass it round the yard three or four times, haul taut, and make it fast to the mast; then the lee one in the same manner. Never make a long gasket fast to its own part round the yard, for it may work loose, and slip out to the yard-arm. Always pass a gasket *over* the yard and down abaft, which will help to bring the sail upon the yard.

A Topgallant Sail is furled in the same manner, except that it usually requires two men, in a large vessel; in which case, each man takes a yard-arm, and they make the bunt up together. If there are buntlines and a jigger, the bunt may be triced well up, by bending the jigger to the bight of a buntline, and having it hauled taut on deck.

To furl a Topsail or Course.—The sail being hauled up, lay out on the yard, the two most experienced men standing in the slings, one on each side the mast, to make the bunt up. The light hands lay out to the yard-arms, and take the leach up and bring it taut along the yard. In this way the clews are reached and handed to the men in the bunt, and the slack of the sail hauled through them and stowed away on and abaft the yard. The bunt being made up fairly on the yard against the mast, and the skin prepared, let it fall a little forward, and stow all the body of the sail, the clews, bolt-rope, and blocks, away in it; then, as many as can get hold, lend a hand to haul it well upon the yard. Overhaul a buntline a little, bend the jigger to it, and trice up on deck. Bring the skin down well abaft, see that the clews are not too taut, pass the bunt gasket, cast the jigger off, and make it fast slack to the tye. Then pass the yard-arm gaskets, hauling the sail well upon the yard, and passing the turns over the yard, and down abaft. If the sail has long gaskets, make them fast to the tye; if short, pass them in turns close together, and make them fast to their own parts, jammed as well as possible.

To Furl a Jib.—Go out upon the weather side of the boom. See your gasket clear for passing. The handiest way usually is, to make it up on its end, take a hitch over the whole with the standing part, and let it hang. Haul the sail well upon the boom, getting the clew, and having the sheet pennant hauled amidships. Cast the hitch off the gasket, take it in your hand, and pass two or three turns, beginning at the head; haul them taut; and so on to the clew. Pass the turns over and to windward. This will help to bring the sail upon the yard and to windward. Make the end fast to the stay, to the withe, or to the boom inside the cap, in any way that shall keep it from slipping back, which it might do if made fast to its own part round the boom. If there is but one hand on the boom, the first turns may be hauled taut enough to keep the sail up for the time; then, after the gasket is fast, go out to the head, and haul each turn well taut, beating the sail down with the hand. Be careful to confine the clew well.

To stow a Jib in Cloth.—Haul the jib down snugly, and get it fairly up on the boom. Overhaul the after leach until you come to the first straight cloth. Gather this cloth over the rest of the sail on the boom, stopping the outer end of the cloth with a rope-yarn round the jib stay. If the jib halyards are double, stop the block inside the sail. Cover the sail well up with the cloth, stopping it at every two feet with the rope-yarns round the sail and boom. If you are to lie in port for a long time, cast off the pennant, stow the clew on the boom, snugly under the cloth, which will be stopped as before with ropeyarns.

To reef a Topsail.—Round in on the weather-brace, ease off the halyards, and clew the yard down by the clewlines and reef-tackles. Brace the yard in nearly to the wind, and haul taut both braces. Haul out the reef-tackles, make fast, and haul taut the buntlines. Before going upon the yard, see that it is well down by the lifts. Let the best men go to the yardarms, and the light hands remain in the slings. Cast adrift the weather earing, pass it *over* the yard-arm outside the lift, down abaft and under the yard, and *up* through the reef-cringle. Haul well out, and take a round-turn with the earing round the cringle. Then pass several turns round the yard and through the cringle, hauling them well taut, passing the turns *over* the yard, down abaft and under, and *up* through the cringle. Having expended nearly all the earing, hitch the remainder round the two first parts, that go outside the lift, jamming them together and passing several turns round them both to expend the rope. The bare end may be hitched to these two parts or to the lift. The men on the yard light the sail out to windward by the reef-points, to help the man at the weather yard-arm in hauling out his earing. As soon as the weather earing is hauled out and made secure by a turn or two, the word is passed—" Haul out to leeward," and the lee earing is hauled out till the band is taut along the yard, and made fast in the same manner. Then the men on the yard tie the reef points with square knots, being careful to take the after points clear of the topgallant sheets.

In reefing, a good deal depends upon the way in which the yard is laid. If the yard is braced too much in, the sail catches flat aback and cannot be hauled out, besides the danger of knocking the men off the foot-ropes. The best way is to shiver the sail well till the yard is down, then brace it in with a slight full, make the braces fast, and luff up occasionally and shake the sail while the men are reefing. If you are going before the wind, you may, by putting your helm either way, and bringing the wind abeam, clew the yard down as the sail lifts, and keep her in this position, with the yard braced sharp up, until the sail is reefed; or, if you are not willing to keep off from your course, and the wind is very fresh, clew down and clew up, and reef as before directed.

All the reefs are taken in the same way except the *close reef*. In close reefing, pass your earing *under* the yard, up abaft and over, and *down* through the cringle. Pass all your turns in the same manner; and bring the reef-band well under the yard in knotting, so as to cover the other reefs.

As soon as the men are off the yard, let go the reef-tackles, clewlines, buntlines, and topgallant sheets; man the halyards, let go the lee brace, slack off the weather one, and hoist away. When well up, trim the yard by the braces, and haul out the bowlines. A reefed sail should never be braced quite sharp up, and if there is a heavy sea and the vessel pitches badly, ease the braces a little, that the yard may play freely, and do not haul the leach too taut.

To REEF A COURSE.—As a course generally has no reef-tackle, you must clew it up as for furling, according to the directions before given, except that the clews are not hauled chock up. Lay out on the yard and haul out the earings, and knot the points as for the first reef of a topsail, seeing them clear of the topsail sheets. If a long course of bad weather is anticipated, as in doubling the southern capes, or crossing the Atlantic in winter, reef-tackles are rove for the courses.

If there are any studdingsail booms on the lower or topsail yards, they must be triced up before reefing.

To TURN OUT REEFS.—For a topsail, haul taut the reef-tackles and buntlines, settle a little on the halyards, if necessary; lay aloft, and cast off all the reef-points, beginning at the bunt and laying out. Be careful to cast all off before slacking up the earing; for, when there is more than one reef, a point may be easily left, if care is not taken. Have one hand at each earing, cast off all the turns but enough to hold it, and when both earings are ready, ease off both together. Pass the end of the earing through the cringle next above its own, and make it fast slack to its own part by a bowline knot. Lay in off the yard, let go reef-tackles, clewlines, buntlines, and topgallant sheets; overhaul them in the top and hoist away, slacking the braces and trimming the yard. The reefs of a course are turned out a good deal in the same manner; slacking up the sheet and tack, if necessary, and, when the earings are cast off, let go clew-garnets, buntlines and leachlines, board the tack, and haul aft the sheet.

To set a Topgallant Studdingsail.—This sail is always set from the top; the sail, together with the tack and halyards in two coils, being kept in the top. If there is but one hand aloft, take the end of the halyards aloft, *abaft* everything, and reeve it *up* through the block at the topgallant mast-head, and *down* through the sheave-hole or block at the topgallant yardarm, *abaft* the sheet, and bring it into the top, forward of the rigging, and make it fast to the forward shroud. Take the end of your tack out on the topsail yard, *under* the brace, reeve it *up* through the block at the end of the topgallant studdingsail boom, bring it in *over* the brace, overhauling a plenty of it so as to let the boom go out, and hitch it to the topmast rigging while you rig your boom out. Cast off the heel-lashing and rig your boom out to the mark, slue the boom with the block up and make fast round the yard. (The easiest way of passing the boom-lashing is to take it over the yard and put a bight up between the head rope and yard; then take the end back over the yard and boom and through the bight, and haul taut. This may be done twice, if necessary, and then hitch it round all parts, between the boom and the yard.) The boom being rigged out and fast, take the end of your tack down into the top and hitch it to the forward shroud. Then take the coil of the tack and throw the other end down on deck, outside of the rigging and backstays. (It is well, in throwing the coil down, to keep hold of the bight with one hand; for otherwise, if they should miss it on deck, you will have to rig in your boom.) Throw down the hauling end of your halyards abaft and inside everything. Now get your sail clear for sending out. Lay the yard across the top, forward of the rigging, with the outer end out. Bend your halyards to the yard by a fisherman's bend, about one-third of the way out. Take your tack under the yard and bend it by a sheet-bend to the outer clew, and pay down the sheet and downhaul through the lubber-hole. All being clear for hoisting, sway away on the halyards on deck, the men in the top guying the sail by the sheet and downhaul, the latter being hauled taut enough to keep the outer clew up to the inner yard-arm. (Sometimes it is well to make up the downhaul, as is done with the downhaul of the topmast studdingsail.) When the sail is above the brace, haul out on the tack, sway the yard, chock up by the halyards, and trim the sheet down. Make the end of the downhaul fast slack.

A weather topgallant or topmast studdingsail should be set abaft the sail, and a lee one forward of the sail. Therefore, in setting a lee topgallant studdingsail, it is well to send it out of the top with a turn in it, that is, with the inner yard-arm slued forward and out, so that when the tack and sheet are hauled upon, the inner yard-arm will swing forward of the topgallant sail.

Small-sized vessels have no downhaul to the topgallant studdingsails. This saves confusion, and is very well if the sail is small.

TO TAKE IN A TOPGALLANT STUDDINGSAIL.—Let go the tack and clew up the downhaul, dipping the yard abaft the leach of the topgallant sail, if it is forward. Lower away handsomely on the halyards, hauling down on the sheet and downhaul. When the yard is below the topsail brace, lower roundly and haul into the top, forward of the rigging.

If the sail is taken in temporarily, stand the yard up and down, and becket it to the middle topmast shroud; make the sail up, hitch the bight of the tack and halyards to the forward shroud, and haul up the sheet and downhaul. If everything is to be stowed away, unreeve the tack and halyards, and coil them away separately in the top; also coil away the sheets and downhaul, and stop all the coils down by hitches passed through the slats of the top. Rig the boom in and make it fast to the tye. Sometimes the halyards are unrove from the yard-arm and rounded up to the span-block, with a knot in their end.

TO SET A TOPMAST STUDDINGSAIL.—The topmast studdingsail halyards are generally kept coiled away in the top. Take the end up, reeve it *up* through the span-block at the cap, and *out* through the block at the topsail yard-arm, and pay the end down to the forecastle, forward of the yard and outside the bowline. Pay the hauling end down through the lubber-hole. Reeve your lower halyards. These are usually kept coiled away in the top, with the pennant, which hooks to the cap of the lower mast. Hook the pennant, reeve the halyards *up* through the pennant block, *out* through the block on the boom-end, and pay the end down to the forecastle. Pay the hauling end down *forward* of the top. (Some vessels keep their topmast studdingsail tacks coiled away at the yard-arm, and hitched down to the boom and yard. This is a clumsy practice, and saves no time or trouble. The best way is to unreeve them whenever the boom is to be rigged in, and coil them away in the bow of the long-boat, or elsewhere. There is no more trouble, and less liability to confusion, in reeving them afresh, than in coiling them away and clearing again on the yard-arms.) Carry your tack outside the backstays and lower rigging, clear of everything, out upon the lower yard under the brace; reeve it *forward* through the tack-block at the boom-end, first sluing the block up, and pay the end down forward of the yard. Rig the boom out to the mark and lash it. Get the studdingsail on the forecastle clear for setting. Bend the halyards to the yard, about one half of the way out. Hitch the end of the downhaul over the inner yard-arm by the eye in its end, reeve it through the lizard on the outer leach, and through the block at the outer clew abaft the sail. Bend the tack to the outer clew, and take a turn with the sheet. Clew the yard down by the downhaul, and make the downhaul up just clear of the block, by a catspaw doubled and the bight of the running part shoved through the bight of all the parts, so that hauling on it may clear it and let the yard go up. Hoist on the halyards until the sail is above the lower yard, guying it by the sheet and downhaul, then haul out on the tack until the clew is chock out to the boom-end, hoist on the halyards, jerking the downhaul clear, and trim down the sheet.

To take in a Topmast Studdingsail.—Lower away handsomely on the halyards, clewing the yard down to the outer clew by the downhaul. Slack up the tack, and lower away on the halyards, hauling down well on the sheet and downhaul, till the sail is in upon the forecastle. The sail may be made up on the forecastle, and the end of the tack and halyards made fast forward, if it is to be soon set again. If not, cast off all, unreeve your tack, hauling from aft, and coil it away. Unreeve the halyards, or round them up to the block at the masthead with a knot in their end. Rig the boom in, and lash it to the slings.

To set a lower Studdingsail.—Before rigging out the topmast studdingsail boom, the lower halyards should always be rove, as before directed. Reeve the inner halyards *out* through a small single block under the slings of the lower yard, and through another about two thirds of the way out, and pay the end down upon the forecastle for bending. Get the studding-sail clear, bend the outer halyards to the yard, and the inner halyards to the inner cringle at the head of the sail. Reeve the outhaul through the block at the swinging boom end, and bend the forward end to the outer clew of the sail. Hook the topping-lift and forward guy to the boom, and top up on it. Haul on the forward guy, and ease off the after one, slacking away a little on the topping-lift, until the boom is trimmed by the lower yard; then make fast the guys and lift. Haul well taut the fore-lift and brace, and belay. Take a turn with one sheet, hoist away on the outer halyards, and when about one third up, clear the downhaul, haul chock out on the outhaul, and hoist well up by the halyards, which will serve as a lift to the topmast studdingsail boom; and then set taut on the inner halyards and trim down the sheet. The practice now is, and it is found most convenient, to set the sail before rigging out the boom; then clap on the outhaul and forward guy, and trim the boom by the lower yard.

To take in a lower Studdingsail.—Let go the outhaul, and haul on the clewline till the outer clew is up to the yard. Then lower away the outer halyards, and haul in on the sheet and clewline. When the sail is in over the rail, lower away the inner halyards. If the booms are to be rigged in, cast off all the gear; making the bending end of the outhaul fast in-board, and unreeving the outer and inner halyards, or running the outer up to the pennant block, and the inner up to the yard block, with knots in their ends. Ease off the forward guy with a turn, haul in on the after guy, topping well up by the lift, and get the boom alongside. Rig in the topmast studdingsail boom before unreeving the outer halyards. It is a convenient practice, when the swinging boom is alongside, to hook the topping-lift to a becket or thimble at the turning in of the fore swifter, and the forward guy to a strap and thimble on the spritsail yard.

In strong winds it is well to have a boom-brace-pennant fitted to the topmast studdingsail boom-end with a single block, making a whip purchase, the hauling part leading to the gangway, and belaying at the same pin with the tack; or else, the brace may lead to the gangway, and the tack be brought in through blocks on the yard, and lead down on deck, beside the mast. The former mode is more usual.

The topmast studdingsail is sometimes made with a reef in it, to be carried with a single reefed topsail; in which case it is reefed on deck to the yard and sent out as before.

CHAPTER X.

GENERAL PRINCIPLES OF WORKING A SHIP.

Action of the water upon the rudder. Headway. Sternway. Action of the wind upon the sails. Head-sails. After-sails. Centre of gravity or rotation. Turning a ship to or from the wind.

A SHIP is acted upon principally by the rudder and sails. When the rudder is fore-and-aft, that is, on a line with the keel, the water runs by it, and it has no effect upon the ship's direction. When it is changed from a right line to one side or the other, the water strikes against it, and forces the stern in an opposite direction. For instance, if the helm is put to the starboard, the rudder is put off the line of the keel, to port. This sends the stern off to the starboard, and, of course, the ship turning on her centre of gravity, her head goes in an opposite direction, to port. If the helm is put to port, the reverse will follow, and the ship's head will turn off her course to starboard. Therefore the helm is always put in the opposite direction from that in which the ship's head is to be moved.

Moving the rudder from a right line has the effect of deadening the ship's way more or less, according as it is put at a greater or less angle with the keel. A ship should therefore be so balanced by her sails that a slight change of her helm may answer the purpose.

If a vessel is going astern, and the rudder is turned off from the line of the keel, the water, striking against the back of the rudder, pushes the stern off in the same direction in which the rudder is turned. For instance, if sternway is on her, and the helm is put to the starboard, the rudder turns to port, the water forces the stern in the same direction, and the ship's head goes off to the starboard. Therefore, when sternway is on a vessel, put the helm in the same direction in which the head is to be turned.

A current or tide running astern, that is, when the ship's head is towards it, will have the same effect on the rudder as if the ship were going ahead; and when it runs forward, it will be the same as though the ship were going astern.

It will now be well to show how the sails act upon a ship, with reference to her centre of rotation. Suppose a vessel to be rigged with three sails, one in the forward part, one at the centre, and the third at the after part, and her left or larboard side to be presented to the wind, which we will suppose to be abeam, or at right angles with the keel. If the head sail only were set, the effect would be that the wind would send the vessel a little ahead and off to the starboard on her centre of rotation, so as to bring her stern slowly round to the wind. If the after sail only were set, the vessel would shoot ahead a little, her stern would go off to the starboard and her head come up into the wind. If only the centre sail were set, the effect would be the same as if all three of the sails were set, and she would go ahead in a straight line. So far, we have supposed the sails to be set *full*; that is, with their tacks forward and their sheets aft. If they were all set *aback*, the vessel would go astern nearly, if the rudder were kept steady, in a straight line. If the head sail only is set and aback, she will go astern and round upon her axis, with her head from the wind, much quicker than if full. So, if the after sail alone were set and aback, she would go astern, and her head would come suddenly into the wind.

These principles of the wind acting upon the sails, and the water upon the rudder, are the foundation of the whole science of working a ship. In large vessels the sails are numerous, but they may all be reduced to three classes, viz., head sails, or those which are forward of the centre of gravity or rotation, having a tendency to send the ship's head off from the wind; after sails, or those abaft the centre of rotation, and which send the stern off and the head toward the wind; and lastly, centre sails, which act equally on each side the centre of rotation, and do not turn the ship off her course one way or the other. These classes of sails, if set aback, tend to stop the headway, and send the ship astern, and also to turn her off her course in the same direction as when set full, but with more rapidity. The further a sail is from the centre of rotation, the greater is its tendency to send the ship off from the line of her keel. Accordingly, a jib is the strongest head sail, and a spanker the strongest after sail.

The centre of rotation is not necessarily at the centre of the ship. On the contrary, as vessels are now built, it may not be much abaft that part of the deck to which the main tack is boarded. For the main breadth, or dead flat, being there, the greatest cavity will also be there, and of course the principal weight of the cargo should centre there, as being the strongest part. Therefore, the centre of rotation will greatly depend upon proper stowage. If the ship is much by the stern, the centre of rotation will be carried aft; and if by the head, it will be carried forward. The cause of this is, that when loaded down by the stern, her after sails have but little effect to move her stern against the water, and a very slight action upon the forward sails will send her head off to leeward, as she is there light and high in the air. Accordingly, to keep her in a straight line, the press of sail is required to be further aft, or, in other words, the centre of rotation is further aft. If a ship is loaded down by the head, the opposite results follow, and more head and less after sail is necessary.

A ship should be so stowed, and have her sails so trimmed, that she may be balanced as much as possible, and not be obliged to carry her helm much off the line of her keel, which tends to deaden her way. If a ship is stowed in her best sailing trim, and it is found, when on a wind, that her head tends to windward, obliging her to carry a strong weather-helm, it may be remedied by taking in some after sail, or adding head sail. So, if she carries a lee helm, that is, if her head tends to fly off from the wind, it is remedied by taking in head or adding after sail. Sometimes a ship is made to carry a weather helm by having too much head-sail set aloft. For, if she lies much over on a wind, the square sails forward have a tendency to press her downwards and raise her proportionally abaft, so that she meets great resistance from the water to leeward under her bows, while her stern, being light, is easily carried off; which, of course, requires her to carry a weather helm.

The general rules, then, for turning a ship are these: to bring her head to the wind, put the helm to leeward and bring the wind to act as much as possible on the after sails, and as little as possible on the head sails. This may be done without taking in any sail, by letting go the head sheets, so that those sails may lose their wind, and by pointing the head yards to the wind, so as to keep the head sails shaking. At the same time keep the after sails full, and flatten in the spanker sheet; or, if this is not sufficient, the after sails may be braced aback, which will send the stern off and the head to windward. But as this makes back sails of them, and tends to send the vessel astern, there should be either head or centre sails enough filled to counteract this and keep headway upon her. On the other hand, to turn the head off from the wind, put the helm to windward, shiver the after sails, and flatten in the head sheets. Brace the head yards aback if necessary, being careful not to let her lose headway if it can be avoided.

The vessel may be assisted very much in going off or coming to, by setting or taking in the jib and spanker; which, if the latter is fitted with brails, are easily handled.

CHAPTER XI.

TACKING, WEARING, BOXING, ETC.

Tacking without fore-reaching. Tacking against a heavy sea. Hauling off all. To trim the yards. Flattening in. Missing stays. Wearing—under courses—under a mainsail—under bare poles. Box-hauling—short round. Club-hauling. Drifting in a tide-way. Backing and filling in do. Clubbing in do.

TACKING.—Have the ship so suited with sails that she may steer herself as nearly as possible, and come to with a small helm. Keep her a good full, so that she may have plenty of headway. *Ready, About!* Send all hands to their stations. The chief mate and one, two, or more of the best men, according to the size of the vessel, on the forecastle, to work the head sheets and bowlines and the fore tack; two or more good men (one usually a petty officer, or an older and trusty seaman) to work the main tack and bowline. The second mate sees the lee fore and main braces clear and ready for letting go, and stands by to let go the lee main braces, which may all be belayed to one pin. Put one hand to let go the weather cross-jack braces, and others to haul in to leeward; the cook works the fore sheet, and the steward the main; station one or more at the spanker sheet and guys; and the rest at the weather main braces.

Ease the helm down gradually; *Helm's a lee!* and let go the jib sheet and fore sheets. As soon as the wind is parallel with the yards, blowing directly upon the leaches of the square sails, so that all is shaking, *Raise tacks and sheets!* and let go the fore and main tacks and main sheet, keeping the fore and main bowline fast. As soon as her head is within a point or a point and a half of the wind, *Mainsail haul!* let go the lee main and weather cross-jack braces, and swing the after yards

F

round. While she is head to the wind, and the after sails are becalmed by the head sails, get the main tack down and sheet aft, and right your helm, using it afterwards as her coming to or falling off requires. As soon as she passes the direction of the wind, shift your jib sheets over the stays, and when the after sails take full, or when she brings the wind four points on the other bow, and you are sure of paying off sufficiently, *Let go and haul!* brace round the head yards briskly, down fore tack and aft the sheet, brace sharp up and haul your bowlines out, and trim down your head sheets.

It is best to haul the mainsail just before you get the wind right ahead, for then the wind, striking the weather leaches of the after sails, forces them round almost without the braces, and you will have time to brace up and get your tack down and sheet aft, when she has payed off on the other side.

If she falls off too rapidly while swinging your head yards, so as to bring the wind abeam or abaft, *'Vast bracing!* Ease off head sheets and put your helm a-lee; and as she comes up, meet her and brace sharp up. If, on the other hand, (as sometimes happens with vessels which carry a strong weather helm,) she does not fall off after the after sails take, be careful not to haul your head yards until she is fully round; and if she should fly up into the wind, let go the main sheet, and, if necessary, brail up the spanker and shiver the cross-jack yards.

In staying, be careful to right your helm before she loses headway.

TO TACK WITHOUT FORE-REACHING, as in a narrow channel, when you are afraid to keep headway. If she comes slowly up to windward, haul down the jib and get your spanker-boom well over to windward. As you raise tacks and sheets, let go the lee fore-topsail brace, being careful to brace up again as soon as she takes aback. Also, hoist the jib, and trim down, if necessary, as soon as she takes on the other side.

TACKING AGAINST A HEAVY HEAD SEA.—You are under short sail, there is a heavy head sea, and you doubt whether she will stay against it. Haul down the fore topmast stay sail, ease down the helm, and raise fore sheet. When within about a point of the wind's eye, let go main tack and sheet, lee braces and after bowlines, and *Mainsail haul!* If she loses her headway at this time, shift your helm. As soon as she brings the wind on the other bow, she will fall off rapidly by reason of her sternway, therefore shift your helm again to meet her, and *Let go and haul!* at once. Brace about the head yards, but keep the weather braces in, to moderate her falling off. When she gets headway, right the helm, and as she comes up to the wind, brace up and haul aft.

TACKING BY HAULING OF ALL.—This can be done only in a smooth sea, with a light working breeze, a smart vessel and strong crew. Man all the braces. Let her come up head to the wind, and fall off on the other tack, shifting the helm if she gathers sternway. When you get the wind about five points on the other bow, *Haul of all!* let go all the braces and bowlines and swing all the yards at once. Right the helm, board tacks and haul aft sheets, brace up and haul aft.

TO TRIM THE YARDS WHEN CLOSE-HAULED.—In smooth water, with a light breeze, brace the lower yards sharp up, and trim the upper yards each a trifle in abaft the one below it. If you have a pretty stiff breeze, brace the topsail yard in about half a point more than the lower yard, and the topgallant yard half a point more than the topsail yard, and so on. If you have a strong breeze and a topping sea, and especially if reduced to short sail, brace in your lower yards a little, and the others proportionally. This will prevent the vessel going off bodily to leeward; and if she labours heavily, the play of the mast would otherwise carry away the braces and sheets, or spring the yards.

MISSING STAYS.—If after getting head to the wind

she comes to a stand and begins to fall off before you have hauled your main yard, flatten in your jib sheets, board fore tack, and haul aft fore sheet; also ease off spanker sheet, or brail up the spanker, if necessary. When she is full again, trim the jib and spanker sheets, and when she has recovered sufficient headway, try it again. If, after coming head to the wind, and after the after yards are swung, she loses headway and refuses to go round, or begins to fall off on the same tack on which she was before, and you have shifted the helm without effect, haul up the mainsail and spanker, square the after yards, shift your helm again a-lee, so as to assist her in falling off, and brace round the head yards so as to box her off. As she fills on her former tack, brace up the after yards, brace round the head yards, sharp up all, board tacks, haul out and haul aft.

WEARING.—Haul up the mainsail and spanker, put the helm up, and, as she goes off, brace in the after yards. If there is a light breeze, the rule is to keep the mizen topsail lifting, and the main topsail full. This will keep sufficient headway on her, and at the same time enable her to fall off. But if you have a good breeze and she goes off fast, keep both the main and mizen topsails lifting. As she goes round, bringing the wind on her quarter and aft, follow the wind with your after yards, keeping the mizen topsail lifting, and the main either lifting or full, as is best. After a vessel has fallen off much, the less headway she has the better, provided she has enough to give her steerage. When you have the wind aft, raise fore tack and sheet, square in the head yards, and haul down the jib. As she brings the wind on the other quarter, brace sharp up the after yards, haul out the spanker, and set the mainsail. As she comes to on the other tack, brace up the head yards, keeping the sails full, board fore tack and aft the sheet, hoist the jib, and meet her with the helm.

TO WEAR UNDER COURSES.—Square the cross-jack yards, ease off main bowline and tack, and haul up the weather clew of the mainsail. Ease off the main sheet, and haul up the lee clew, and the buntlines and leach-lines. Square the main yards and put the helm a-weather. As she falls off, let go the fore bowline, ease off the fore sheet, and brace in the fore yard. When she gets before the wind, board the fore and main tacks on the other side, and haul aft the main sheet, but keep the weather braces in. As she comes to on the other side, ease the helm, trim down the fore sheet, brace up and haul aft.

To wear under a Mainsail.—Vessels lying-to under this sail generally wear by hoisting the fore topmast staysail, or some other head sail. If this cannot be done, brace the cross-jack yards to the wind, and, if necessary, send down the mizen topmast and the cross-jack yard. Brace the head yards full. Take an opportunity when she has headway, and will fall off, to put the helm up. Ease off the main sheet, and, as she falls off, brace in the main yard a little. When the wind is abaft the beam, raise the main tack. When she is dead before it, get the other main tack down as far as possible; and when she has the wind on the other quarter, ease the helm, haul aft the sheet, and brace up.

To wear under bare Poles.—Some vessels, which are well down by the stern, will wear in this situation, by merely pointing the after yards to the wind, or sending down the mizen topmast and the cross-jack yard, and filling the head yards; but vessels in good trim will not do this. To assist the vessel, veer a good scope of hawser out of the lee quarter, with a buoy, or something for a stop-water, attached to the end. As the ship sags off to leeward, the buoy will be to windward, and will tend to bring the stern round to the wind. When she is before it, haul the hawser aboard.

Box-hauling.—Put the helm down, light up the head sheets and slack the lee braces, to deaden her way. As she comes to the wind, raise tacks and sheets, and haul up the mainsail and spanker. As soon as she comes head to the wind and loses her headway, square the after yards, brace the head yards sharp aback, and flatten in the head sheets. The helm, being put down to bring her up, will now pay her off, as she has sternway on. As she goes off, keep the after sails lifting, and square in the head yards. As soon as the sails on the foremast give her headway, shift the helm. When she gets the wind on the other quarter, haul down the jib, haul out the spanker, set the mainsail, and brace the after yards sharp up. As she comes to on the other tack, brace up the head yards, meet her with the helm, and set the jib.

Box-hauling short round; sometimes called *wearing short round*.—Haul up the mainsail and spanker, put the helm hard a-weather, square the after yards, brace the head yards sharp aback, and flatten in the head sheets. As she gathers sternway, shift the helm. After this, proceed as in box-hauling by the former method. The first mode is preferable when you wish to stop headway as soon as possible; as a vessel under good way will range ahead some distance after the sails are all thrown flat aback.

Few merchant vessels are strongly enough manned to perform these evolutions; but they are often of service, as they turn a vessel round quicker on her heel, and will stop her from fore-reaching when near in shore or when close aboard another vessel.

Club-hauling.—This method of going about is resorted to when on a lee shore, and the vessel can neither be tacked nor box-hauled. Cock-bill your lee anchor, get a hawser on it for a spring, and lead it to the lee quarter; range your cable, and unshackle it abaft the windlass. *Helm's a-lee!* and *Raise tacks and sheets!* as for going in stays. The moment she loses headway, let go the anchor and *Mainsail haul!* As soon as the anchor brings her head to the wind, let the chain cable go, holding on to the spring; and when the after sails take full, cast off or cut the spring, and *Let go and haul!*

DRIFTING IN A TIDE-WAY.—As a vessel is deeper aft than forward, her stern will always tend to drift faster than her head. If the current is setting out of a river or harbour, and the wind the opposite way, or only partly across the current, you may work out by tacking from shore to shore; or you may let her drift out, broadside to the current; or, keeping her head to the current by sufficient sail, you may let her drift out stern first; or, lastly, you may *club* her down. If the wind is partly across the current, cast to windward. If you work down by tacking, and the wind is at all across the current, be careful of the lee shore, and stay in season, since, if you miss stays, you may not be able to save yourself by wearing or box-hauling, as you might on the weather shore. If the channel is very narrow, or there are many vessels at anchor, the safest way is to bring her head to the current, brace the yards full, and keep only sail enough to give her steerage, that you may sheer from side to side. If there is room enough, you will drift more rapidly by bringing her broadside to the current, keeping the topsails shaking, and counteract the force of the current upon the stern by having the spanker full and the helm a-lee. You can at any time shoot her ahead, back her astern, or bring her head to the current, by filling the head yards, taking in the spanker, and setting the jib; filling the after yards, taking in the jib, and setting the spanker; or by bracing all aback.

BACKING AND FILLING IN A TIDE-WAY.—Counter-brace your yards as in lying-to, and drift down broadside to the current. Fill away and shoot ahead, or throw all aback and force her astern, as occasion may require. When you approach the shore on either side, fill away till she gets sufficient headway, and put her in stays or wear her round.

CLUBBING IN A TIDE-WAY.—Drift down with your anchor under your foot, heaving in or paying out on your cable as you wish to increase or deaden her way. Have a spring on your cable, so as to present a broadside to the current. This method is a troublesome and dangerous one, and rarely resorted to. An anchor will seldom drag clear, through the whole operation.

CHAPTER XII.

GALES OF WIND, LYING-TO, GETTING ABACK, BY THE LEE, &c.

Lying-to—choice of sails. Scudding. Heave-to after scudding. Taken aback. Chapelling. Broaching-to. By the lee.

LYING-TO.—The best single sail to lie-to under, is generally thought to be a close-reefed maintopsail. The fore or the main spencer (sails which are used very much now instead of main and mizen staysails) may be used to advantage, according as a ship requires sail more before or abaft the centre of gravity. If a ship will bear more than one sail, it is thought best to separate the pressure. Then set the fore and main spencers; or (if she carries staysails instead) the main and mizen staysail: or, if she is easier under lofty sail, the fore and main topsails close-reefed. A close-reefed main topsail, with three lower storm staysails; or, with the two spencers, fore topmast staysail, and reefed spanker, is considered a good arrangement for lying-to. If the fore topmast staysail and balance-reefed spanker can be added to the two close-reefed topsails, she will keep some way, will go less to leeward, and can be easily wore round. Close-reefed topsails are used much more now for lying-to than the courses. As ships are now built, with the centre of gravity farther forward, and the foremast stepped more aft, they will lie-to under head sail better than formerly. Some vessels, which are well down by the stern, will lie-to under a reefed foresail, as this tends to press her down forward; whereas, if she had much after sail, she would have all the lateral resistance of the water aft, and would come up in the wind. In carrying most head or after sail, you must be determined by the trim of the vessel, her tendency to come to or go off, and as to whether the sail you use will act as a lifting or a burying sail.

A topsail has an advantage over a spencer or lower staysail for lying-to, since it steadies the ship better, and counteracts the heavy weather roll, which a vessel will give under low and small fore-and-aft sails.

SCUDDING.—The most approved sail for scudding is the close-reefed maintopsail, with a reefed foresail. The course alone might get becalmed under the lee of a high sea, and the vessel, losing her way, would be overtaken by the sea from aft; whereas the topsail will always give her way enough and lift her. The foresail is of use in case she should be brought by the lee. Many officers recommend that the fore topmast staysail, or fore storm staysail, should always be set in scudding, to pay her off if she should broach-to, and with the sheets hauled flat aft.

It has been thought that with the wind quartering and a heavy sea, a vessel is more under command with a close-reefed fore topsail and maintopmast staysail. The foretopmast staysail may also be hoisted. If the ship flies off and gets by the lee, the foretopsail is soon braced about, and, with the maintopmast staysail sheet shifted to the other side, the headway is not lost.

TO HEAVE-TO AFTER SCUDDING.—Secure everything about decks, and watch a smooth time. Suppose her to be scudding under a close-reefed maintopsail and reefed foresail; haul up the foresail, put the helm down, brace up the after yards, and set the mizen staysail. As she comes to, set the main staysail, meet her with the helm, brace up the head yards, and set the fore or foretopmast staysail.

If your vessel labours much, ease the lee braces and the halyards, that everything may work fairly aloft, and let her have a plenty of helm, to come to and fall off freely with the sea. The helmsman will often let the wheel fly off to leeward, taking care to meet her easily and in season. The sails should be so arranged as to require little of the rudder.

TAKEN ABACK.—It will frequently happen, when sailing close-hauled, especially in light winds, from a shift of wind, from its dying away, or from inattention, that the ship will come up into the wind, shaking the square sails forward. In this case, it will often be sufficient to put the helm hard up, flatten in the head sheets, or haul their bights to windward, and brail up the spanker. If this will not recover her, and she continues to come to, box her off. Raise fore tack and sheet, brail up the spanker, up mainsail, brace the head-yards aback, haul the jib sheets to windward, and haul out the lee bowlines. When the after sails fill, *Let go and haul!* This manœuvre of boxing can only be performed in good weather and light winds, as it usually gives a vessel sternway.

If the wind has got round upon the other bow, and it is too late for box-hauling, square the yards fore and aft, keeping your helm so as to pay her off under sternway; and, as the sails fill, keep the after yards shaking, and haul up the spanker and mainsail, squaring the head-yards, and shifting your helm as she gathers headway.

CHAPELLING.—This operation is performed when, instead of coming to, you are taken aback in light winds. Put the helm up, if she has headway, haul up the mainsail and spanker, and square the after yards. Shift the helm as she gathers sternway, and when the after sails fill, and she gathers headway, shift your helm again. When she brings the wind aft, brace up the after yards, get the main tack down and sheet aft, and haul out the spanker as soon as it will take. The head braces are not touched, but the yards remain braced as before. The former mode of wearing, by squaring the head-yards when the after sails are full, has great advantages over chapelling, as the vessel will go off faster when the wind is abeam and abaft, and will come to quicker when the wind gets on the other side.

BROACHING-TO.—This is when a vessel is scudding, and comes up into the wind and gets aback. For such an accident, the foretopmast staysail is set, which will act as an off-sail, so that by keeping the helm up, with the maintopsail (if set) braced into the wind, she will pay off again without getting sternway. If the close-reefed foretopsail is carried instead of the main, it can be easily filled.

BROUGHT BY THE LEE.—This is when a vessel is scudding with the wind quartering, and falls off so as to bring the wind on the other side, laying the sails aback. This is more likely to occur than broaching-to, especially in a heavy sea. Suppose the vessel to be scudding under a close-reefed maintopsail and reefed foresail, with the wind on her larboard quarter. She falls off suddenly and brings the wind on the starboard quarter, laying all aback. Put your helm hard a-starboard, raise fore tack and sheet, and fill the foresail, shivering the maintopsail. When she brings the wind aft again, meet her with the helm, and trim the yards for her course.

CHAPTER XIII.

ACCIDENTS.

On beam-ends. Losing a rudder. A squall. A man overboard. Collision. Rules for vessels passing one another.

ON BEAM-ENDS.—A vessel is usually thrown upon her beam-ends by a sudden squall taking her, when under a press of sail, and shifting the ballast. She must be righted, if possible, without cutting away the masts. For, beside sacrificing them, the object can seldom be accomplished in that way, if the ballast and cargo have shifted. Carry a hawser from the lee quarter, with spars and other good stop-waters bent to it. As the ship drifts well to leeward, the hawser will bring her stern to the wind; but it may not cast her on the other side. If a spring can be got upon the hawser from the lee bow, and hauled upon, and the stern fast let go, this will bring the wind to act upon the flat part of the deck and pay her stern off, and assist the spring, when the sails may be trimmed to help her in righting. If she can be brought head to the wind, and the sails be taken aback, she may cast on the other tack. When there is anchoring ground, the practice is to let go the lee anchor, which may take the sails aback and cast her. Then the ballast and cargo may be righted.

If there is no anchoring ground, a vessel may still be kept head to the wind, by paying a chain cable out of the lee hawse-hole; or by bending a hawser to a large spar, which may be kept broadside-to by a span, to the centre of which the hawser is bent. The same operation may be applied to a vessel overset, and is preferable to wearing by a hawser. Make fast the hawser forward to the lee bow, carry the other end aft to windward and bend it to the spar, and launch the spar overboard. By this means, or by letting go an anchor, though there be no bottom to be reached, a vessel may often be recovered.

LOSING A RUDDER.—The first thing to be done on losing a rudder, is to bring the ship to the wind by bracing up the after yards. Meet her with the head yards as she comes to. Take in sail forward and aft, and keep her hove-to by her sails. A vessel may be made to steer herself for a long time, by carefully trimming the yards and slacking up the jib sheets or the spanker sheet a little, as may be required.

Having got the ship by the wind, get up a hawser, middle it, and take a slack clove-hitch at the centre. Get up a cable, reeve its end through this hitch, and pay the cable out over the taffrail. Having paid out about fifty fathoms, jam the hitch and rack it well, so that it cannot slip; pay out on the cable until the hitch takes the water; then lash the cable to the centre of the taffrail; lash a spare spar under it across the stern, with a block well secured at each end, through which reeve the ends of the hawser, one on each quarter, and reeve them again through blocks at the sides, abreast of the wheel. By this, a ship may be steered until a temporary rudder can be constructed.

A rudder may be fitted by taking a spare topmast, or other large spar, and cutting it flat in the form of a stern-post. Bore holes at proper distances in that part which is to be the fore part of the preventer or additional stern-post; then take the thickest plank on board, and make it as near as possible into the form of a rudder; bore holes at proper distances in the fore part of it and in the after part of the preventer stern-post, to correspond with each other, and reeve rope grommets through those holes in the rudder and after part of the stern-post, for the rudder to play upon. Through the preventer stern-post, reeve guys, and at the fore part of them fix tackles, and then put the machine overboard. When it is in a proper position, or in a line with the ship's stern-post, lash the upper part of the preventer post to the upper part of the ship's stern-post; then hook tackles at or near the main chains, and bowse taut on the guys to confine it to the lower part of the preventer stern-post. Having holes bored through the preventer and proper stern-post, run an iron bolt through both (taking care not to touch the rudder), which will prevent the false stern-post from rising or falling. By the guys on the after part of the rudder and tackles affixed to them, the ship may be steered, taking care to bowse taut the tackles on the preventer stern-post, to keep it close to the proper stern-post.

A SQUALL.—If you see a squall approaching, take in the light sails, stand by to clew down, and keep her off a little, if necessary. If you are taken by one, unprepared, with all sail set and close-hauled, put the helm hard up, let go the spanker sheet and outhaul, and the main sheet. Clew up royals and topgallant sails, haul down flying-jib, haul up the mainsail, and clew down the mizen topsail. When you are before the wind, clew down the topsail yards, and haul out the reef-tackles. You may run before the squall until it moderates, or furl the light sails, bring by the wind, and reef.

A MAN OVERBOARD *.—The moment the cry is heard, put the helm down and bring her up into the wind, whether she is on the wind or free, and deaden her headway. Throw overboard instantly life buoys, or, if there are none at hand, take a grating, the carpenter's bench, or any pieces of plank or loose spars there may be about decks; and let two or three hands clear away a quarter boat. The best plan is, if the vessel was on the wind, to haul the mainsail up and brace aback the after yards and raise the head sheets; then, having her main yard aback, she will drift down directly toward the man. Keep your head sails full to steady her, while the after ones stop her headway.

If you are sailing free, with studdingsails set, clew up the lower studdingsail, brace up the head yards, haul forward the fore tack, and keep the head yards full, while you luff up to back the after ones. Lower away the boat as soon as it is safe, and, as the vessel will have turned nearly round, direct the boat with reference to her position when the accident happened and her progress since.

COLLISION.—If two vessels approach one another, both having a free wind, each keeps to the right. That is, the one with her starboard tacks aboard keeps on or luffs; and the other, if it is necessary to alter her course, keeps off. So, if two vessels approach one another close-hauled on different tacks, and it is doubtful which is to windward, the vessel on the starboard tack keeps on her course, and the other gives way and keeps off. That is, each goes to the right, and the vessel with her starboard

---

* See Totten's Naval Text Book, Letter xx.

tacks aboard has the preference. The only exception to this is, that if the vessel on the larboard tack is so much to windward that, in case both persist, the vessel on the starboard tack will strike her to leeward and abaft the beam; then the vessel on the starboard tack must give way, as she can do it more easily than the other.

Another rule is, that if one vessel is going dead before the wind and the other going free on the starboard tack, the latter must luff and go under the stern of the former.

CHAPTER XIV.

HEAVING-TO BY COUNTER-BRACING. SPEAKING. SOUNDING. HEAVING THE LOG.

COUNTER-BRACING.—This is done whenever, with a breeze, a vessel wishes to remain stationary, for the purpose of speaking another vessel, sounding, lowering a boat, or the like. If you do not wish to stop your way entirely, haul up the mainsail, square the main yards aback, keeping the fore and cross-jack yards full, and the foresail, spanker and jib set. If you wish to stop her way still more, back the cross-jack yards also, haul up the foresail, and put the helm a-lee. She will then fall off and come to, which you may regulate by the jib and spanker sheets; and she may be ranged a little ahead, or deadened, by filling or backing the cross-jack yards.

You may, on the other hand, back the head yards and fill the after yards. The former method is called heaving-to with the maintopsail to the mast, and the latter, with the foretopsail to the mast.

SPEAKING.—When two vessels speak at sea, the one to windward heaves her maintopsail to the mast, and the one to leeward her fore. This is in order that the weather one may the more readily fill without falling off so as to run afoul of the other, and that the lee one may box her head off and keep clear of the ship to windward. The weather one either throws all aback and drops astern, or fills her after yards and shoots ahead. The lee one shivers her after yards and boxes off.

If the weather ship comes too near the lee one, before the latter has time to wear, the weather ship squares her head yards, drops her mainsail, braces her cross-jack yards sharp aback, and puts her helm a-weather. This gives her sternway, and the after sails and helm keep her to the wind.

If three vessels communicate at sea, the weather and middle ones back their main topsails, and the lee one her fore; then, in case of necessity, the weather one fills her after yards and shoots ahead, the middle one throws all aback and drops astern, and the lee one shivers her after sails and falls off.

SOUNDING.—The marks upon the lead-lines have been given previously, at pages 5, 6. To sound with the hand-lead, a man stands in the weather main channels with a breast-rope secured to the rigging, and throws the lead forward, while the vessel has headway on. If the depth corresponds with the marks upon the line, as if it is 5, 7, or 10 fathoms, he calls out, "By the *mark five!*" &c. If it is a depth the fathoms of which have no mark upon the line, as 6, 8, or 9, he calls out, "By the *deep six!*" &c. If he judges the depth to be a quarter or a half more than a particular fathom, as, for instance, 5, he calls out "And a quarter," or, "And a half, five!" &c. If it is 5 and three quarters, he would say, "Quarter less six!" and so on.

TO SOUND BY THE DEEP-SEA-LEAD.—Have the line coiled down in a tub or rack, clear for running, abreast of the main rigging. Carry the end of the line forward on the weather side, outside of everything, to the cat-head or the spritsail yard-arm, and bend it to the lead, which must be armed with tallow. One man holds the lead for heaving, and the others range themselves along the side, at intervals, each with a coil of the line in his hand. An officer, generally the chief mate, should stand by to get the depth. All being ready, the word is given, "*Stand by! Heave!*" As soon as the man heaves the lead, he calls out "*Watch, ho! Watch!*" and each man, as the last fake of the coil goes out of his hand, repeats, *Watch, ho! Watch!*" The line then runs out until it brings up by the lead's being on bottom, or until there is enough out to show that there is no bottom to be reached. The officer notes the depth by the line, which is then snatched, and the men haul it aboard, and coil it away fair. If the lead has been on the bottom, the arming of tallow will bring up some of it; by which the character of the soundings may be ascertained.

The soundings, however, cannot be taken until the vessel's way has been stopped or deadened. For this purpose, before heaving the lead, either luff up and keep all shaking, or brace aback the main or mizen topsail, or both, according to your headway, keeping the head yards full. If you are going free with studding-sails set, you may clew up the lower and boom end the topmast studdingsails, bring her up to the wind, and keep the sails lifting, without getting them aback.

It has been laid down as a rule, that if the vessel sags much to leeward, as when under short sail in a gale of wind, pass the line from the weather side round the stern, clear of everything, and heave the lead from the lee side; otherwise she would leave the lead too far to windward for measurement, or for recovering it again. But in this mode there is great danger of the line getting caught on the bottom or at the rudder-heel. It must be very deep water if a vessel cannot be managed so as to get soundings to windward.

HEAVING THE LOG.—One man holds the log-reel, upon which the log-line is wound, another holds the glass, and the officer holds the line; and, having coiled up a little of the stray line, he throws the log-ship overboard astern, or from the lee quarter. As he throws the log-ship, he calls out, "Watch!" To which the man with the glass answers, "Watch." As soon as the mark for the stray line goes off the reel, he calls out, "Turn!" and the man turns the glass, answering, "Turn," or "Done." The instant the sand has run out, he calls "Out!" or "Stop!" and the officer stops the line and notes the marks. It is then wound up again on the reel.

CHAPTER XV.

COMING TO ANCHOR.

Getting ready for port. Coming to anchor—close-hauled—free. Mooring. Flying moor. Clearing hawse. To anchor with a slip-rope. Slipping a cable. Coming-to at a slipped cable.

GETTING READY FOR PORT.—Get your anchors off the bows, and let them hang by the cat-stoppers and shank-painters. Bend your cables and overhaul a few ranges forward of the windlass, according to the depth of the anchorage and the strength of the tide or wind, and range the remainder that you expect to use along the decks, abaft the windlass. Have the boats ready for lowering, and a spare hawser, with some stout rope for kedging or warping, at hand, coiled on the hatches.

COMING TO ANCHOR.—If you have the wind free and all sail set, take in your studdingsails, make them up and stow them away, rig in the booms and coil away the gear, and have all ready in good season. You may then, as you draw in toward the anchorage, take in your royals and flying jib, furling the royals if you have time. The topgallant sails are next taken in, and the foresail hauled up. The topgallant sails may be furled or not, according to the strength of the wind and the number of hands. If you are before the wind, your mainsail will be hauled up, or, if the sheet is aft, haul up the lee clew-garnet. Get your ship under her topsails, jib and spanker. When near the ground, clew up the fore and main topsails, put the helm down, haul down the jib and flatten in the spanker. If you have too much headway, back the mizen topsail. Cock-bill your anchor and stream the buoy. When she has lost her headway, let go the anchor. Let hands stand by to give her chain, as she needs it.

If you come into anchoring ground close-hauled, haul in the weather fore and main braces, and clew up. If the wind is light, you may square the fore and main yards before clewing up. This will deaden her way. If the wind is fresh, it would make it difficult to clew up the sails. Haul down the jib, and come to by the spanker, or mizen topsail and spanker. If the wind is light, she may need the mizen topsail; if not, it may be taken in, and she may be brought to by the spanker. If she has too much headway or there is a tide setting her in, throw all aback.

MOORING.—A vessel is said to be moored when she rides with more than one anchor, in different directions. The common method of mooring is, when you have come to with one anchor, to pay out chain and let her drop astern until you have out double the scope you intend to ride by. Then let go your other anchor. Slack up the cable of the latter anchor, and heave in on that of the first, until you have the same scope to each anchor. You may also moor by lowering the anchor and lashing it to the stern of the long-boat, and coiling away the full scope in the bottom of the boat. You may then pull off and pick out your own berth, and let go.

If you wish to drop your second anchor in any other place than directly to leeward of the first, you may, without using your long-boat, warp the vessel over the berth intended for your second anchor.

You should always moor so that you may ride with an open hawse in the direction from which you are liable to the strongest winds. If you have chain cables, you may moor with both cables bent to a swivel just clear of the hawse-hole, one chain coming in-board. In moderate weather, and where you are not in a strong tide-way, it will generally be sufficient to let go one anchor, since, if you have out a good scope of chain, you will ride by the bight of it, and it will require a very heavy blow to bring a strain upon the anchor.

In mooring, you should always have a shackle near the hawse-hole, for clearing hawse. If it is just abaft the windlass, it will be convenient in case you wish to slip your cable.

A FLYING MOOR, sometimes called a RUNNING MOOR.—Have both anchors ready for letting go, with double the scope of chain you intend to ride by ranged for the weather anchor, and the riding scope of the lee chain. There are two ways of making a flying moor. One is to clew up everything and let go the first anchor while she has sufficient headway to run out the whole double range. When it is all out, or just before, luff sharp up, brace aback to stop her way, and let go the other anchor. Then heave in on the first and light out on the second, until there is the same scope to each. This mode is almost impracticable in a merchant vessel, where there is but one deck, and where the chain may have to be paid out over a windlass, since the headway would in most cases be soon stopped.

The other mode is, to lay all flat aback, and the moment the headway ceases, let go your first anchor, paying out chain as she drops astern, until double your riding scope is out. Then let go your second anchor and heave in on the first.

CLEARING HAWSE.—When a vessel is moored, she may swing so as to get a *foul hawse;* that is, so as to bring one cable across the other. If one cable lies over the other, it is called *a cross*. When they make another cross, it is called an *elbow*. Three crosses make a *round turn*. The turns may be kept out of a cable by tending the vessel when she swings, and casting her stern one side or the other, by the helm, jib and spanker. To clear hawse, trice the slack cable up by a line or a whip purchase and hook, below the turns. Lash the two cables together just below the lowest turn. Pass a line round the cable from outside, following each turn, and in through the hawse-hole of the slack cable, and bend it to the shackle. Unshackle and bend a line to the end. Rouse the cable out through the hawse-hole, slacking up on the end line, and tricing up if necessary. Take out the turns by the first line passed in, and haul in again on the end line. Shackle the chain again, heave taut, and cast off the lashings.

To Anchor with a Slip-rope.—This is necessary when you are lying in an open roadstead, where you must stand out to sea upon a gale coming up, without taking time to get your anchor. You must ride at one anchor. Having come to, take a hawser round from the quarter on the same side with your anchor, outside of everything, and bend its end to the cable just below the hawse-hole. Have a buoy triced up forward clear of everything, and carry the buoy-rope in through the hawse-hole, and round the windlass, with three turns, (the first turn being *outside* the others,) and bend it to the shackle, which is to be cast off when the cable is slipped. Have another buoy bent to the end of the hawser which is to be used for the slip-rope.

To Slip a Cable.—When ready to slip, everything having been prepared as above, unshackle the chain abaft the windlass, and hoist the topsails, reefed, if necessary. Stream the buoy for the end of the chain, and that at the end of the slip-rope aft. Take good turns with the slip-rope round the timber-heads, at the quarter. Hoist the fore-topmast staysail and back the fore-topsail, hauling in the braces on the same side with the cable, so that she may cast to the opposite side. Fill the after yards, and let go the end of the cable. Hold on to the slip-rope aft, until her head is fairly off; then let go, brace full the head-yards, and set the spanker.

Coming-to at a Slipped Cable.—Keep a look-out for your buoys. Having found them, heave-to to windward of them, send a boat with a strong warp and bend it to the slip-rope buoy, take the other end to the capstan and walk the ship up to the buoy. Take the slip-rope through the chock, forward, and heave on it until you get the chain, where the slip-rope was bent to it, under foot. Make well fast the slip-rope, then fish the buoy at the end of the chain, haul up on that buoy-rope, and get the end of the chain. Rouse it in through the hawse-hole and shackle it. Heave taut, until the bend of the slip-rope is above the water, then take the other end round aft and make it fast at the quarter-port again. Pass in the buoy-rope for the end of the chain, and you are all ready for slipping again.

CHAPTER XVI.

GETTING UNDER WAY.

To unmoor. Getting under way from a single anchor. To cat and fish. To get under way with a wind blowing directly out, and riding head to it ;—with a rock or shoal close astern ;—when riding head to wind and tide, and to stand out close-hauled ;—wind-rode, with a weather tide ; —tide-rode, casting to windward ;—tide-rode, wearing round.

UNMOOR.—Pay out on your riding cable, heaving in the slack of the other. When the other is short, trip it, cat and fish, and heave in on your riding cable. Instead of this method, the anchor which you are not riding by may be weighed, if it is a small one, by the long-boat. Send the long-boat out over the anchor, take aboard the buoy-rope, carrying it over the roller in the boat's stern, or through the end of a davit, clap the watch-tackle to it, and weigh it out of the ground. This done, and the buoy-rope and tackle secured to the boat, heave in on the chain on board, which will bring the anchor alongside, the boat approaching at the same time. When under the bow, cast off the fasts to the boat, heave up the anchor, cat and fish.

GETTING UNDER WAY FROM A SINGLE ANCHOR.—It

is the duty of the chief mate to see all ready forward for getting under way; the rigging fair for making sail, the cat and fish tackles rove, and the fish-davit at hand. Heave short on your chain and pawl the windlass. Loose all the sails, if the wind is light, and sheet home and hoist up topsails, topgallant sails, and royals. If there is a stiff breeze, set topsails alone, whole or reefed. You should always, if it will answer, cast on the opposite side from your anchor; that is, if you are riding by your starboard anchor, cast to port. Brace your head-yards aback and your after-yards full for the tack you mean to cast upon. The sails being set, man the windlass again, give her a sheer with the helm, and trip your anchor. The mate reports when it is away. As soon as it is away, hoist the jib. The fore-topsail aback will pay her head off. Put the helm for stern-board. When her head is off enough, fill away the head-yards and haul out the spanker, shifting the helm for headway. Trim the yards for your course, and make sail on her. If the wind is light and the sea smooth, you may cat and fish your anchor after you get under way; but it is best in a rough sea to keep the vessel hove-to until the anchor is catted and fished.

To CAT AND FISH AN ANCHOR.—When the anchor is lifted and brought under foot, pawl the windlass, keeping a good hold on the chain. Overhaul down the cat-block and hook it to the ring of the anchor. Stretch along the cat-fall and let all hands tally on. Set taut on the cat-tackle and pay out a little chain. Hoist away the anchor to the cat-head, and belay the fall. Pass the cat-stopper through the ring of the anchor, through the chock, belay it to the cat-tail, and seize it to its own part. Overhaul down the fish-tackle, hook the lower block to the pennant, and hook the fish-hook to the inner fluke of the anchor. Rig out your fish-davit across the forecastle, and put the bight of the pennant into the sheave-hole. Get a guy over it, near the outer end, to keep it down, and another at the inner end, to keep it out. Get the shoe over the side, to fend off the bill of the anchor. Hoist the fluke well up, pass the shank-painter under the inner arm and shank, bring it inboard, and belay and stop it to the timber-heads. Rig in the davit, unreeve the cat-fall and fish-tackle.

A vessel may sometimes be got under way to advantage with the jib and spanker; particularly if the wind is blowing directly out of the harbour. Heave the anchor up at once. When it has broken ground, hoist the jib, and, as she pays off, haul out the spanker. Keep her under this sail until the anchor is catted and fished, then make sail and stand out.

TO GET UNDER WAY, WITH A WIND BLOWING DIRECTLY OUT, AND RIDING HEAD TO IT.—Suppose the ship to have her starboard anchor down. Heave short and clear away the jib, and put the helm to port. Heave again until the anchor is up to the bows. Cat and fish. When the anchor is a-weigh, hoist the jib. Let her pay off under the jib. When she gathers headway, shift the helm, and let fall the sails. When she gets before it, sheet home and hoist the topsails, set the foresail, and haul down the jib. Make sail aloft.

TO GET UNDER WAY, RIDING HEAD TO THE WIND, WITH A ROCK OR SHOAL CLOSE ASTERN.—Suppose you wish to cast the ship on the starboard tack. Heave in a safe scope on the chain, and run out a kedge with a hawser from the starboard bow. Cast off the yard-arm gaskets and mast-head the topsails, keeping the bunts fast. Heave taut on the hawser, and brace the yards up for the starboard tack fore and aft, hauling the jib sheet to windward. Heave up the anchor, taking in the slack of the hawser, cat it, pass the stopper, and have all ready for letting go. Haul ahead on the hawser, and as soon as the kedge is short apeak or comes home, sheet home the topsails, run up the jib, and put the helm a-starboard. As soon as the jib fills, run the kedge up and take it in. When the topsails take and she gathers headway, draw the jib, set the spanker, board fore and main tacks, haul aft sheets and right the helm. If she falls off too rapidly when the topsails take, give her the spanker and mainsail, easing off the jib sheet. When she comes to, haul aft the jib sheet and board the fore tack. If, when the kedge is a-weigh, she falls off on the wrong side, let go the anchor.

To get under Way, riding head to Wind and Tide, and to stand out close-hauled.—Suppose you wish to cast to port. Heave short, keeping the helm a-starboard. Set the topsails. Brace up the after yards for the starboard tack, and back the head yards. Man the windlass and heave up the anchor. When the anchor is a-weigh, hoist the jib. When she has paid off sufficiently, fill away the head yards, shift the helm for headway, set the spanker, and make sail. . Cat and fish, either before or after filling away.

If you have no room to cast on either side, but have a vessel on each quarter, heave short, set the topsails, jib, and spanker, brace all the yards half up for the starboard tack, weigh the anchor, and put the helm to port. The tide acting on the rudder will sheer her head to starboard. When the sails take aback and give her sternway, the rudder and aftersails will act against the head sails, and she will drift fairly down between the two vessels. Keep her off or to, by the spanker and jib. When you are clear, cast to port; or, haul up the spanker, shiver the after yards, and let her go off before it.

To get under Way wind-rode, with a Weather Tide; that is, a tide setting to windward.—Suppose you wish to cast to port. Heave short, loose the sails, and set the topsails. Square the after yards, and haul in the starboard head-braces. Heave again, and when you are a-weigh, put the helm to port and hoist the jib. When she has payed off enough, fill away the head yards and shift the helm for headway.

To get under Way, tide-rode, casting to windward.—Suppose the wind to be a little on the starboard bow, and you wish to cast to starboard, standing out on the larboard tack. Having hove short and set the topsails, brace up the after yards for the larboard tack, and brace the head yards aback. Weigh the anchor, keeping your helm to port, and hauling the spanker boom well over to starboard. When she comes head to the wind, hoist the jib, with the sheet to port. Shift the helm for sternway. As she falls off, draw the jib, fill the head yards, and shift the helm for headway.

TO GET UNDER WAY, TIDE-RODE, WEARING ROUND.—Suppose you have the wind on your starboard quarter, and are obliged to wear her round and stand out on the larboard tack. Set the topsails, square the head yards, and shiver the after yards. When the anchor is a-weigh, put the helm hard a-starboard, and give her the foresail, if necessary. Having headway, she will go round on her keel, and you may proceed as in wearing.

If a vessel is in a confined situation, without room to cast by her sails or by the tide, she may be cast by a spring upon her cable, leading in at that which will be the weather quarter. The spring may be bent to the ring of the anchor before it is let go, or it may be seized to the cable just outside the hawse-hole.

It will be remembered that when a vessel is riding head to the tide, the helm is to be put as though she had headway; and when the tide sets from astern, as though she had sternway. But you should be reminded that when you have the wind and tide both ahead, if the vessel, after you weigh your anchor, goes astern faster than the current, the helm must be used as for sternboard.

DICTIONARY OF SEA TERMS.

Aback. The situation of the sails when the wind presses their surfaces against the mast, and tends to force the vessel astern.
Abaft. Toward the stern of a vessel.
Aboard. Within a vessel.
About. On the other tack.
Abreast. Alongside of. Side by side.
Accommodation. (See Ladder.)
A-cock-bill. The situation of the yards when they are topped up at an angle with the deck. The situation of an anchor when it hangs to the cathead by the ring only.
Adrift. Broken from moorings or fasts. Without fasts.
Afloat. Resting on the surface of the water.
Afore. Forward. The opposite of abaft.
Aft—After. Near the stern.
Aground. Touching the bottom.
Ahead. In the direction of the vessel's head. *Wind ahead* is from the direction toward which the vessel's head points.
A-hull. The situation of a vessel when she lies with all her sails furled and her helm lashed a-lee.
A-lee. The situation of the helm when it is put in the opposite direction from that in which the wind blows.
All-aback. When all the sails are aback.
All Hands. The whole crew.
All in the wind. When all the sails are shaking.
Aloft. Above the deck.
Aloof. At a distance.
Amain. Suddenly. At once.
Amidships. In the centre of the vessel; either with reference to her length or to her breadth.
Anchor. The machine by which, when dropped to the bottom, the vessel is held fast.
Anchor-watch. (See Watch.)
An-end. When a mast is perpendicular to the deck.
A-Peek. When the cable is hove taut so as to bring the vessel nearly over her anchor. The *yards* are *a-peek* when they are topped up by contrary lifts.

APRON. A piece of timber fixed behind the lower part of the stem, just above the fore end of the keel. A covering to the vent or lock of a cannon.

ARM. YARD-ARM. The extremity of a yard. Also, the lower part of an anchor, crossing the shank and terminating in the flukes.

ARMING. A piece of tallow put in the cavity and over the bottom of a lead-line.

A-STERN. In the direction of the stern. The opposite of a-head.

A-TAUNT. (See TAUNT.)

ATHWART. Across.
Athwart-ships. Across the line of the vessel's keel.
Athwart-hawse. Across the direction of a vessel's head. Across her cable.

ATHWART-SHIPS. Across the length of a vessel. In opposition to fore-and-aft.

A-TRIP. The situation of the anchor when it is raised clear of the ground. The same as a-weigh.

AVAST, or 'VAST. An order to stop; as, "Avast heaving!"

A-WEATHER. The situation of the helm when it is put in the direction from which the wind blows.

A-WEIGH. The same as a-trip.

AWNING. A covering of canvas over a vessel's deck, or over a boat, to keep off sun or rain.

BACK. *To back an anchor,* is to carry out a smaller one ahead of the one by which the vessel rides, to take off some of the strain.
To back a sail, is to throw it aback.
To back and fill, is alternately to back and fill the sails.

BACKSTAYS. Stays running from a masthead to the vessel's side, slanting a little aft. (See STAYS.)

BAGPIPE. *To bagpipe the mizen,* is to lay it aback by bringing the sheet to the weather mizen rigging.

BALANCE-REEF. A reef in a spanker or fore-and-aft mainsail, which runs from the outer head-earing, diagonally, to the tack. It is the closest reef, and makes the sail triangular, or nearly so.

BALE. *To bale a boat,* is to throw water out of her.

BALLAST. Heavy material, as iron, lead, or stone, placed in the bottom of the hold, to keep a vessel from upsetting.
To freshen ballast, is to shift it. Coarse gravel is called *shingle ballast.*

BANK. *To double bank* an oar, is to have it pulled by two men.

BAR. A bank or shoal at the entrance of a harbour.
Capstan-bars are heavy pieces of wood by which the capstan is hove round.

BARE-POLES. The condition of a ship when she has no sail set.

BARGE. A large double-banked boat, used by the commander of a vessel, in the navy.

BARK, or BARQUE. (See PLATE 4.) A three-masted vessel, having her fore and main masts rigged like a ship's, and her mizen mast like the main mast of a schooner, with no sail upon it but a spanker.

BARNACLE. A shell-fish often found on a vessel's bottom.

BATTENS. Thin strips of wood put around the hatches, to keep the tarpaulin down. Also, put upon rigging to keep it from chafing. A large batten widened at the end, and put upon rigging, is called a *Scotchman*.

BEACON. A post or buoy placed over a shoal or bank to warn vessels off. Also as a signal-mark on land.

BEAMS. Strong pieces of timber stretching across the vessel, to support the decks.

On the weather or lee beam, is in a direction to windward or leeward, at right angles with the keel.

On beam ends. The situation of a vessel when turned over so that her beams are inclined toward the vertical.

BEAR. An object *bears* so and so, when it is in such a direction from the person looking.

To bear down upon a vessel, is to approach her from the windward.

To bear up, is to put the helm up and keep a vessel off from her course, and move her to leeward.

To bear away, is the same as to *bear up*; being applied to the vessel instead of to the tiller.

To bear-a-hand. To make haste.

BEARING. The direction of an object from the person looking. The *bearings* of a vessel, are the widest part of her below the plank-shear. That part of her hull which is on the water-line when she is at anchor and in her proper trim.

BEATING. Going toward the direction of the wind, by alternate tacks.

BECALM. To intercept the wind. A vessel or highland to windward is said to *becalm* another. So one sail *becalms* another.

BECKET. A piece of rope placed so as to confine a spar or another rope. A handle made of rope, in the form of a circle, (as the handle of a chest,) is called a *becket*.

BEES. Pieces of plank bolted to the outer end of the bowsprit, to reeve the foretopmast stays through.

BELAY. To make a rope fast by turns round a pin or coil, without hitching or seizing it.

BEND. To make fast.

To bend a sail, is to make it fast to the yard.

To bend a cable, is to make it fast to the anchor.

A bend, is a knot by which one rope is made fast to antoher.

BENDS. (See PLATE 3.) The strongest part of a vessel's side, to which the beams, knees, and foot-hooks are bolted. The part between the water's edge and the bulwarks.

BENEAPED. (See NEAPED.)

BENTICK SHROUDS. Formerly used, and extending from the futtock-staves to the opposite channels.

BERTH. The place where a vessel lies. The place in which a man sleeps.

BETWEEN-DECKS. The space between any two decks of a ship.

BIBBS. Pieces of timber bolted to the hounds of a mast, to support the trestle trees.

BIGHT. The double part of a rope when it is folded; in contradistinction from the ends. Any part of a rope may be called the bight, except the ends. Also, a bend in the shore, making a small bay or inlet.

BILGE. That part of the floor of a ship upon which she would rest if aground; being the part near the keel which is more in a horizontal than a perpendicular line.

Bilge-ways. Pieces of timber bolted together and placed under the bilge in launching.

Bilged. When the bilge is broken in.

Bilge Water. Water which settles in the bilge.

Bilge. The largest circumference of a cask.

BILL. The point at the extremity of the fluke of an anchor.

BILLET-HEAD. (See HEAD.)

BINNACLE. A box near the helm, containing the compass.

BITTS. Perpendicular pieces of timber going through the deck, placed to secure anything to. The cables are fastened to them, if there is no windlass. There are also *bitts* to secure the windlass, and on each side of the heel of the bowsprit.

BITTER, or BITTER-END. That part of the cable which is abaft the bitts.

BLACKWALL HITCH. (See PLATE 5 and page 41.)

BLADE. The flat part of an oar which goes into the water.

BLOCK. A piece of wood, with sheaves or wheels in it, through which the ropes are rove.

BLUFF. A *bluff-bowed* or *bluff-headed* vessel is one which is full and square forward.

BOARD. The stretch a vessel makes upon one tack, when she is beating.

Stern-board. When a vessel goes stern foremost.

By the board. Said of masts when they fall over the side.

BOAT-HOOK. An iron hook with a long staff, held in the hand, by which a boat is kept fast to a wharf, or vessel.

BOATSWAIN. (Pronounced *bo-s'n.*) A warrant officer in the navy, who has charge of the rigging, and calls the crew to duty.

BOBSTAYS. Used to confine the bowsprit down to the stem or cutwater.

BOLSTERS. Pieces of soft wood, covered with canvas, placed on the trestle-trees, for the eyes of the rigging to rest upon.

BOLTS. Long cylindrical bars of iron or copper, used to secure or unite the different parts of a vessel.

BOLT-ROPE. The rope which goes round a sail, and to which the canvas is sewed.

BONNET. An additional piece of canvas attached to the foot of a jib, or a schooner's foresail, by lacings. Taken off in bad weather.

BOOM. A spar used to extend the foot of a fore-and-aft sail or studding-sail.

Boom-irons. Iron rings on the yards, through which the studding-sail booms traverse.

BOOT-TOPPING. Scraping off the grass, or other matter, which may be on a vessel's bottom, and daubing it over with tallow, or some mixture.

BOUND. *Wind-bound.* When a vessel is kept in port by a head wind.

BOW. The rounded part of a vessel, forward.

BOWER. A working anchor, the cable of which is bent and reeved through the hawse-hole.

Best bower is the larger of the two bowers. (See page 4.)

BOW-GRACE. A frame of old rope or junk, placed round the bows and sides of a vessel, to prevent the ice from injuring her.

BOWLINE. (Pronounced *bo-lin.*) A rope leading forward from the leach of a square sail, to keep the leach well out when sailing close-hauled. A vessel is said to be *on a bowline*, or *on a taut bowline*, when she is close-hauled.

Bowline-bridle. The span on the leach of the sail to which the bowline is toggled.

Bowline-knot. (See PLATE 5, page 40.)

BOWSE. To pull upon a tackle.

BOWSPRIT. (Pronounced *bo-sprit.*) A large and strong spar, standing from the bows of a vessel. (See PLATE 1.)

BOX-HAULING. Wearing a vessel by backing the head sails. (See page 69.)

BOX. *To box the compass*, is to repeat the thirty-two points of the compass in order.

BRACE. A rope by which a yard is turned about.

To brace a yard, is to turn it about horizontally.

To brace up, is to lay the yard more fore and aft.

To brace in, is to lay it nearer square.

To brace aback. (See ABACK.)

To brace to, is to brace the head yards a little aback, in tacking or wearing.

BRAILS. Ropes by which the foot or lower corners of fore-and-aft sails are hauled up.

BRAKE. The handle of a ship's pump.

BREAK. *To break bulk*, is to begin to unload.
   To break ground, is to lift the anchor from the bottom.
   To break shear, is when a vessel, at anchor, in tending, is forced the wrong way by the wind or current, so that she does not lie so well for keeping herself clear of her anchor.

BREAKER. A small cask containing water.

BREAMING. Cleaning a ship's bottom by burning.

BREAST-FAST. A rope used to confine a vessel sideways to a wharf, or to some other vessel.

BREAST-HOOKS. Knees placed in the forward part of a vessel, across the stem, to unite the bows on each side. (See PLATE 3.)

BREAST-ROPE. A rope passed round a man in the chains, while sounding.

BREECH. The outside angle of a knee-timber.

BREECHING. A strong rope used to secure the breech of a gun to the ship's side.

BRIDLE. Spans of rope attached to the leaches of square sails, to which the bowlines are made fast.
   Bridle-port. The foremost port, used for stowing the anchors.

BRIG. A square-rigged vessel, with two masts. An *hermaphrodite brig* has a brig's foremast, and a schooner's mainmast. (See PLATE 4.)

BROACH-TO. To fall off so much, when going free, as to bring the wind round on the other quarter, and take the sails aback.

BROADSIDE. The whole side of a vessel.

BROKEN-BACKED. The state of a vessel when she is so loosened as to droop at each end.

BUCKLERS. Blocks of wood made to fit in the hawse-holes, or holes in the half-ports, when at sea. Those in the hawse-holes are sometimes called *hawse-blocks*.

BULGE. (See BILGE.)

BULK. The whole cargo, when stowed.
   Stowed in bulk, is when goods are stowed loose, instead of being stowed in casks or bags. (See BREAK-BULK.)

BULK-HEAD. Temporary partitions of boards to separate different parts of a vessel.

BULL. A sailor's term for a small keg, holding a gallon or two.

BULL'S-EYE. (See page 45.) A small piece of stout wood with a hole in the centre for a stay or rope to reeve through, without any sheave, and with a groove round it for the strap, which is usually of iron. Also a piece of thick glass inserted in the deck, to let light below.

BULWARKS. The wood-work round a vessel, above her deck, consisting of boards fastened to stanchions and timber-heads.

BUM-BOATS. Boats which lie alongside a vessel in port with provisions and fruit to sell.

BUMPKIN. Pieces of timber projecting from the vessel to board the fore tack to; and from each quarter for the main brace-blocks.

BUNT. The middle of a sail.

BUNTINE. (Pronounced *buntin*.) Thin woollen stuff of which a ship's colours are made.

BUNTLINES. Ropes used for hauling up the body of a sail.

BUOY. A floating cask, or piece of wood, attached by a rope to an anchor, to show its position. Also floated over a shoal, or other dangerous place, as a beacon.

To stream a buoy, is to drop it into the water before letting go the anchor.

A buoy is said to *watch,* when it floats upon the surface of the water.

BURTON. A tackle, rove in a particular manner.

A single Spanish burton has three single blocks, or two single blocks and a hook in the bight of one of the running parts.

A double Spanish burton has three double blocks. (See page 46.)

BUTT. The end of a plank where it unites with the end of another.

Scuttle-butt. A cask with a hole cut in its bilge, and kept on deck to hold water for daily use.

BUTTOCK. That part of the convexity of a vessel abaft, under the stern, contained between the counter above and the after part of the bilge below, and between the quarter on the side and the stern-post. (See PLATE 3.)

BY. *By the head.* Said of a vessel when her head is lower in the water than her stern. If her stern is lower, she is *by the stern.*

By the lee. (See LEE. See RUN.)

CABIN. The after part of a vessel, in which the officers live.

CABLE. A large, strong rope, made fast to the anchor, by which the vessel is secured. It is usually 120 fathoms in length.

CABLE-TIER. (See TIER.)

CABOOSE. A house on deck, where the cooking is done. Commonly called the *Galley*.

CALK. (See CAULK.)

CAMBERED. When the floor of a vessel is higher at the middle than towards the stem and stern.

CAMEL. A machine used for lifting vessels over a shoal or bar.

CAMFERING. Taking off an angle or edge of a timber.

CAN-HOOKS. Slings with flat hooks at each end, used for hoisting barrels or light casks, the hooks being placed round the chimes, and the purchase hooked to the centre of the slings. Small ones are usually wholly of iron.

CANT-PIECES. Pieces of timber fastened to the angles of fishes and side-trees, to supply any part that may prove rotten.

H

Cant-timbers. Timbers at the two ends of a vessel, raised obliquely from the keel.

Lower Half Cants. Those parts of frames situated forward and abaft the square frames, or the floor-timbers which cross the keel.

Canvas. The cloth of which sails are made. No. 1. is the coarsest and strongest.

Cap. A thick, strong block of wood with two holes through it, one square and the other round, used to confine together the head of one mast and the lower part of the mast next above it. (See Plate 1.)

Capsize. To overturn.

Capstan. A machine placed perpendicularly in the deck, and used for a strong purchase in heaving or hoisting. Men-of-war weigh their anchors by capstans. Merchant-vessels use a windlass. (See Bar.)

Careen. To heave a vessel down upon her side by purchases upon the masts. To lie over, when sailing on the wind.

Carlings. Short and small pieces of timber running between the beams.

Carrick-bend. A kind of knot. (See Plate 5, and page 41.)

Carrick-bitts are the windlass bitts.

Carry-away. To break a spar, or part a rope.

Cast. To pay a vessel's head off, in getting under way, on the tack she is to sail upon.

Cat. The tackle used to hoist the anchor up to the cat-head.

Cat-block, the block of this tackle.

Cat-harpin. An iron leg used to confine the upper part of the rigging to the mast.

Cat-head. Large timbers projecting from the vessel's side, to which the anchor is raised and secured.

Cat's-paw. A kind of hitch made in a rope. (See Plate 5, and page 41.) A light current of air seen on the surface of the water during a calm.

Caulk. To fill the seams of a vessel with oakum.

Cavil. (See Kevel.)

Ceiling. The inside planking of a vessel.

Chafe. To rub the surface of a rope or spar.

Chafing-gear is the stuff put upon the rigging and spars to prevent their chafing.

Chains. (See Plate 1.) Strong links or plates of iron, the lower ends of which are bolted through the ship's side to the timbers. Their upper ends are secured to the bottom of the dead-eyes in the channels. Also, used familiarly for the Channels, which see. The chain-cable of a vessel is called familiarly her *chain.*

Rudder-chains lead from the outer and upper end of the rudder to the quarters. They are hung slack.

CHAIN-PLATES. Plates of iron bolted to the side of a ship, to which the chains and dead-eyes of the lower rigging are connected.

CHANNELS. Broad pieces of plank bolted edgewise to the outside of a vessel. Used for spreading the lower rigging. (See CHAINS.)

CHAPELLING. Wearing a ship round, when taken aback, without bracing the head-yards. (See page 74.)

CHECK. A term sometimes used for slacking off a little on a brace, and then belaying it.

CHEEKS. The projections on each side of a mast, upon which the trestle-trees rest. The sides of the shell of a block.

CHEERLY! Quickly, with a will.

CHESS-TREES. Pieces of oak, fitted to the sides of a vessel, abaft the fore chains, with a sheave in them, to board the main tack to. Now out of use.

CHIMES. The ends of the staves of a cask, where they come out beyond the head of the cask.

CHINSE. To thrust oakum into seams with a small iron.

CHOCK. A wedge used to secure anything with, or for anything to rest upon. The long-boat rests upon two large *chocks*, when it is stowed.

Chock-a-block. When the lower block of a tackle is run close up to the upper one, so that you can hoist no higher. This is also called hoisting up *two-blocks*.

CISTERN. An apartment in the hold of a vessel, having a pipe leading out through the side, with a cock, by which water may be let into her.

CLAMPS. Thick planks on the inside of vessels, to support the ends of beams. Also, crooked plates of iron fore-locked upon the trunnions of cannon. Any plate of iron made to turn, open, and shut so as to confine a spar or boom, as, a studdingsail boom, or a boat's mast.

CLASP-HOOK. (See CLOVE-HOOK.)

CLEAT. A piece of wood used in different parts of a vessel to belay ropes to.

CLEW. The lower corner of square sails, and the after corner of a fore-and-aft sail.

To clew up, is to haul up the clew of a sail.

CLEW-GARNET. A rope that hauls up the clew of a foresail or mainsail in a square-rigged vessel.

CLEWLINE. A rope that hauls up the clew of a square-sail. The *clew-garnet* is the clewline of a course.

CLINCH. A half-hitch, stopped to its own part.

CLOSE-HAULED. Applied to a vessel which is sailing with her yards braced up so as to get as much as possible to windward. The same as *on a taut bowline, full and by, on the wind,* &c.

Clove-hitch. Two half-hitches round a spar or other rope. (See Plate 5 and page 39.)

Clove-hook. An iron clasp, in two parts, moving upon the same pivot, and overlapping one another. Used for bending chain-sheets to the clews of sails.

Club-haul. To bring a vessel's head round on the other tack, by letting go the lee anchor, and cutting or slipping the cable. (See page 70.)

Clubbing. Drifting down a current with an anchor out. (See page 71.)

Coaking. Uniting pieces of spar by means of tabular projections, formed by cutting away the solid of one piece into a hollow, so as to make a projection in the other, in such a manner that they may correctly fit, the butts preventing the pieces from drawing asunder.

Coaks are fitted into the beams and knees of vessels to prevent their drawing.

Coal Tar. Tar made from bituminous coal.

Coamings. Raised work round the hatches, to prevent water going down into the hold.

Coat. *Mast-coat* is a piece of canvas, tarred or painted, placed round a mast or bowsprit, where it enters the deck.

Cock-bill. To cock-bill a yard or anchor. (See A-cock-bill.)

Cock-pit. An apartment in a vessel of war, used by the surgeon during an action.

Codline. An eighteen thread line.

Coxswain. (Pronounced *cox'n*.) The person who steers a boat and has charge of her.

Coil. To lay a rope up in a ring, with one turn or fake over another. *A coil* is a quantity of rope laid up in that manner.

Collar. An eye in the end or bight of a shroud or stay, to go over the mast-head.

Come. *Come home*, said of an anchor when it is broken from the ground and drags.

To come up a rope or tackle, is to slack it off.

Companion. A wooden covering over the staircase to a cabin.

Companion-way, the staircase to the cabin.

Companion-ladder. The ladder leading from the poop to the main deck.

Compass. The instrument which tells the course of a vessel.

Compass-timbers are such as are curved or arched.

Concluding-line. A small line leading through the centre of the steps of a rope or Jacob's ladder.

Conning, or **Cunning.** Directing the helmsman in steering a vessel.

Counter. (See Plate 3.) That part of a vessel between the bottom of the stern and the wing-transom and buttock.

COUNTER—*continued.*
   Counter-timbers are short timbers put in to strengthen the counter.
   To counter-brace yards, is to brace the head-yards one way and the after-yards another.

COURSES. The common term for the sails that hang from a ship's lower yards. The foresail is called the *fore course* and the mainsail the *main course.*

CRANES. Pieces of iron or timber at the vessel's sides, used to stow boats or spars upon. A machine used at a wharf for hoisting.

CRANK. The condition of a vessel when she is inclined to lean over a great deal and cannot bear much sail. This may be owing to her construction or to her stowage.

CREEPER. An iron instrument, like a grapnell, with four claws, used for dragging the bottom of a harbour or river, to find anything lost.

CRINGLE. A short piece of rope with each end spliced into the bolt-rope of a sail, confining an iron ring or thimble.

CROSS-BARS. Round bars of iron, bent at each end, used as levers to turn the shank of an anchor.

CROSS-CHOCKS. Pieces of timber fayed across the dead-wood amidships, to make good the deficiency of the heels of the lower futtocks.

CROSS-JACK (pronounced *croj-jack*). The cross-jack yard is the lower yard on the mizen mast. (See PLATE 1.)

CROSS-PAWLS. Pieces of timber that keep a vessel together while in her frames.

CROSS-PIECE. A piece of timber connecting two bitts.

CROSS-SPALES. Pieces of timber placed across a vessel, and nailed to the frames, to keep the sides together until the knees are bolted.

CROSS-TREES. (See PLATE 1.) Pieces of oak supported by the cheeks and trestle-trees, at the mast heads, to sustain the tops on the lower mast, and to spread the topgallant rigging at the topmast head.

CROW-FOOT. A number of small lines rove through the uvrou to suspend an awning by.

CROWN of an anchor, is the place where the arms are joined to the shank.
   To crown a knot, is to pass the strands over and under each other above the knot. (See PLATE 5, page 37.)

CRUTCH. A knee or piece of knee timber, placed inside of a vessel to secure the heels of the cant-timbers abaft. Also, the chock upon which the spanker-boom rests when the sail is not set.

CUCKOLD'S NECK. A knot by which a rope is secured to a spar, the two parts of the rope crossing each other, and seized together.

CUDDY. A cabin in the fore part of a boat.

CUNTLINE. The space between the bilges of two casks, stowed side by side. Where one cask is set upon the cuntline between two others, they are stowed *bilge and cuntline.*

CUT-WATER. The foremost part of a vessel's prow, which projects forward of the bows.

CUTTER. A small boat. Also, a kind of sloop.

DAGGER. A piece of timber crossing all the puppets of the bilge-ways to keep them together.

Dagger-knees. Knees placed obliquely, to avoid a port.

DAVITS. Pieces of timber or iron, with sheaves or blocks at their ends, projecting over a vessel's sides or stern, to hoist boats up to. Also, a spar with a roller or sheave at its end, used for fishing the anchor, called a *fish-davit.*

DEAD-EYE. A circular block of wood, with three holes through it, for the lanyards of rigging to reeve through, without sheaves, and with a groove round it for an iron strap. (See page 45).

DEAD-FLAT. One of the bends amidships.

DEAD-LIGHT. Ports placed in the cabin windows in bad weather.

DEAD RECKONING. A reckoning kept by observing a vessel's courses and distances by the log, to ascertain her position.

DEAD-RISING, or RISING-LINE. Those parts of a vessel's floor, throughout her whole length, where the floor timber is terminated upon the lower futtock.

DEAD-WATER. The eddy under a vessel's counter.

DEAD-WOOD. Blocks of timber, laid upon each end of the keel where the vessel narrows.

DECK. The planked floor of a vessel, resting upon her beams.

DECK-STOPPER. A stopper used for securing the cable forward of the windlass or capstan, while it is overhauled. (See STOPPER.)

DEEP-SEA-LEAD (pronounced *dipsey*). (See page 5.) The lead used in sounding at great depths.

DEPARTURE. The easting or westing made by a vessel. The bearing of an object on the coast from which a vessel commences her dead reckoning.

DERRICK. A single spar, supported by stays and guys, to which a purchase is attached, used to unload vessels, and for hoisting.

DOG. A short iron bar, with a fang or teeth at one end, and a ring at the other. Used for a purchase, the fang being placed against a beam or knee, and the block of a tackle hooked to the ring.

DOG-VANE. A small vane, made of feathers or buntin, to show the direction of the wind.

DOG-WATCHES. Half watches of two hours each, from 4 to 6 and from 6 to 8 P. M. (See WATCH.)

DOLPHIN. A rope or strap round a mast to support the puddening, where the lower yards rest in the slings. Also, a spar or buoy with a large ring in it, secured to an anchor, to which vessels may bend their cables.

DOLPHIN-STRIKER. The martingale. (See PLATE 1.)

DOUSE. To lower suddenly.

DOWELLING. A method of coaking, by letting pieces into the solid, or uniting two pieces together by tenons.

DOWNHAUL. A rope used to haul down jibs, staysails, and studdingsails.

DRABLER. A piece of canvas laced to the bonnet of a sail, to give it more drop.

DRAG. A machine with a bag net, used for dragging on the bottom for anything lost.

DRAUGHT. The depth of water which a vessel requires to float her.

DRAW. A sail *draws* when it is filled by the wind.

To *draw a jib*, is to shift it over the stay to leeward, when it is aback.

DRIFTS. Those pieces in the sheer-draught where the rails are cut off.

DRIVE. To scud before a gale, or to drift in a current.

DRIVER. A spanker.

DROP. The depth of a sail, from head to foot, amidships.

DRUM-HEAD. The top of the capstan.

DUB. To reduce the end of a timber.

DUCK. A kind of cloth, lighter and finer than canvas; used for small sails.

DUNNAGE. Loose wood or other matters, placed on the bottom of the hold, above the ballast, to stow cargo upon.

EARING. A rope attached to the cringle of a sail, by which it is bent or reefed.

EIKING. A piece of wood fitted to make good a deficiency in length.

ELBOW. Two crosses in a hawse. (See page 109.)

ESCUTCHEON. The part of a vessel's stern where her name is written.

EVEN-KEEL. The situation of a vessel when she is so trimmed that she sits evenly upon the water, neither end being down more than the other.

EUPLUVE. A piece of wood, by which the legs of the crow-foot to an awning are extended. (See UNION.)

EYE. The circular part of a shroud or stay, where it goes over a mast.

Eye-bolt. A long iron bar, having an eye at one end, driven through a vessel's deck or side into a timber or beam, with the eye remaining out, to hook a tackle to. If there is a ring through this eye, it is called a *ring-bolt*.

An *Eye-splice* is a certain kind of splice made with the end of a rope. (See PLATE 5 and page 36.)

Eye—*continued*.
   Eyelet-hole. A hole made in a sail for a cringle or roband to go through.
   The Eyes of a vessel. A familiar phrase for the forward part.

Face-pieces. Pieces of wood wrought on the fore part of the knee of the head.

Facing. Letting one piece of timber into another, with a rabbet.

Fag. A rope is *fagged* when the end is untwisted.

Fair-leader. A strip of board or plank, with holes in it, for running rigging, to lead through. Also, a block or thimble used for the same purpose.

Fake. One of the circles or rings made in coiling a rope.

Fall. That part of a tackle to which the power is applied in hoisting.

False Keel. Pieces of timber secured under the main keel of vessels.

Fancy-line. A line rove through a block at the jaws of a gaff, used as a downhaul. Also, a line used for cross-hauling the lee topping-lift.

Fashion-pieces. The aftermost timbers, terminating the breadth and forming the shape of the stern.

Fast. A rope by which a vessel is secured to a wharf. There are *bow* or *head*, *breast*, *quarter*, and *stern* fasts.

Fathom. Six feet.

Feather. *To feather an oar* in rowing, is to turn the blade horizontally with the top aft as it comes out of the water.

Feather-edged. Planks which have one side thicker than another.

Fenders. Pieces of rope or wood hung over the side of a vessel or boat, to protect it from chafing. The fenders of a neat boat are usually made of canvas and stuffed.

Fid. A block of wood or iron, placed through the hole in the heel of a mast, and resting on the trestle-trees of the mast below. This supports the mast. Also, a wooden pin, tapered, used in splicing large ropes, in opening eyes, &c.

Fiddle-block. A long shell, having one sheave over the other, and the lower smaller than the upper.

Fiddle-head. (See Head.)

Fife-rail. The rail going round a mast.

Figure-head. A carved head or full-length figure, over the cut-water.

Fillings. Pieces of timber used to make the curve fair for the mouldings, between the edges of the fish-front and the sides of the mast.

Filler. (See Made Mast.)

Finishing. Carved ornaments of the quarter-galley, below the second counter, and above the upper lights.

FISH. To raise the flukes of an anchor upon the gunwale. Also, to strengthen a spar when sprung or weakened, by putting in or fastening on another piece.
Fish-front, Fishes-sides. (See MADE MAST.)
FISH-DAVIT. The davit used for fishing an anchor.
FISH-HOOK. A hook with a pennant, to the end of which the fish-tackle is hooked.
FISH-TACKLE. The tackle used for fishing an anchor.
FLARE. When the vessel's sides go out from the perpendicular. In opposition to *falling-home* or *tumbling-in.*
FLAT. A sheet is said to be hauled *flat,* when it is hauled down close.
Flat-aback, when a sail is blown with its after surface against the mast.
FLEET. To come up a tackle and draw the blocks apart, for another pull, after they have been hauled *two-blocks.*
Fleet ho! The order given at such times. Also, to shift the position of a block or fall, so as to haul to more advantage.
FLEMISH COIL. (See FRENCH-FAKE.)
FLEMISH-EYE. A kind of eye-splice. (See PLATE 5 and page 36.)
FLEMISH-HORSE. An additional foot-rope at the end of topsail yards.
FLOOR. The bottom of a vessel, on each side of the keelson.
FLOOR TIMBERS. Those timbers of a vessel which are placed across the keel. (See PLATE 3.)
FLOWING SHEET. When a vessel has the wind free, and the lee clews eased off.
FLUKES. The broad triangular plates at the extremity of the arms of an anchor, terminating in a point called the *bill.*
FLY. That part of a flag which extends from the Union to the extreme end. (See UNION.)
FOOT. The lower end of a mast or sail. (See FORE-FOOT.)
FOOT-ROPE. The rope stretching along a yard, upon which men stand when reefing or furling, formerly called *horses.*
FOOT.WALING. The inside planks or lining of a vessel, over the floor-timbers.
FORE. Used to distinguish the forward part of a vessel, or things in that direction; as, *fore mast, fore hatch,* in opposition to *aft* or *after.*
FORE-AND-AFT. Lengthwise with the vessel. In opposition to *athwart ships.* (See SAILS.)
FORECASTLE. That part of the upper deck forward of the fore-mast; or, as some say, forward of the after part of the fore channels. (See PLATE 1.) Also, the forward part of the vessel, under the deck, where the sailors live, in merchant vessels.
FORE-FOOT. A piece of timber at the forward extremity of the keel, upon which the lower end of the stem rests. (See PLATE 3.)
FORE-GANGER. A short piece of rope grafted on a harpoon, to which the line is bent.

Fore Lock. A flat piece of iron, driven through the end of a bolt, to prevent its drawing.

Fore Mast. The forward mast of all vessels. (See **Plate 1.**)

Fore-reach. To shoot ahead, especially when going in stays.

Fore-runner. A piece of rag, terminating the stray-line of the log-line.

Forge. *To forge ahead,* to shoot ahead ; as, in coming to anchor, after the sails are furled. (See **Fore-reach.**)

Formers. Pieces of wood used for shaping cartridges or wads.

Fother, or **Fodder.** To draw a sail, filled with oakum, under a vessel's bottom, in order to stop a leak.

Foul. The term for the opposite of clear.

Foul Anchor. When the cable has a turn round the anchor.

Foul Hawse. When the two cables are crossed or twisted outside the stem.

Founder. A vessel *founders* when she fills with water and sinks.

Fox. (See page 43.) Made by twisting together two or more rope-yarns.

A Spanish fox is made by untwisting a single yarn and laying it up the contrary way.

Frap. To pass ropes round a sail to keep it from blowing loose. Also, to draw ropes round a vessel which is weakened, to keep her together.

Free. A vessel is going *free,* when she has a fair wind and her yards braced in. A vessel is said to be *free,* when the water has been pumped out of her.

Freshen. To relieve a rope, by moving its place; as, to *freshen the nip* of a stay, is to shift it, so as to prevent its chafing through.

To freshen ballast, is to alter its position.

French-fake. To coil a rope with each fake outside of the other, beginning in the middle. If there are to be riding fakes, they begin outside and go in ; and so on. This is called a *Flemish coil.*

Full-and-by. Sailing close-hauled on a wind.

Full-and-by ! The order given to the man at the helm to keep the sails full and at the same time close to the wind.

Furl. To roll a sail up snugly on a yard or boom, and secure it.

Futtock-plates. Iron plates crossing the sides of the top-rim perpendicularly. The dead eyes of the topmast rigging are fitted to their upper ends, and the futtock-shrouds to their lower ends.

Futtock-shrouds. Short shrouds, leading from the lower ends of the futtock-plates to a bend round the lower mast, just below the top.

Futtock-staff. A short piece of wood or iron, seized across the upper part of the rigging, to which the catharpin legs are secured.

FUTTOCK-TIMBERS. (See PLATE 3.) Those timbers between the floor and naval timbers, and the top-timbers. There are two —the *lower*, which is over the floor, and the *middle*, which is over the naval timber. The naval timber is sometimes called the *ground futtock*.

GAFF. A spar, to which the head of a fore-and-aft sail is bent. (See PLATE 1.)

GAFF-TOPSAIL. A light sail set over a gaff, the foot being spread by it.

GAGE. The depth of water of a vessel. Also, her position as to another vessel, as having the *weather* or *lee gage*.

GALLEY. The place where the cooking is done.

GALLOWS-BITTS. A strong frame raised amidships, to support spare spars, &c., in port.

GAMMONING. (See PLATE 1.) The lashing by which the bowsprit is secured to the cut-water.

GANG-CASKS. Small casks, used for bringing water on board in boats.

GANGWAY. (See PLATE 1.) That part of a vessel's side, amidships, where people pass in and out of the vessel.

GANTLINE. (See GIRTLINE.)

GARBOARD-STREAK. (See PLATE 3.) The range of planks next the keel, on each side.

GARLAND. A large rope, strap or grommet, lashed to a spar when hoisting it in board.

GARNET. A purchase on the main stay, for hoisting cargo.

GASKETS. Ropes or pieces of plaited stuff, used to secure a sail to the yard or boom when it is furled. They are called a *bunt*, *quarter*, or *yard-arm gasket*, according to their position on the yard.

GIMBLET. To turn an anchor round by its stock. To turn anything round on its end.

GIRT. The situation of a vessel when her cables are too taut.

GIRTLINE. A rope rove through a single block aloft, making a whip purchase. Commonly used to hoist rigging by, in fitting it.

GIVE WAY! An order to men in a boat to pull with more force, or to begin pulling. The same as, *Lay out on your oars!* or, *Lay out!*

GLUT. A piece of canvas sewed into the centre of a sail, near the head. It has an eyelet-hole in the middle for the bunt-jigger or becket to go through.

GOB-LINE, or GAUB-LINE. A rope leading from the martingale inboard. The same as *back-rope*.

GOODGEON. (See GUDGEON.)

GOOSE-NECK. An iron ring fitted to the end of a yard or boom, for various purposes.

GOOSE-WINGED. The situation of a course when the buntlines and lee clew are hauled up, and the weather clew down.

Gores. The angles at one or both ends of such cloths as increase the breadth or depth of a sail.

Goring-cloths. Pieces cut obliquely and put in to add to the breadth of a sail.

Grafting. (See page 43.) A manner of covering a rope by weaving together yarns.

Grains. An iron, with four or more barbed points to it, used for striking small fish.

Grapnel. A small anchor, with several claws, used to secure boats.

Grappling Irons. Crooked irons, used to seize and hold fast another vessel.

Grating. Open lattice work of wood. Used principally to cover hatches in good weather.

Greave. To clean a ship's bottom by burning.

Gripe. The outside timber of the forefoot, under water, fastened to the lower stem-piece. (See Plate 3.) A vessel *gripes* when she tends to come up into the wind.

Gripes. Bars of iron, with lanyards, rings, and clews, by which a large boat is lashed to the ring-bolts of the deck. Those for a quarter-boat are made of long strips of matting, going round her and set taut by a lanyard.

Grommet. (See Plate 5 and page 37.) A ring formed of rope, by laying round a single strand.

Ground Tackle. General term for anchors, cables, warps, springs, &c.; everything used in securing a vessel at anchor.

Ground-tier. The lowest tier of casks in a vessel's hold.

Guess-warp, or **Guess-rope.** A rope fastened to a vessel or wharf, and used to tow a boat by; or to haul it out to the swinging boom-end, when in port.

Gun-tackle Purchase. A purchase made by two single blocks. (See page 45.)

Gunwale. (Pronounced *gun-nel.*) The upper rail of a boat or vessel.

Guy. A rope attaching to anything to steady it, and bear it one way and another in hoisting.

Gybe. (Pronounced *jibe.*) To shift over the boom of a fore-and-aft sail.

Hail. To speak or call to another vessel, or to men in a different part of a ship.

Halyards. Ropes or tackles used for hoisting and lowering yards, gaffs, and sails.

Half-hitch. (See Plate 5 and page 39.)

Hammock. A piece of canvas, hung at each end, in which seamen sleep.

Hand. To *hand* a sail is to *furl* it.
  Bear a hand: make haste.
  Lend a hand: assist.

HAND—*continued*.
 Hand-over-hand: hauling rapidly on a rope, by putting one hand before the other alternately.
HAND-LEAD. (See page 5.) A small lead, used for sounding in rivers and harbours.
HANDSOMELY. Slowly, carefully. Used for an order, as, "Lower handsomely!"
HANDSPIKE. A long wooden bar, used for heaving at the windlass.
HANDY BILLY. A watch-tackle.
HANKS. Rings or hoops of wood, rope, or iron, round a stay, and seized to the luff of a fore-and-aft sail.
HARPINGS. The fore part of the wales, which encompass the bows of a vessel, and are fastened to the stem. (See PLATE 3.)
HARPOON. A spear used for striking whales and other fish.
HATCH, or HATCHWAY. An opening in the deck to afford a passage up and down. The coverings over these openings are also called *hatches*.
 Hatch-bar is an iron bar going across the hatches to keep them down.
HAUL. *Haul her wind*, said of a vessel when she comes up close upon the wind.
HAWSE. The situation of the cables before a vessel's stem when moored. Also the distance upon the water a little in advance of the stem; as, a vessel sails *athwart the hawse*, or anchors *in the hawse* of another.
 Open hawse. When a vessel rides by two anchors, without any cross in her cables.
HAWSE-HOLE. The hole in the bows through which the cable runs.
HAWSE-PIECES. Timbers through which the hawse-holes are cut.
HAWSE-BLOCK. A block of wood fitted into a hawse-hole at sea.
HAWSER. A large rope used for various purposes, as warping, for a spring, &c.
HAWSER-LAID, or CABLE-LAID rope, is rope laid with nine strands against the sun. (See PLATE 5 and page 34.)
HAZE. A term for punishing a man by keeping him unnecessarily at work upon disagreeable or difficult duty.
HEAD. The work at the prow of a vessel. If it is a carved figure, it is called a *figure-head*; if simple carved work, bending over and out, a *billet-head*; and if bending in, like the handle of a violin, a *fiddle-head*. Also, the upper end of a mast, called a *mast-head*. (See BY-THE-HEAD. See FAST.)
HEAD-LEDGES. Thwartship pieces that frame the hatchways.
HEAD-SAILS. A general name given to all sails that set forward of the fore-mast.
HEART. A block of wood in the shape of a heart, for stays to reeve through.
HEART-YARNS. The centre yarns of a strand.

HEAVE SHORT. To heave in on the cable until the vessel is nearly over her anchor.

HEAVE-TO. To put a vessel in the position of lying to. (See LIE-TO.)

HEAVE IN STAYS. To go about in tacking.

HEAVER. A short wooden bar, tapering at each end. Used as a purchase.

HEEL. The after part of the keel. Also the lower end of a mast or boom. Also the lower end of the stern post.

To heel, is to lie over on one side.

HEELING. The square part of the lower end of a mast, through which the fid-hole is made.

HELM. The machinery by which a vessel is steered, including the rudder, tiller, wheel, &c. Applied more particularly, perhaps, to the tiller.

HELM-PORT. The hole in the counter through which the rudder-head passes.

HELM-PORT TRANSOM. A piece of timber placed across the lower counter, inside at the height of the helm-port, and bolted through every timber, for the security of that port. (See PLATE 3.)

HIGH AND DRY. The situation of a vessel when she is aground, above water mark.

HITCH. A peculiar manner of fastening ropes. (See PLATE 5 and page 39.)

HOG. A flat, rough broom, used for scrubbing the bottom of a vessel.

HOGGED. The state of a vessel when by any strain she is made to droop at each end, bringing her centre up.

HOLD. The interior of a vessel where the cargo is stowed.

HOLD-WATER. To stop the progress of a boat by keeping the oar-blades in the water.

HOLY-STONE. A large stone, used for cleaning a ship's decks.

HOME. The sheets of a sail are said to be *home*, when the clews are hauled chock out to the sheave-holes. An anchor *comes home* when it is loosened from the ground, and is hove in toward the vessel.

HOOD. A covering for a companion hatch.

HOOD-ENDS, or HOODING-ENDS, or WHOODEN-ENDS. Those ends of the planks which fit into the rabbets of the stem or stern-post.

HOOK-AND-BUTT. The scarfing, or laying the ends of timbers over each other.

HORNS. The jaws of booms. Also the ends of cross-trees.

HORSE. (See FOOT-ROPE.)

HOUNDS. Those projections at the mast-head serving as shoulders for the top or trestle-trees to rest upon.

House. To *house* a mast, is to lower it about half its length, and secure it by lashing its heel to the mast below. (See page 27.)
   To house a gun, is to run it in clear of the port and secure it.
Housing, or House-line. (Pronounced *houze-lin*.) A small cord made of three small yarns, and used for seizings.
Hull. The body of a vessel. (See A-hull.)

In-and-out. A term sometimes used for the scantline of the timbers, the moulding way, and particularly for those bolts that are driven into the hanging and lodging knees, through the sides, which are called *in-and-out bolts*.
Inner-post. A piece brought on at the fore side of the main-post, and generally continued as high as the wing-transom, to seat the other transoms upon.
Irons. A ship is said to be in *irons* when, in working, she will not cast one way or the other.
Jack. A common term for the *jack-cross-trees*. (See Union.)
Jack-block. A block used in sending topgallant masts up and down.
Jack-cross-trees. (See Plate 1.) Iron cross-trees at the head of long topgallant masts.
Jack-staff. A short staff, raised at the bowsprit cap, upon which the Union Jack is hoisted.
Jack-stays. Ropes stretched taut along a yard to bend the head of the sail to. Also long strips of wood or iron, used now for the same purpose.
Jack-screw. A purchase, used for stowing cotton.
Jacob's Ladder. A ladder made of rope, with wooden steps.
Jaws. The inner ends of booms or gaffs, hollowed in.
Jeers. Tackles for hoisting the lower yards.
Jewel-blocks. Single blocks at the yard-arms, through which the studdingsail halyards lead.
Jib. (See Plate 2.) A triangular sail, set on a stay, forward.
   Flying-jib sets outside of the jib; and the *jib-o'-jib* outside of that.
Jib-boom. (See Plate 1.) The boom rigged out beyond the bowsprit, to which the tack of the jib is lashed.
Jigger. A small tackle used about decks or aloft.
Jolly-boat. A small boat, usually hoisted at the stern.
Junk. Condemned rope, cut up and used for making mats, swabs, oakum, &c.
Jury-mast. A temporary mast, rigged at sea, in place of one lost.

Keckling. Old rope wound round cables, to keep them from chafing. (See Rounding.)
Kedge. A small anchor, with an iron stock, used for warping.
   To kedge, is to warp a vessel ahead by a kedge and hawser.

KEEL. (See PLATE 3.) The lowest and principal timber of a vessel, running fore-and-aft its whole length, and supporting the whole frame. It is composed of several pieces, placed lengthwise, and scarfed and bolted together. (See FALSE KEEL.)

KEEL-HAUL. To haul a man under a vessel's bottom, by ropes at the yard-arms on each side. Formerly practised as a punishment in ships of war.

KEELSON. (See PLATE 3.) A timber placed over the keel on the floor timbers, and running parallel with it.

KENTLEDGE. Pig-iron ballast, laid each side of the keelson.

KEVEL, or CAVIL. A strong piece of wood, bolted to some timber or stanchion, used for belaying large ropes to.

KEVEL-HEADS. Timber-heads used as kevels.

KINK. A twist in a rope.

KNEES. (See PLATE 3.) Crooked pieces of timber, having two arms, used to connect the beams of a vessel with her timbers. (See DAGGER.)

Lodging-knees, are placed horizontally, having one arm bolted to a beam, and the other across two of the timbers.

Knee of the head, is placed forward of the stem, and supports the figure-head.

KNIGHT-HEADS, or BOLLARD-TIMBERS. The timbers next the stem on each side, and continued high enough to form a support for the bowsprit. (See PLATE 3.)

KNITTLES, or NETTLES. (See page 43.) The halves of two adjoining yarns in a rope, twisted up together, for pointing or grafting. Also, small line used for seizings and for hammock-clews.

KNOCK-OFF! An order to leave off work.

KNOT. A division on the log-line, answering to a mile of distance. (See page 5.)

LABOUR. A vessel is said to labour when she rolls or pitches heavily.

LACING. Rope used to lash a sail to a gaff, or a bonnet to a sail. Also, a piece of compass or knee timber, fayed to the back of the figure-head and the knee of the head, and bolted to each.

LAND-FALL. The making land after being at sea.

A good land-fall, is when a vessel makes the land as intended.

LAND HO! The cry used when land is first seen.

LANYARDS. Ropes rove through dead-eyes for setting up rigging. Also, a rope made fast to anything to secure it, or as a handle, is called a *lanyard.*

LARBOARD. The left side of a vessel, looking forward.

LARBOWLINES. The familar term for the men in the larboard watch.

LARGE. A vessel is said to be going *large*, when she has the wind free.

LATCHINGS. Loops on the head-rope of a bonnet, by which it is laced to the foot of the sail.

LAUNCH. A large boat. The LONG-BOAT.

LAUNCH HO! High enough!

LAY. To come or to go; as, *Lay aloft! Lay forward! Lay aft!* Also the direction in which the strands of a rope are twisted; as, from left to right, or from right to left.

LEACH. The border or edge of a sail, at the sides.

LEACHLINE. A rope used for hauling up the leach of a sail.

LEAD. A piece of lead, in the shape of a cone or pyramid, with a small hole at the base, and a line attached to the upper end, used for sounding. (See HAND-LEAD, DEEP-SEA-LEAD.)

LEADING-WIND. A fair wind. More particularly applied to a wind abeam or quartering.

LEAK. A hole or breach in a vessel, at which the water comes in.

LEDGES. Small pieces of timber placed athwart-ships under the decks of a vessel, between the beams.

LEE. The side opposite to that from which the wind blows; as, if a vessel has the wind on her starboard side, that will be the *weather*, and the larboard will be the *lee* side.

A lee shore is the shore upon which the wind is blowing.

Under the lee of anything, is when you have that between you and the wind.

By the lee. The situation of a vessel going free, when she has fallen off so much as to bring the wind round her stern, and to take her sails aback on the other side.

LEE-BOARD. A board fitted to the lee side of flat-bottomed boats, to prevent their drifting to leeward.

LEE-GAGE. (See GAGE.)

LEEWAY. What a vessel loses by drifting to leeward. When sailing close-hauled with all sail set, a vessel should make no leeway. If the topgallant sails are furled, it is customary to allow one point; under close-reefed topsails, two points; when under one close-reefed sail, four or five points.

LEEFANGE. An iron bar, upon which the sheets of fore-and-aft sails traverse. Also, a rope rove through the cringle of a sail which has a bonnet to it, for hauling in, so as to lace on the bonnet. Not much used.

LEEWARD. (Pronounced *lu-ard*.) The lee side. In a direction opposite to that from which the wind blows, which is called *windward.* The opposite of *lee* is *weather*, and of *leeward* is *windward;* the first two being adjectives.

LIE-TO, is to stop the progress of a vessel at sea, either by counter-bracing the yards, or by reducing sail so that she will make little or no headway, but will merely come to and fall off by the counteraction of the sails and helm.

LIFE-LINES. Ropes carried along yards, booms, &c., or at any part of the vessel, for men to hold on by.

LIFT. A rope or tackle, going from the yard-arms to the mast-head, to support and move the yard. Also, a term applied to the sails when the wind strikes them on the leaches and raises them slightly.

LIGHT. To move or lift anything along; as, to "*Light* out to windward!" that is, haul the sail over to windward. The *light sails* are all above the topsails, also the studdingsails and flying jib.

LIGHTER. A large boat, used in loading and unloading vessels.

LIMBERS, or LIMBER-HOLES. Holes cut in the lower part of the floor-timbers, next the keelson, forming a passage for the water fore-and-aft.

Limber-boards are placed over the limbers, and are moveable.

Limber-rope. A rope rove fore-and aft through the limbers, to clear them if necessary.

Limber-streak. The streak of foot-waling nearest the keelson.

LIST. The inclination of a vessel to one side; as, a *list* to port, or a *list* to starboard.

LIZARD. A piece of rope, sometimes with two legs, and one or more iron thimbles spliced into it. It is used for various purposes. One with two legs, and a thimble to each, is often made fast to the topsail tye, for the buntlines to reeve through. A single one is sometimes used on the swinging-boom topping-lift.

LOCKER. A chest or box to stow anything away in.

Chain-locker. Where the chain cables are kept.

Boatswain's locker. Where tools and small stuff for working upon rigging are kept.

LOG, or LOG-BOOK. A journal kept by the chief officer, in which the situation of the vessel, winds, weather, courses, distances, and everything of importance that occurs, is noted down.

Log. A line with a piece of board, called the *log-ship*, at-tached to it, wound upon a reel, and used for ascertaining the ship's rate of sailing. (See page 57.)

LONG-BOAT. The largest boat in a merchant-vessel. When at sea, it is carried between the fore and main masts.

LONGERS. The longest casks, stowed next the keelson.

LONG-TIMBERS. Timbers in the cant-bodies, reaching from the dead-wood to the head of the second futtock.

LOOF. That part of a vessel where the planks begin to bend as they approach the stern.

Loom. That part of an oar which is within the row-lock. Also, to appear above the surface of the water; to appear larger than nature, as in a fog.

Lubber's Hole. A hole in the top, next the mast.

Luff. To put the helm so as to bring the ship up nearer to the wind.

Spring-a-luff! Keep your luff! &c. Orders to luff. Also, the roundest part of a vessel's bow. Also the forward leach of fore-and-aft sails.

Luff-tackle. A purchase composed of a double and single block. (See page 46.)

Luff-upon-Luff. A luff-tackle applied to the fall of another.

Lugger. A small vessel carrying lug-sails.

Lug-sail. A sail used in boats and small vessels, bent to a yard which hangs obliquely to the mast.

Lurch. The sudden rolling of a vessel to one side.

Lying-to. (See Lie-to.)

Made. A *made mast* or *block* is one composed of different pieces. A ship's lower mast is a made spar, her topmast is a whole spar.

Mall, or Maul (pronounced *mawl*). A heavy iron hammer used in driving bolts. (See Top-maul.)

Mallet. A small maul, made of wood; as, *caulking-mallet*; also, *serving-mallet*, used in putting service on a rope.

Manger. A coaming just within the hawse-hole.

Man-ropes. Ropes used in going up and down a vessel's side.

Marl. To wind or twist a small line or rope round another.

Marline (pronounced *mar-lin*). Small two-stranded stuff, used for marling. A finer kind of spunyarn.

Marling-hitch. A kind of hitch used in marling.

Marlingspike. An iron pin, sharpened at one end, and having a hole in the other for a lanyard. Used both as a fid and a heaver.

Marry. To join ropes together by a worming over both.

Martingale. A short, perpendicular spar, under the bowsprit-end, used for guying down the head-stays. (See Dolphin-striker.)

Mast. A spar set upright from the deck, to support rigging, yards, and sails. Masts are whole or *made*.

Mat. Made of strands of old rope, and used to prevent chafing.

Mate. An officer under the master.

Maul. (See Mall.)

Mend. *To mend service*, is to add more to it.

Meshes. The places between the lines of a netting.

Mess. Any number of men who eat or lodge together.

Messenger. A rope used for heaving in a cable by the capstan.

Midships. The timbers at the broadest part of the vessel. (See Amidships.)

Miss-stays. To fail of going about from one tack to another. (See page 65.)

Mizen-mast. The aftermost mast of a ship. (See Plate 1.) The spanker is sometimes called the *mizen.*

Monkey Block. A small single block strapped with a swivel.

Moon-sail. A small sail sometimes carried in light winds, above a skysail.

Moor. To secure by two anchors. (See page 83.)

Mortice. A *morticed block* is one made out of a whole block of wood with a hole cut in it for the sheave; in distinction from a *made block.* (See page 44.)

Moulds. The patterns by which the frames of a vessel are worked out.

Mouse. To put turns of rope yarn or spun yarn round the end of a hook and its standing part, when it is hooked to anything, so as to prevent its slipping out.

Mousing. A knot or puddening, made of yarns, and placed on the outside of a rope.

Muffle. Oars are muffled by putting mats or canvas round their looms in the row-locks.

Munions. The pieces that separate the lights in the galleries.

Naval Hoods, or **Hawse Bolsters.** Plank above and below the hawse-holes.

Neap Tides. Low tides, coming at the middle of the moon's second and fourth quarters. (See Spring Tides.)

Neaped, or **Beneaped.** The situation of a vessel when she is aground at the height of the spring tides.

Near. Close to wind. "Near!" the order to the helmsman when he is too near the wind.

Netting. Network of rope or small lines. Used for stowing away sails or hammocks.

Nettles. (See Knittles.)

Ninepin Block. A block in the form of a ninepin, used for a *fair leader* in the rail.

Nip. A short turn in a rope.

Nippers. A number of yarns marled together, used to secure a cable to the messenger.

Nock. The forward upper end of a sail that sets with a boom.

Nun-buoy. A buoy tapering at each end.

Nut. Projections on each side of the shank of an anchor, to secure the stock to its place.

Oakum. Stuff made by picking rope-yarns to pieces. Used for caulking, and other purposes.

Oar. A long wooden instrument with a flat blade at one end, used for propelling boats.

OFF-AND-ON. To stand on different tacks towards and from the land.
OFFING. Distance from the shore.
ORLOP. The deck beneath the lower deck of a ship of the line on which the cables are stowed.
OUT-HAUL. A rope used for hauling out the clew of a boom sail.
OUT-RIGGER. A spar rigged out to windward from the tops or cross-trees, to spread the breast-backstays. (See page 14.)
OVERHAUL. *To overhaul a tackle*, is to let go the fall and pull on the leading parts so as to separate the blocks.
To overhaul a rope, is generally to pull a part through a block so as to make slack.
To overhaul rigging, is to examine it.
OVER-RAKE. Said of heavy seas which come over a vessel's head when she is at anchor, head to the sea.

PAINTER. A rope attached to the bows of a boat, used for making her fast.
PALM. A piece of leather fitted over the hand, with an iron for the head of a needle to press against in sewing upon canvas. Also, the fluke of an anchor.
PANCH. (See PAUNCH.)
PARBUCKLE. To hoist or lower a spar or cask by single ropes passed round it.
PARCEL. (See page 34.) To wind tarred canvas (called *parcelling*) round a rope.
PARCELLING. (See PARCEL.)
PARLIAMENT-HEEL. The situation of a vessel when she is careened.
PARRAL. The rope by which a yard is confined to a mast at its centre.
PART. To break a rope.
PARTNERS. A framework of short timber fitted to the hole in a deck, to receive the heel of a mast or pump, &c.
PAZAREE. A rope attached to the clew of the foresail and rove through a block on the swinging boom. Used for guying the clews out when before the wind.
PAUNCH MAT. A thick mat, placed at the slings of a yard or elsewhere.
PAWL. A short bar of iron, which prevents the capstan or windlass from turning back.
To pawl, is to drop a pawl and secure the windlass or capstan.
PAY-OFF. When a vessel's head falls off from the wind.
To pay, to cover over with tar or pitch.
To pay out. To slack up on a cable and let it run out.
PEAK. The upper outer corner of a gaff-sail.
PEAK. (See A-PEAK.)
A *stay-peak* is when the cable and forestay form a line.
A *short stay-peak* is when the cable is too much in to form this line.

PENDANT, or PENNANT. A long narrow piece of bunting, carried at the mast-head.

Broad pennant, is a swallow-tailed piece, carried in the same way, in a commodore's vessel.

Pennant. A rope to which a purchase is hooked. A long strap fitted at one end to a yard or mast-head, with a hook or block at the other end, for a brace to reeve through, or to hook a tackle to.

PILLOW. A block which supports the inner end of the bowsprit.

PIN. The axis on which a sheave turns. Also, a short piece of wood or iron to belay ropes to.

PINK-STERN. A high, narrow stern.

PINNACE. A boat, in size between the launch and a cutter.

PINTLE. A metal bolt used for hanging a rudder.

PITCH. A resin taken from pine, and used for filling up the seams of a vessel.

PLANKS. Thick, strong boards, used for covering the sides and decks of vessels.

PLAT. A braid of foxes. (See Fox.)

PLATE. (See CHAIN-PLATE.)

PLUG. A piece of wood, fitted into a hole in a vessel or boat, so as to let in or keep out water.

POINT. To take the end of a rope and work it over with knittles. (See page 43. See REEF-POINTS.)

POLE. Applied to the highest mast of a ship, usually painted ; as, *sky-sail pole.*

POOP. A deck raised over the after part of the spar deck. A vessel is *pooped* when the sea breaks over her stern.

POPPETS. Perpendicular pieces of timber fixed to the fore-and-aft part of the bilge-ways in launching.

PORT. Used instead of *larboard.*

To port the helm, is to put it to the larboard.

PORT, or PORT-HOLE. Holes in the side of a vessel, to point cannon out of. (See BRIDLE.)

PORTOISE. The gunwale. The yards are *a-portoise* when they rest on the gunwale.

PORT-SILLS. (See SILLS.)

PREVENTER. An additional rope or spar, used as a support.

PRICK. A quantity of spunyarn or rope laid close up together.

PRICKER. A small marlinspike, used in sail-making. It generally has a wooden handle.

PUDDENING. A quantity of yarns, matting, or oakum, used to prevent chafing.

PUMP-BRAKE. The handle to the pump.

PURCHASE. A mechanical power which increases the force applied.

To purchase, is to raise by a purchase.

QUARTER. The part of a vessel's side between the after part of the main chains and the stern. The *quarter* of a yard is between the slings and the yard-arm.

The wind is said to be *quartering*, when it blows in a line between that of the keel and the beam, and abaft the latter.

QUARTER-BLOCK. A block fitted under the quarters of a yard on each side the slings, for the clewlines and sheets to reeve through.

QUARTER-DECK. That part of the upper deck abaft the main-mast.

QUARTER-MASTER. A petty officer in a man-of-war, who attends the helm and binnacle at sea, and watches for signals, &c., when in port.

QUICK-WORK. That part of a vessel's side which is above the chain-wales and decks. So called in ship-building.

QUILTING. A coating about a vessel, outside, formed of ropes woven together.

QUOIN. A wooden wedge for the breech of a gun to rest upon.

RACE. A strong rippling tide.

RACK. To seize two ropes together, with cross-turns. Also, a *fair-leader* for running rigging.

RACK-BLOCK. A course of blocks made from one piece of wood, for fair-leaders.

RAKE. The inclination of a mast from the perpendicular.

RAMLINE. A line used in mast-making to get a straight middle line on a spar.

RANGE OF CABLE. A quantity of cable, more or less, placed in order for letting go the anchor or paying out.

RATLINES. (Pronounced *rat-lins*.) Lines running across the shrouds, horizontally, like the rounds of a ladder, and used to step upon in going aloft.

RATTLE DOWN RIGGING. To put ratlines upon rigging. It is still called rattling *down*, though they are now rattled *up;* beginning at the lowest. (See page 11.)

RAZEE. A vessel of war which has one deck cut down.

REEF. To reduce a sail by taking in upon its head, if a square sail, and its foot, if a fore-and-aft sail.

REEF-BAND. A band of stout canvas sewed on the sail across, with points in it, and earings at each end for reefing.

A *reef* is all of the sail that is comprehended between the head of the sail and the first reef-band, or between two reef-bands.

REEF-TACKLE. A tackle used to haul the middle of each leach up toward the yard, so that the sail may be easily reefed.

REEVE. To pass the end of a rope through a block, or any aperture.

Relieving Tackle. A tackle hooked to the tiller in a gale of wind, to steer by, in case anything should happen to the wheel or tiller-ropes.

Render. To pass a rope through a place. A rope is said to *render* or not, according as it goes freely through any place.

Rib-bands. Long, narrow, flexible pieces of timber nailed to the outside of the ribs, so as to encompass the vessel lengthwise.

Ribs. A figurative term for a vessel's timbers.

Ride at anchor. To lie at anchor. Also, to bend or bear down by main strength and weight; as, to ride down the main tack.

Riders. Interior timbers placed occasionally opposite the principal ones, to which they are bolted, reaching from the keelson to the beams of the lower deck. Also, casks forming the second tier in a vessel's hold.

Rigging. The general term for all the ropes of a vessel. (See Running, Standing.) Also, the common term for the shrouds with their ratlines; as, the *main rigging, mizen rigging,* &c.

Right. To *right* the helm, is to put it amidships.

Rim. The edge of a top.

Ring. The iron ring at the upper end of an anchor, to which the cable is bent.

Ring-bolt. An eye-bolt with a ring through the eye. (See Eye-bolt.)

Ring-tail. A small sail, shaped like a jib, set abaft the spanker in light winds.

Roach. A curve in the foot of a square sail, by which the clews are brought below the middle of the foot. The *roach* of a fore-and-aft sail is in its forward leach.

Road, or **Roadstead.** An anchorage at some distance from the shore.

Robands. (See Rope-bands.)

Rolling-tackle. Tackles used to steady the yards in a heavy sea.

Rombowline. Condemned canvas, rope, &c.

Rope-bands, or **Robands.** Small pieces of two or three yarn, spunyarn, or marline, used to confine the head of the sail to the yard or gaff.

Rope-yarn. A thread of hemp, or other stuff, of which a rope is made. (See page 33.)

Rough-tree. An unfinished spar.

Round in. To haul in on a rope, especially a weather-brace.

Round up. To haul up on a tackle.

Rounding. A service of rope, hove round a spar or larger rope.

Rowlocks, or **Rollocks.** Places cut in the gunwale of a boat for the oar to rest in while pulling.

Royal. A light sail next above a topgallant sail. (See Plate 2.)

ROYAL YARD. The yard from which the royal is set. The fourth from the deck. (See PLATE 1.)

RUBBER. A small instrument used to rub or flatten down the seams of a sail in sail-making.

RUDDER. The machine by which a vessel or boat is steered.

RUN. The after part of a vessel's bottom, which rises and narrows in approaching the stern-post.

By the run. To let go *by the run,* is to let go altogether, instead of slacking off.

RUNG-HEADS. The upper ends of the floor timbers.

RUNNER. A rope used to increase the power of a tackle. It is rove through a single block which you wish to bring down, and a tackle is hooked to each end, or to one end, the other being made fast.

RUNNING RIGGING. The ropes that reeve through blocks, and are pulled and hauled, such as braces, halyards, &c.; in opposition to the *standing rigging,* the ends of which are securely seized, such as stays, shrouds, &c. (See page 33.)

SADDLES. Pieces of wood hollowed out to fit on the yards, to which they are nailed, having a hollow in the upper part for the boom to rest in.

SAG. To *sag to leeward,* is to drift off bodily to leeward.

SAILS are of two kinds : *square sails,* which hang from yards, their foot lying across the line of the keel, as the courses, topsails, &c.; and *fore-and-aft sails,* which set upon gaffs, or on stays, their foot running with the line of the keel, as jib, spanker, &c.

SAIL HO! The cry used when a sail is first discovered at sea.

SAVE-ALL. A small sail sometimes set under the foot of a lower studdingsail. (See WATER SAIL.)

SCANTLING. A term applied to any piece of timber, with regard to its breadth and thickness, when reduced to the standard size.

SCARF. To join two pieces of timber at their ends by shaving them down and placing them over-lapping.

SCHOONER. (See PLATE 4.) A small vessel with two masts and no tops.

A *fore-and-aft schooner* has only fore-and-aft sails.

A *topsail schooner* carries a square fore topsail, and frequently, also, topgallant sail and royal. There are some schooners with three masts. They also have no tops.

A *maintopsail schooner* is one that carries square topsails, fore and aft.

SCORE. A groove in a block or dead-eye.

SCOTCHMAN. A large batten placed over the turnings-in of rigging. (See BATTEN.)

SCRAPER. A small, triangular iron instrument, with a handle fitted to its centre, and used for scraping decks and masts.

SCROWL. A piece of timber bolted to the knees of the head, in place of a figure-head.

SCUD. To drive before a gale, with no sail, or only enough to keep the vessel ahead of the sea. Also, low, thin clouds that fly swiftly before the wind.

SCULL. A short oar.

To scull, is to impel a boat by one oar at the stern.

SCUPPERS. Holes cut in the water-ways for the water to run from the decks.

SCUTTLE. A hole cut in a vessel's deck, as, a hatchway. Also, a hole cut in any part of a vessel.

To scuttle, is to cut or bore holes in a vessel to make her sink.

SCUTTLE-BUTT. (See BUTT.)

SEAMS. The intervals between planks in a vessel's deck or side.

SEIZE. To fasten ropes together by turns of small stuff.

SEIZINGS. (See page 42.) The fastenings of ropes that are seized together.

SELVAGEE. A skein of rope-yarns or spunyarn, marled together. Used as a neat strap. (See page 42.)

SEND. When a ship's head or stern pitches suddenly and violently into the trough of the sea.

SENNIT, or SINNIT. (See page 42.) A braid, formed by plaiting rope-yarns or spunyarn together. Straw, plaited in the same way for hats, is called sennit.

SERVE. (See page 35.) To wind small stuff, as rope-yarns, spun-yarn, &c., round a rope, to keep it from chafing. It is wound and hove round taut by a serving-board or mallet.

SERVICE, is the stuff so wound round.

SET. To *set up rigging*, is to tauten it by tackles. The seizings are then put on afresh.

SHACKLES. Links in a chain cable which are fitted with a moveable bolt, so that the chain can be separated.

SHAKES. The staves of hogsheads taken apart.

SHANK. The main piece in an anchor, at one end of which the stock is made fast, and at the other the arms.

SHANK-PAINTER. A strong rope by which the lower part of the shank of an anchor is secured to the ship's side.

SHARP UP. Said of yards when braced as near fore-and-aft as possible.

SHEATHING. A casing or covering on a vessel's bottom.

SHEARS. Two or more spars, raised at angles and lashed together near their upper ends, used for taking in masts. (See page 44.)

SHEAR HULK. An old vessel fitted with shears, &c., and used for taking out and putting in the masts of other vessels.

SHEAVE. The wheel in a block upon which the rope works.

Sheave-hole, the place cut in a block for the ropes to reeve through.

Sheep-shank. A kind of hitch or bend, used to shorten a rope temporarily. (See Plate 5 and page 42.)

Sheer, or Sheer-strake. The line of plank on a vessel's side, running fore-and-aft under the gunwale. Also, a vessel's position when riding by a single anchor.

Sheet. A rope used in setting a sail, to keep the clew down to its place. With square sails, the sheets run through each yard-arm. With boom sails, they haul the boom over one way and another. They keep down the inner clew of a studding-sail and the after clew of a jib. (See Home.)

Sheet Anchor. A vessel's largest anchor: not carried at the bow.

Shell. The case of a block.

Shingle. (See Ballast.)

Ship. A vessel with three masts, with tops and yards to each. (See Plate 4.) To enter on board a vessel. To fix anything in its place.

Shiver. To shake the wind out of a sail by bracing it so that the wind strikes upon the leach.

Shoe. A piece of wood used for the bill of an anchor to rest upon, to save the vessel's side. Also, for the heels of shears, &c.

Shoe-block. A block with two sheaves, one above the other, the one horizontal and the other perpendicular.

Shore. A prop or stanchion, placed under a beam. To *shore*, to prop up.

Shrouds. A set of ropes reaching from the mast-heads to the vessel's sides, to support the masts.

Sills. Pieces of timber put in horizontally between the frames to form and secure any opening; as, for ports.

Sister Block. A long piece of wood with two sheaves in it, one above the other, with a score between them for a seizing, and a groove around the block, lengthwise.

Skids. Pieces of timber placed up and down a vessel's side, to bear any articles off clear that are hoisted in.

Skin. The part of a sail which is outside and covers the rest when it is furled. Also, familiarly, the sides of the hold; as, an article is said to be stowed *next the skin*.

Skysail. A light sail next above the royal. (See Plate 2.)

Sky-scraper. A name given to a skysail when it is triangular.

Slabline. A small line used to haul up the foot of a course.

Slack. The part of a rope or sail that hangs down loose.

Slack in stays, said of a vessel when she works slowly in tacking.

Sleepers. The knees that connect the transoms to the after timbers on the ship's quarter.

Sling. To set a cask, spar, gun, or other article, in ropes, so as to put on a tackle and hoist or lower it.

SLINGS. The ropes used for securing the centre of a yard to the mast.
    Yard-slings are now made of iron. Also, a large rope fitted so as to go round any article which is to be hoisted or lowered.

SLIP. To let a cable go and stand out to sea. (See page 85.)

SLIP-ROPE. A rope bent to the cable just outside the hawse-hole, and brought in on the weather quarter, for slipping. (See page 85.)

SLOOP. A small vessel with one mast. (See PLATE 4.)

SLOOP OF WAR. A vessel of any rig, commanded by a commander in the navy.

SLUE. To turn anything round or over.

SMALL STUFF. The term for spunyarn, marline, and the smallest kinds of rope, such as ratline-stuff, &c.

SNAKE. To pass small stuff across a seizing, with marling hitches at the outer turns.

SNATCH-BLOCK. A single block, with an opening in its side below the sheave, or at the bottom, to receive the bight of a rope.

SNOTTER. A rope going over a yard-arm, with an eye, used to bend a tripping-line to in sending down topgallant and royal yards in vessels of war.

SNOW. A kind of brig, formerly used.

SNUB. To check a rope suddenly.

SNYING. A term for a circular plank, edgewise, to work in the bows of a vessel.

So! An order to 'vast hauling upon anything when it has come to its right position.

SOLE. A piece of timber fastened to the foot of the rudder, to make it level with the false keel.

SOUND. To get the depth of water by a lead and line. (See page 80.) The pumps are *sounded* by an iron *sounding rod*, marked with a scale of feet and inches.

SPAN. A rope with both ends made fast, for a purchase to be hooked to its bight.

SPANKER. The after sail of a ship or bark. It is a fore-and-aft sail, setting with a boom and gaff. (See PLATE 2.)

SPAR. The general term for all masts, yards, booms, gaffs, &c.

SPELL. The common term for a portion of time given to any work.
    To spell, is to relieve another at his work.
    Spell ho! An exclamation used as an order or request to be relieved at work by another.

SPENCER. A fore-and-aft sail, set with a gaff and no boom, and hoisting from a small mast called a *spencer-mast*, just abaft the fore and main masts. (See PLATES 2 and 4.)

Spill. To shake the wind out of a sail by bracing it so that the wind may strike its leach and shiver it.

Spilling Line. A rope used for spilling a sail. Rove in bad weather.

Spindle. An iron pin upon which the capstan moves. Also, a piece of timber forming the diameter of a made mast. Also, any long pin or bar upon which anything revolves.

Spirketing. The planks from the water-ways to the port-sills.

Splice. (See Plate 5 and page 35.) To join two ropes together by interweaving their strands.

Spoon-drift. Water swept from the tops of the waves by the violence of the wind in a tempest, and driven along before it, covering the surface of the sea.

Spray. An occasional sprinkling dashed from the top of a wave by the wind, or by its striking an object.

Spring. To crack or split a mast.

To spring a leak, is to begin to leak.

To spring a luff, is to force a vessel close to the wind, in sailing.

Spring-stay. A preventer-stay, to assist the regular one. (See Stay.)

Spring Tides. The highest and lowest course of tides, occurring every new and full moon.

Sprit. A small boom or gaff, used with some sails in small boats. The lower end rests in a becket or snotter by the foot of the mast, and the other end spreads and raises the outer upper corner of the sail, crossing it diagonally. A sail so rigged in a boat is called a *sprit-sail*.

Sprit-sail yard. (See Plate 1.) A yard lashed across the bowsprit or knight-heads, and used to spread the guys of the jib and flying jib-boom. There was formerly a sail bent to it called a *sprit-sail*.

Spunyarn. (See page 35.) A cord formed by twisting together two or three rope-yarns.

Spurling-line. A line communicating between the tiller and tell-tale.

Spurs. Pieces of timber fixed on the bilge-ways, their upper ends being bolted to the vessel's sides above the water. Also, curved pieces of timber, serving as half beams, to support the decks where whole beams cannot be placed.

Spur-shoes. Large pieces of timber that come abaft the pump-well.

Square. Yards are *squared* when they are horizontal and at right angles with the keel. Squaring by the lifts makes them horizontal; and by the braces, makes them at right angles with the vessel's line. Also, the proper term for the length of yards. A vessel has square yards when her yards are unusually long. A sail is said to be very *square* in the head when it is long on the head.

SQUARE—*continued*.

To square a yard, in working a ship, means to bring it in square by the braces.

SQUARE-SAIL. A temporary sail set at the fore-mast of a schooner or sloop when going before the wind. (See SAIL.)

STABBER. A PRICKER.

STAFF. A pole or mast used to hoist flags upon.

STANCHIONS. (See PLATE 3.) Upright posts of wood or iron, placed so as to support the beams of a vessel. Also, upright pieces of timber, placed at intervals along the sides of a vessel, to support the bulwarks and rail, and reaching down to the bends, by the side of the timbers, to which they are bolted. Also, any fixed, upright support; as to an awning, or for the man-ropes.

STAND BY! An order to be prepared.

STANDARD. An inverted knee, placed above the deck, instead of beneath it; as, *bitt-standard*, &c.

STANDING. The *standing part* of a rope is that part which is fast, in opposition to the part that is hauled upon; or the main part, in opposition to the end.

The *standing part* of a tackle is that part which is made fast to the blocks, and between that and the next sheave, in opposition to the hauling and leading parts.

STANDING RIGGING. (See page 33.) That part of a vessel's rigging which is made fast and not hauled upon. (See RUNNING.)

STARBOARD. The right side of a vessel, looking forward.

STARBOWLINES. The familiar term for the men in the starboard watch.

START. To *start a cask*, is to open it.

STAY. To tack a vessel, or put her about, so that the wind, from being on one side, is brought upon the other, round the vessel's head. (See TACK, WEAR.)

To stay a mast, is to incline it forward or aft, or to one side or the other, by the stays and backstays. Thus, a mast is said to be *stayed* too much forward or aft, or too much to port, &c.

STAYS. Large ropes, used to support masts, and leading from the head of some mast down to some other mast, or to some part of the vessel. Those which lead forward are called *fore-and-aft stays*; and those which lead down to the vessel's sides, *backstays*. (See BACKSTAYS.)

In stays, or *hove in stays*, the situation of a vessel when she is *staying* or going about from one tack to the other.

STAYSAIL. A sail which hoists upon a stay.

STEADY! An order to keep the helm as it is.

STEERAGE. That part of the between-decks which is just forward of the cabin.

STEEVES. A bowsprit *steeves* more or less, according as it is raised more or less from the horizontal.

STEEVE—*continued.*
The *steeve* is the angle it makes with the horizon. Also, a long heavy spar, with a place to fit a block at one end, and used in stowing certain kinds of cargo, which need be driven in close.

STEM. (See PLATE 3.) A piece of timber reaching from the forward end of the keel, to which it is scarfed, up to the bowsprit, and to which the two sides of the vessel are united.

STEMSON. A piece of compass timber, fixed on the after part of the apron inside. The lower end is scarfed into the keelson, and receives the scarf of the stem, through which it is bolted.

STEP. A block of wood secured to the keel, into which the heel of the mast is placed.

To step a mast, is to put it in its step.

STERN. (See PLATE 3.) The after end of a vessel. (See BY THE STERN.)

STERN-BOARD. The motion of a vessel when going stern foremost.

STERN-FRAME. The frame composed of the stern-post transom and the fashion-pieces.

STERN-POST. (See PLATE 3.) The aftermost timber in a ship, reaching from the after end of the keel to the deck. The stem and stern-post are the two extremes of a vessel's frame.

Inner stern-post. A post on the inside, corresponding to the stern-post.

STERN-SHEETS. The after part of a boat, abaft the rowers, where the passengers sit.

STIFF. The quality of a vessel which enables it to carry a great deal of sail without lying over much on her side. The opposite to *crank.*

STIRRUPS. Ropes with thimbles at their ends, through which the foot-ropes are rove, and by which they are kept up toward the yards.

STOCK. A beam of wood, or a bar of iron, secured to the upper end of the shank of an anchor, at right angles with the arms. An iron stock usually goes with the key, and unships.

STOCKS. The frame upon which a vessel is built.

STOOLS. Small channels for the dead eyes of the backstays.

STOPPER. A stout rope with a knot at one end and sometimes a hook at the other, used for various purposes about decks; as, making fast a cable, so as to overhaul. (See CAT STOPPER, DECK STOPPER.)

STOPPER BOLTS. Ring-bolts to which the deck stoppers are secured.

STOP. A fastening of small stuff. Also, small projections on the outside of the cheeks of a lower mast, at the upper parts of the hounds.

STRAND. (See page 33.) A number of rope-yarns twisted together. Three, four, or nine strands twisted together form a rope.

STRAND—*continued.*
  A rope is *stranded* when one of its strands is parted or broken by chafing or by a strain.
  A vessel is *stranded* when she is driven on shore.
STRAP. A piece of rope spliced round a block to keep its parts well together. Some blocks have iron straps, in which case they are called *iron-bound.*
STREAK, or STRAKE. A range of planks running fore and aft on a vessel's side.
STREAM. The *stream anchor* is one used for warping, &c., and sometimes as a lighter anchor to moor by, with a hawser. It is smaller than the *bowers*, and larger than the *kedges.*
  To stream a buoy, is to drop it into the water.
STRETCHERS. Pieces of wood placed across a boat's bottom, inside, for the oarsmen to place their feet against, in rowing. Also, cross pieces placed between a boat's sides to keep them apart when hoisted up and griped.
STRIKE. To lower a sail or colours.
STUDDINGSAILS. (See PLATE 2.) Light sails set outside the square sails on booms rigged out for that purpose. They are only carried with a fair wind and in moderate weather.
SUED, or SEWED. The condition of a ship when she is high and dry on shore. If the water leaves her two feet, she sues, or is sued, two feet.
SUPPORTERS. The knee-timbers under the cat-heads.
SURF. The breaking of the sea upon the shore.
SURGE. A large, swelling wave.
  To *surge* a rope or cable, is to slack it up suddenly where it renders round a pin, or round the windlass or capstan.
  Surge ho! The notice given when a cable is to be *surged.*
SWAB. A mop, formed of old rope, used for cleaning and drying decks.
SWEEP. To drag the bottom for an anchor. Also, large oars, used in small vessels to force them ahead.
SWIFT. To bring two shrouds or stays close together by ropes.
SWIFTER. The forward shroud to a lower mast. Also, ropes used to confine the capstan bars to their places when shipped.
SWIG. A term used by sailors for the mode of hauling off upon the bight of a rope when its lower end is fast.
SWIVEL. A long link of iron, used in chain cables, made so as to turn upon an axis and keep the turns out of a chain.
SYPHERING. Lapping the edges of planks over each other for a bulk-head.

TABLING. Letting one beam-piece into another. (See SCARFING.) Also, the broad hem on the borders of sails, to which the bolt-rope is sewed.

TACK. To put a ship about, so that from having the wind on one side, you bring it round on the other by the way of her head. The opposite of *wearing*.
A vessel is on the *starboard tack*, or has her *starboard tacks on board*, when she has the wind on her starboard side.
The rope or tackle by which the weather clew of a course is hauled forward and down to the deck.
The *tack* of a fore-and-aft sail is the rope that keeps down the lower forward clew; and of a studdingsail, the lower outer clew. The tack of the lower studding sail is called the *outhaul*. Also, that part of a sail to which the tack is attached.

TACKLE. (Pronounced *tay-cle*.) A purchase formed by a rope rove through one or more blocks.

TAFFRAIL, or TAFFEREL. The rail round a ship's stern.

TAIL. A rope spliced into the end of a block, and used for making it fast to rigging or spars. Such a block is called a *tail-block*.
A ship is said to *tail* up or down stream, when at anchor, according as her stern swings up or down with the tide; in opposition to *heading* one way or another, which is said of a vessel when under way.

TAIL-TACKLE. A watch-tackle. (See page 46.)

TAIL-ON! or TALLY ON! An order given to take hold of a rope and pull.

TANK. An iron vessel placed in the hold to contain the vessel's water.

TAR. A liquid gum, taken from pine and fir trees, and used for caulking, and to put upon yarns in rope-making, and upon standing rigging, to protect it from the weather.

TARPAULIN. A piece of canvas, covered with tar, used for covering hatches, boats, &c. Also, the name commonly given to a sailor's hat when made of tarred or painted cloth.

TAUNT. High or tall. Commonly applied to a vessel's masts.
All-a-taunt-o. Said of a vessel when she has all her light and tall masts and spars aloft.

TAUT. Tight.

TELL-TALE. A compass hanging from the beams of the cabin, by which the heading of a vessel may be known at any time. Also, an instrument connected with the barrel of the wheel, and traversing so that the officer may see the position of the wheel.

TEND. To watch a vessel at anchor at the turn of tides, and cast her by the helm, and some sail if necessary, so as to keep turns out of her cables.

TENON. The heel of a mast, made to fit into the step.

THICK-AND-THIN BLOCK. A block having one sheave larger than the other. Sometimes used for quarter-blocks.

THIMBLE. An iron ring, having its rim concave on the outside for a rope or strap to fit snugly round.

K

THOLE-PINS. Pins in the gunwale of a boat, between which an oar rests when pulling, instead of a rowlock.

THROAT. The inner end of a gaff, where it widens and hollows in to fit the mast. (See JAWS.) Also, the hollow part of a knee.

The *throat* brails, halyards, &c., are those that hoist or haul up the gaff or sail near the throat. Also, the angle where the arm of an anchor is joined to the shank.

THRUM. To stick short strands of yarn through a mat or piece of canvas, to make a rough surface.

THWARTS. The seats going across a boat, upon which the oarsmen sit.

THWARTSHIPS. (See ATHWARTSHIPS.)

TIDE. To *tide up or down* a river or harbour, is to work up or down with a fair tide and head wind or calm, coming to anchor when the tide turns.

TIDE-RODE. The situation of a vessel, at anchor, when she swings by the force of the tide. In opposition to *wind-rode*.

TIER. A range of casks. Also, the range of the fakes of a cable or hawser.

The *cable tier* is the place in a hold or between decks where the cables are stowed.

TILLER. A bar of wood or iron, put into the head of the rudder, by which the rudder is moved.

TILLER-ROPES. Ropes leading from the tiller-head round the barrel of the wheel, by which a vessel is steered.

TIMBER. A general term for all large pieces of wood used in ship-building. Also, more particularly, long pieces of wood in a curved form, bending outward, and running from the keel up, on each side, forming the *ribs* of a vessel. The keel, stem, sternposts, and timbers form a vessel's outer frame. (See PLATE 3.)

TIMBER-HEADS. (See PLATE 3.) The ends of the timbers that come above the decks. Used for belaying hawsers and large ropes.

TIMENOGUY. A rope carried taut between different parts of the vessel, to prevent the sheet or tack of a course from getting foul, in working ship.

TOGGLE. A pin placed through the bight or eye of a rope, block-strap, or bolt, to keep it in its place, or to put the bight or eye of another rope upon, and thus to secure them both together.

TOMPION. A bung or plug placed in the mouth of a cannon.

TOP. A platform placed over the head of a lower mast, resting on the trestle-trees, to spread the rigging, and for the convenience of men aloft. (See PLATE 1.)

To *top* up a yard or boom, is to raise up one end of it by hoisting on the lift.

Top-block. A large iron-bound block, hooked into a bolt under the lower cap, and used for the top-rope to reeve through in sending up and down topmasts.

Top-light. A signal-lantern carried in the top.

Top-lining. A lining on the after part of sails, to prevent them from chafing against the top-rim.

Topmast. (See Plate 1.) The second mast above the deck. Next above the lower mast.

Topgallant Mast. (See Plate 1.) The third mast above the deck.

Top-rope. The rope used for sending topmasts up and down.

Topsail. (See Plate 2.) The second sail above the deck.

Topgallant Sail. (See Plate 2.) The third sail above the deck.

Topping-lift. (See Plate 1.) A lift used for topping up the end of a boom.

Top Timbers. The highest timbers on a vessel's side, being above the futtocks. (See Plate 3.)

Toss. To throw an oar out of the rowlock, and raise it perpendicularly on its end, and lay it down in the boat, with its blade forward.

Touch. A sail is said to *touch*, when the wind strikes the leach so as to shake it a little.

Luff and touch her! The order to bring the vessel up and see how near she will go to the wind.

Tow. To draw a vessel along by means of a rope.

Train-tackle. The tackle used for running guns in and out.

Transoms. (See Plate 3.) Pieces of timber going across the stern-post, to which they are bolted.

Transom-knees. Knees bolted to the transoms and after timbers.

Traveller. An iron ring, fitted so as to slip up and down a rope.

Treenails, or Trunnels. Long wooden pins, used for nailing a plank to a timber.

Trend. The lower end of the shank of an anchor, being the same distance on the shank from the throat that the arm measures from the throat to the bill.

Trestle-trees. Two strong pieces of timber, placed horizontally and fore-and-aft on opposite sides of a mast-head, to support the cross-trees and top, and for the fid of the mast above to rest upon.

Triatic Stay. A rope secured at each end to the heads of the fore and main masts, with thimbles spliced into its bight, to hook the stay tackles to.

Trice. To haul up by means of a rope.

Trick. The time allotted to a man to stand at the helm.

Trim. The condition of a vessel, with reference to her cargo and ballast. A vessel is *trimmed* by the head or by the stern.

In ballast trim, is when she has only ballast on board.

Also, to arrange the sails by the braces with reference to the wind.

TRIP. To raise an anchor clear of the bottom.

TRIPPING LINE. A line used for tripping a topgallant or royal yard in sending it down.

TRUCK. A circular piece of wood, placed at the head of the highest mast on a ship. It has small holes or sheaves in it for signal halyards to be rove through. Also, the wheel of a gun-carriage.

TRUNNIONS. The arms on each side of a cannon by which it rests upon the carriage, and on which, as an axis, it is elevated or depressed.

TRUSS. The rope by which the centre of a lower yard is kept in toward the mast.

TRYSAIL. A fore-and-aft sail, set with a boom and gaff, and hoisting on a small mast abaft the lower mast, calling a *trysail-mast*. This name is generally confined to the sail so carried at the mainmast of a full-rigged brig; those carried at the foremast and at the mainmast of a ship or bark being called *spencers*, and those that are at the mizenmast of a ship or bark, *spankers*.

TUMBLING HOME. Said of a ship's sides when they fall in above the bends. The opposite of *wall-sided*.

TURN. Passing a rope once or twice round a pin or kevel, to keep it fast. Also, two crosses in a cable.

To turn in or *turn out*, nautical terms for going to rest in a berth or hammock, and getting up from them.

Turn up! The order given to send the men up from between decks.

TYE. A rope connected with a yard, to the other end of which a tackle is attached for hoisting.

UNBEND. To cast off or untie. (See BEND.)

UNION. The upper inner corner of an ensign. The rest of the flag is called the *fly*. The *union* of the U. S. ensign is a blue field with white stars, and the *fly* is composed of alternate white and red stripes.

Union-down. The situation of a flag when it is hoisted upside down, bringing the union down instead of up. Used as a signal of distress.

Union-jack. A small flag, containing only the union without the fly, usually hoisted at the bowsprit-cap.

UNMOOR. To heave up one anchor so that the vessel may ride at a single anchor. See MOOR.

UNSHIP. (See SHIP.)

UVROE. (See EUVROU.)

VANE. A fly worn at the mast-head, made of feathers or buntine, traversing on a spindle, to show the direction of the wind. (See DOG VANE.)

Vang. (See Plate 1.) A rope leading from the peak of the gaff of a fore-and-aft sail to the rail on each side, and used for steadying the gaff.

'Vast. (See Avast.)

Veer. Said of the wind when it changes. Also to slack a cable and let it run out. (See Pay.)

To veer and haul, is to haul and slack alternately on a rope, as in warping, until the vessel or boat gets headway.

Viol, or **Voyal.** A larger messenger sometimes used in weighing an anchor by a capstan. Also the block through which the messenger passes.

Waist. That part of the upper deck between the quarter-deck and forecastle.

Waisters. Green hands, or broken-down seamen, placed in the waist of a man-of-war.

Wake. The track or path a ship leaves behind her in the water.

Wales. Strong planks in a vessel's sides running her whole length fore and aft.

Wall. A knot put on the end of a rope. (See Plate 5, page 37.)

Wall-sided. A vessel is *wall-sided* when her sides run up perpendicularly from the bends. In opposition to *tumbling home* or *flaring out.*

Ward-room. The room in a vessel of war in which the commissioned officers live.

Ware, or **Wear.** To turn a vessel round, so that from having the wind on one side, you bring it upon the other, carrying her stern round by the wind. In *tacking,* the same result is produced by carrying a vessel's head round by the wind.

Warp. To move a vessel from one place to another by means of a rope made fast to some fixed object, or to a kedge.

A *warp* is a rope used for warping. If the warp is bent to a kedge which is let go, and the vessel is hove ahead by the capstan or windlass, it would be called *kedging.*

Wash-boards. Light pieces of board placed above the gunwale of a boat.

Watch. (See page 178.) A division of time on board ship. There are seven watches in a day, reckoning from 12 M. round through the 24 hours, five of them being of four hours each, and the two others, called *dog watches,* of two hours each, viz., from 4 to 6, and from 6 to 8 P.M. (See Dog Watch.) Also a certain portion of a ship's company, appointed to stand a given length of time. In the merchant service all hands are divided into two watches, larboard and starboard, with a mate to command each.

A *buoy* is said to *watch* when it floats on the surface.

WATCH-AND-WATCH. The arrangement by which the watches are alternated every other four hours. In distinction from keeping all hands during one or more watches. (See page 178.)

Anchor watch, a small watch of one or two men, kept while in port.

WATCH-HO! WATCH! The cry of the man that heaves the deep-sea lead.

WATCH-TACKLE. (See page 46.) A small luff purchase with a short fall, the double block having a tail to it, and the single one a hook. Used for various purposes about decks.

WATER-SAIL. A *save all*, set under the swinging-boom.

WATER-WAYS. Long pieces of timber, running fore and aft on both sides, connecting the deck with the vessel's sides. The *scuppers* are made through them to let the water off. (See PLATE 3.)

WEAR. (See WARE.)

WEATHER. In the direction from which the wind blows. (See WINDWARD, LEE.)

A ship carries a *weather-helm* when she tends to come up into the wind, requiring you to put the helm up.

Weather gage. A vessel has the *weather gage* of another when she is to windward of her.

A *weatherly ship*, is one that works well to windward, making but little leeway.

WEATHER-BITT. To take an additional turn with a cable round the windlass-end.

WEATHER ROLL. The roll which a ship makes to windward.

WEIGH. To lift up; as, to weigh an anchor or a mast.

WHEEL. The instrument by which a ship is steered; being a barrel, (round which the tiller-ropes go,) and a wheel with spokes.

WHIP. (See page 46.) A purchase formed by a rope rove through a single block.

To whip, is to hoist by a whip. Also, to secure the end of a rope from fagging by a seizing of twine.

Whip-upon-whip. One whip applied to the fall of another.

WINCH. A purchase formed by a horizontal spindle or shaft with a wheel or crank at the end. A small one with a wheel is used for making ropes or spunyarn.

WINDLASS. The machine used in merchant vessels to weigh the anchor by.

WIND-RODE. The situation of a vessel at anchor when she swings and rides by the force of the wind, instead of the tide or current. (See TIDE-RODE.)

WING. That part of the hold or between-decks which is next the side.

WINGERS. Casks stowed in the wings of a vessel.

WING-AND-WING. The situation of a fore-and-aft vessel when she is going dead before the wind, with her foresail hauled over on one side and her mainsail on the other.

WITHE, or WYTHE. An iron instrument fitted on the end of a boom or mast, with a ring to it through which another boom or mast is rigged out and secured.

WOOLD. To wind a piece of rope round a spar.

WORK UP. To draw the yarns from old rigging and make them into spunyarn, foxes, sennet, &c. Also, a phrase for keeping a crew constantly at work upon needless matters, and in all weathers, and beyond their usual hours, for punishment.

WORM. (See page 34.) To fill up between the lays of a rope with small stuff wound round spirally. Stuff so wound round is called *worming*.

WRING. To bend or strain a mast by setting the rigging up too taut.

WRING-BOLTS. Bolts that secure the planks to the timbers.

WRING-STAVES. Strong pieces of plank used with the ring-bolts.

YACHT. (Pronounced *yot*.) A vessel of pleasure or state.

YARD. (See PLATE 1.) A long piece of timber, tapering slightly toward the ends, and hung by the centre to a mast, to spread the square sails upon.

YARD-ARM. The extremities of a yard.

YARD-ARM AND YARD-ARM. The situation of two vessels, lying alongside one another, so near that their yard-arms cross or touch.

YARN. (See ROPEYARN.)

YAW. The motion of a vessel when she goes off from her course.

YEOMAN. A man employed in a vessel of war to take charge of a store-room; as, boatswain's yeoman, the man that has charge of the stores of rigging, &c.

YOKE. A piece of wood placed across the head of a boat's rudder, with a rope attached to each end, by which the boat is steered.

PART II.

CHAPTER I.*

THE MASTER.

Beginning of the voyage. Shipping the crew. Outfit. Provisions. Watches. Navigation. Log-book. Observations. Working ship. Day's work. Discipline.

IN the third part of this work, it will be seen that the shipmaster is a person to whom, both by the general marine law of all commercial nations and by the special statutes of the United States, great powers are confided, and upon whom heavy responsibilities rest. The ship-

---

* There is no special code of statute laws either in the United States or Great Britain, for the maintenance of discipline, or the provisioning and treatment of the crews of trading ships when beyond the precincts of admiralty jurisdiction; but certain usages on these points have by long custom become established and recognized by courts of justice. It is very desirable that a comprehensive code should be devised and compiled, so as to set disputed points at rest; for although a *general* rule is admitted by the mariners of both countries, it is by no means a *universal* one, the custom varying in different trades, according to circumstances; and this is more particularly the case in the merchant service of this country than in that of the United States—the discipline being more stringent, and distinctions of rank more rigidly observed by the republicans than ourselves. The duties of each rating described in this chapter appear to be well defined, and worthy of imitation: our ship-owners and masters would, therefore, do well to adopt them, with such modifications as may be necessary to suit particular trades: and this may be done by inserting a clause to that effect, in the form of agreement now required to be entered into between master and crew before proceeding on a voyage, described at Schedules B & D of 5 & 6 W. 4, cap. 19.

master will find there what are his legal rights, duties and remedies as to owner, ship and crew, and the various requirements as to the papers with which he is to furnish his ship, and the observances of revenue and other regulations.

It is proposed to give here, rather more perhaps for the information of others than of the master himself, the ordinary and every-day duties of his office, and the customs which long usage has made almost as binding as laws.

There is a great difference in different ports, and among the various owners, as to the part the master is to take in supplying and manning the vessel. In many cases the owner puts on board all the stores for the ship's use and for the crew, and gives the master particular directions, sometimes in writing, as to the manner in which he is to dispense them. These directions are more or less liberal, according to the character of the owner; and, in some cases, the dispensing of the stores is left to the master's discretion. In other instances, the master makes out an inventory of all the stores he thinks it expedient to have put on board, and they are accordingly supplied by the owner's order.

In the manner of shipping the crew, there is as great a difference as in that of providing the stores. Usually, the whole thing is left to shipping-masters, who are paid so much a head for each of the crew, and are responsible for their appearance on board at the time of sailing. When this plan is adopted, neither the master nor owner, except by accident, knows anything of the crew before the vessel goes to sea. The shipping-master opens the articles at his office, procures the men, sees that they sign in due form, pays them their advance, takes care that they, or others in their place, are on board at the time of sailing, and sends in a bill for the whole to the owner. In other cases, the master selects his crew, and occasionally the owner does it, if he has been at sea himself, and understands seamen; though a shipping-master is still employed, to see them on board, and for other purposes.* In the ordinary course of short voyages, where crews are shipped frequently, and there is not much motive for making a selection, the procuring a crew may be left entirely to the agency of a faithful shipping-master; but upon long voyages, the comfort and success of which may depend much upon the character of a crew, the master or owner should interest himself to select able-bodied and respectable men, to explain to them the nature and length of the voyage they are going upon, what clothing they will want, and the work that will be required of them, and should see that they have proper and sufficient accommodations and provisions for their comfort. The master or owner should also, though this duty is often neglected, go to the forecastle and see that it is cleaned out, whitewashed, or painted, put in a proper habitable condition, and furnished with every reasonable convenience. It would seem best that the master should have something to do with the selection of the provisions for his men, as he will usually be more interested in securing their good-will and comfort than the owner would be.

By the master or owner's thus interesting himself for the crew, a great deal of misunderstanding, complaint, and ill-will may be avoided, and the beginning, at least, of the voyage be made under good auspices.

Unless the master is also supercargo, his duties, before

---

* In the British service, the practice is for owners of vessels going on voyages round the Cape of Good Hope to employ an agent, generally called a crimp, to engage the greatest part of the crew. If forty or fifty men are wanted, double that number are brought on board, out of which the chief-mate selects a sufficient company; the agent then receives a note for two months' wages, which he has, for the most part, advanced to the seamen, either in cash or slops (clothes), and also his procuration fee, varying from 5s. to 20s. per man, if he have not engaged to provide the crew for a specified sum.

sailing, are mostly confined to looking after the outfit of the vessel, and seeing that she is in sea order.

Everything being in readiness, the custom-house and other regulations complied with, and the crew on board, the vessel is put under the charge of the pilot to be carried out clear of the land. While the pilot is on board the master has little else to do than to see that everything is in order, and that the commands of the pilot are executed. As soon as the pilot leaves the ship, the entire control and responsibility are thrown upon the master. When the vessel is well clear of the land, and things are put into some order, it is usual for the master to call all hands aft, and say something to them about the voyage upon which they have entered. After this, the crew are divided into watches. The watches are the divisions of the crew into two equal portions. The periods of time occupied by each part of the crew, while on duty, are also called watches.

There are two watches,—the larboard, commanded by the chief mate, and the starboard, by the second mate. The master himself stands no watch, but comes and goes at all times, as he chooses. The starboard is sometimes called the captain's watch, probably from the fact that in the early days of the service, when vessels were smaller, there was usually but one mate, and the master stood his own watch; and now, in vessels which have no second mate, the master keeps the starboard watch. In dividing into watches, the master usually allows the officers to choose the men, one by one, alternately; but sometimes makes the division himself, upon consulting with his officers. The men are divided as equally as possible, with reference to their qualities as able seamen, ordinary seamen, or boys (as all green hands are called, whatever their age may be); but if the number is unequal, the larboard watch has the odd one, since the chief mate does not go aloft and do other duty in his watch, as the second mate does in his. The cook always musters with the larboard watch, and the steward with the starboard. If there is a carpenter, and the larboard watch is the largest, he generally goes aloft with the starboard watch; otherwise, with the larboard.

As soon as the division is made, if the day's work is over, one watch is set, and the other is sent below. Among the numerous customs of the ocean, which can hardly be accounted for, it is one that on the first night of the outward passage the starboard watch should take the first four hours on deck, and on the first night of the homeward passage the larboard should do the same. The sailors explain this by the old phrase, that the master takes the ship out and the mate takes her home.

The master takes the bearing and distance of the last point of departure upon the land, and from that point the ship's reckoning begins, and is regularly kept in the log-book. The chief mate keeps the log-book, but the master examines and corrects the reckoning every day. The master also attends to the chronometer, and takes all the observations, with the assistance of his officers, if necessary. Every day, a few minutes before noon, if there is any prospect of being able to get the sun, the master comes upon deck with his quadrant or sextant, and the chief mate also usually takes his. The second mate does not, except upon a Sunday, or when there is no work going forward. As soon as the sun crosses the meridian, eight bells are struck, and a new sea day begins. The reckoning is then corrected by the observation under the master's superintendence.

The master also takes the lunar observations, usually with the assistance of both his officers; in which case the master takes the angle of the moon with the star or sun, the chief mate takes the altitude of the sun or star, and the second mate the altitude of the moon.

In regulating the hours of duty and sleep, the meal times, the food, &c., the master has absolute power; yet the customs are very nearly the same in all vessels. The hour of breakfast is seven bells in the morning (half after seven), dinner at noon, and supper whenever the day's work is over. If the voyage is a long one, the crew are usually put upon an allowance of bread, beef, and water. The dispensing of the stores and regulating of the allowance lies, of course, with the master, though the duty of opening the casks, weighing, measuring, &c., falls upon the second mate. The chief mate enters in the log-book every barrel or cask of provisions that is broached. The steward takes charge of all the provisions for the use of the cabin, and keeps them in the pantry, over which he has the direct control. The average of allowance in merchant vessels is six pounds of bread a week, and three quarts of water, and one pound and a half of beef, or one and a quarter of pork, a day, to each man*.

The entire control of the navigation and working of the ship lies with the master. He gives the course and general directions to the officer of the watch, who enters upon a slate, at the end of the watch, the course made, and the number of knots, together with any other observations. The officer of the watch is at liberty to trim the yards, to make alterations in the upper sails, to take in and set royals, topgallant sails, &c.; but no important

---

* For want of some fixed scale of allowance in the British merchant service, great discontent frequently arises on the part of the crew, particularly on long voyages. In coasting vessels, where the work is hard and constant, the allowance of beef and bread is unlimited; but on long voyages it would be well to adopt the scale established for the Royal Navy, which is found amply sufficient; and this should form part of the contract, and be entered as a special clause in the articles of agreement. On the next page is the scale alluded to. In trading as well as the Queen's vessels, exciseable articles are allowed in sufficient quantity for the voyage out and home, duty free. This regulation, as regards spirits, coffee, tea, &c., places our shipowners on a par with foreigners in the cost of outfit as to these articles; but they still have to complain that the principal stores of provision, such as beef, pork, and bread, are considerably dearer in this country than abroad—a dis-

alteration can be made, as, for instance, reefing a topsail, without the special order of the master, who, in such cases, always comes upon deck and takes command in person. When on deck, the weather side of the quarter-deck belongs to him, and as soon as he appears the officer of the watch will always leave it, and go over to leeward, or forward into the waist. If the alteration to be made is slight, the master usually tells the officer to take in or set such a sail, and leaves to him the particular ordering as to the braces, sheets, &c., and the seeing all things put in their place. The principal manœuvres of the vessel, as tacking, wearing, reefing topsails, getting under way, and coming to anchor, require all hands. In these cases the master takes command, and gives his orders in person, standing upon the quarter-deck. The chief mate superintends the forward part of the vessel, under the master, and the second mate assists in the waist. The master never goes aloft, nor does any work with his

advantage which presses heavily on the British shipowners in their competition with foreigners.

Days of the week.	Bread, lb.	Beer, gall.	Sugar, oz.	Cocoa, oz.	Tea, oz.	Beef, lb.	Pork, lb.	Flour, lb.	Pease, pint.	Oatmeal, pint.	Vinegar, pint.
Sunday.	1	1	1½	1	¼	¾		¾			
Monday.	1	1	1½	1	¼		¾		½		
Tuesday.	1	1	1½	1	¼	¾		¾			
Wednesday.	1	1	1½	1	¼		¾		½	½	½
Thursday.	1	1	1½	1	¼	¾		¾			
Friday.	1	1	1½	1	¼		¾		½		
Saturday.	1	1	1½	1	¼	¾		¾			
Sunday.	1	1	1½	1	¼		¾		½		
Monday.	1	1	1½	1	¼	¾		¾			
Tuesday.	1	1	1½	1	¼		¾		½		½
Wednesday.	1	1	1½	1	¼	¾		¾		½	
Thursday.	1	1	1½	1	¼		¾		½		
Friday.	1	1	1½	1	¼	¾		¾			
Saturday.	1	1	1½	1	¼		¾		½		
Proportion for 14 days.	14	14	21	14	3½	5¼	5¼	5¼	3½	1	1

hands, unless for his own pleasure. If the officer of the watch thinks it necessary to reef the topsails, he calls the master, who upon coming on deck takes command, and, if he thinks proper, orders all hands to be called. The crew, officers, and all, then take their stations, and await the orders of the master, who works the ship in person, giving all the commands, even the most minute, and looks out for trimming the yards and laying the ship for reefing. The chief mate commands upon the forecastle, under the master, and does not go aloft. The second mate goes aloft with the crew.

In tacking and wearing, the master gives all the orders as to trimming the yards, &c., though the chief mate is expected to look out for the head yards. So, in getting under way, and in coming to anchor, the master takes the entire personal control of everything, the officers acting under him in their several stations.

In the ordinary day's work, however, which is carried on in a vessel, the state of things is somewhat different. This the master does not superintend personally; but gives general instructions to the chief mate, whose duty it is to see to their execution. To understand this distinction, the reader will bear in mind that there are two great divisions of duty and labour on shipboard. One, the *working and navigating of the vessel:* that is, the keeping and ascertaining the ship's position, and directing her course, the making and taking in sail, trimming the sails to the wind, and the various nautical manœuvres and evolutions of a vessel. The other branch is, the work done upon the hull and rigging to keep it in order, such as the making and fitting of new rigging, repairing of old, &c.; all which, together with making of small stuffs to be used on board, constitute the *day's work and jobs* of the crew. As to the latter, the master usually converses with the chief mate upon the state of the vessel and rigging, and tells him, more or less particularly, what he wishes to have done. It then becomes the duty of this officer to see the thing accomplished.

If, for instance, the master tells the chief mate to stay the topmasts more forward, the chief mate goes upon the forecastle, sets the men to work, one upon one thing and another upon another, sees that the stays and backstays are come up with, has tackles got upon the rigging, sights the mast, &c. If the master sees anything which he disapproves of, and has any preferences in the modes of doing the work, he should call the officer aft and speak to him; and if, instead of this, he were to go forward and give orders to the men, it would be considered an interference, and indeed an insult to the officer*. So with any other work doing upon the ship or rigging, as rattling down, turning in and setting up rigging, bending and unbending sails, and all the knotting, splicing, serving, &c., and the making of small stuffs, which constitute the day's work and *jobs* of a vessel. If the chief officer is a competent man, the master is not expected to trouble himself with the details of any of these things; and, indeed, if he were to do so to a great extent, it would probably lead to difficulty.

Where there are passengers, as in regular line of packet ships (or, as they are familiarly called, *liners*), between New York and Liverpool, or Havre, for instance, the master has even less to do with the day's work; since the navigation and working of the ship, with proper attention to his passengers, are as much as can reasonably be required of him.

The master has the entire control of the cabin. The mates usually live in a state-room by themselves, or, if they live in the cabin, they yet feel that the master is the head of the house, and are unwilling to interfere with his hours and occupations. The chief mate dines with the master, and the second mate looks out for the ship while they are below, and dines at the second table.

---

* This is not sufficiently attended to in British merchant ships. The master should consider that a contrary course lessens the authority of his chief officer over the crew, and eventually his own.

In the *liners*, however, the mates dine together, and the master looks out for the ship while they are at dinner, and dines with his passengers at a later hour.

As the master stands no watch, he comes and goes as he pleases, and takes his own hours for rest. In fine weather, he is not necessarily much on deck, but should be ready at all times, especially in bad weather, to be up at a moment's notice.

Everything of importance that occurs, as the seeing a sail or land, or the like, must be immediately reported to the master. And in heaving-to for speaking, the master takes the entire charge of working the vessel, and speaks the other sail in person.

As will be found in the third Part of this book, the master has the entire control of the discipline of the ship, and no subordinate officer has authority to punish a seaman, or to use force, without the master's order, except in cases of necessity not admitting of delay. He has also the complete direction of the internal arrangements and economy of the vessel; and upon his character, and upon the course of conduct he pursues, depend in a great measure the character of the ship and the conduct of both officers and men. He has a power and an influence, both direct and indirect, which may be the means of much good or much evil. If he is profane, passionate, tyrannical, indecent, or intemperate, more or less of the same qualities will spread themselves or break out among officers and men, which, perhaps would have been checked, if not in some degree removed, had the head of the ship been a man of high personal character. He may make his ship almost anything he chooses, and may render the lives and duties of his officers and men pleasant and profitable to them, or may introduce disagreements, discontent, tyranny, resistance, and, in fact, make the situation of all on board as uncomfortable as that in which any human beings can well be placed. Every master of a vessel who will lay this to heart, and consider his great responsibility, may not only be a benefactor to the numbers whom the course of many years will bring under his command, but may render a service to the whole class, and do much to raise the character of the calling.

CHAPTER II.

THE CHIEF MATE.

Care of rigging and ship's furniture. Day's work. Working ship. Coming to anchor. Getting under way. Reefing. Furling. Duties in port. Account of cargo. Stowage. Station. Log-book. Navigation.

THE chief mate, or, as he is familiarly called on board ship, *the mate*, is the active superintending officer. In the previous chapter, upon the duties of the master, it will be seen that, in all matters relating to the care of and work done upon the ship and rigging, the master gives general orders to the mate, who attends personally to their execution in detail. Indeed, in the *day's work* on board ship, the chief mate is the only officer who appears in command. The second mate works like a common seaman, and the men never know what is to be done until they receive their orders in detail from the chief mate. It is his duty to carry on the work, to find every man something to do, and to see that it is done. He appoints the second mate his work, as well as the common seamen theirs; and if the master is dissatisfied with anything, or wishes a change, he should speak to the chief mate, and let him make the change, and not interfere with the men individually. It is also the duty of this officer to examine all parts of the rigging, report anything of importance to the master and take his orders, or, if it be a small and common matter, he will have the repairs or changes made at his own pleasure, as a thing of course. He must also see that there is a supply of small stuffs for the work, and have them made up when necessary, and also that there are instruments ready for every kind of labour, or for any emergency. In bad weather, he must have spare rope, blocks, tackles, sennit, earings, &c., on hand; or rather, see that they are provided, the more immediate care of these things, when provided, belonging to the second mate.

From this description of a chief mate's duty, it will be seen that he ought always to be not only a vigilant and active man, but also well acquainted with all kinds of seaman's work, and a good judge of rigging.

In the working of the ship, when all hands are called and the master is on deck, the chief mate's place is on the forecastle, where, under the general direction of the master, who never need leave the quarter-deck, he commands the forward part of the vessel, and is the organ of communication with the men aloft. In getting under way and coming to anchor, it is his duty to attend to the ground tackle, and see everything ready forward. The master, for instance, tells him to have the ship ready for getting under weigh, and to heave short on the cable. He then goes forward, orders all hands to be called, sees everything secured about decks, tackles got up and boats hoisted in and lashed, fish and cat tackles, pennant, davit, &c., and spare hawsers and rope, in readiness, orders the men to the windlass, (the second mate taking a handspike with the rest,) and stationing himself between the knight-heads, looks out for the cable, ordering and encouraging the men. When the cable is hove short, he informs the master, and, at the word from him, orders the men aloft to loose the sails, and gives particular directions to them when aloft, as to the sails, gaskets, overhauling rigging, &c. The sails being loosed, he awaits the order from the master, which would be addressed to him rather than to the men, and has the windlass manned and the anchor hove up, giving notice to the master as soon as it is a-weigh. When the vessel is under way, the master begins to take more immediate control, ordering the yards to be braced and filled, sail to be set, and the like. The chief mate also sees to the catting and fishing of the anchors, to having the decks cleared up and everything secured.

In coming to anchor, very nearly the same duty falls upon the chief officer. He must see the anchors and cables ready for letting go, the master ordering how much chain is to be overhauled. He must look out that the boats are ready for lowering, the rigging clear for letting go, hauling and clewing, and that spare hawsers, kedges, warps, &c., are at hand. If anything goes wrong forward, he alone is looked to for an explanation. As the vessel draws in toward her anchoring ground, the master gives all the orders as to trimming the yards and taking in sail; and at all times, when on deck, has the entire charge of the man at the helm, it being the mate's duty only to see that a good seaman is there, and that the helm is relieved. As to the sails, the master will, for instance, order—" Clew up the fore and main topsails!" The chief mate then gives the particular orders as to lowering and letting go the halyards, clewing down and up, overhauling rigging, &c. If both topsails were taken in at once, the second mate would attend to the main, unless the master should choose to look out for it himself. All being ready for letting go, the master gives the order—" Let go the anchor!" and the chief mate sees that it is done, has the chain payed out, reports how much is out, sees that the buoys *watch*, and the like. In furling the sails, the whole superintendence comes upon the mate, as the master would probably only tell him to have them furled. He has the rigging hauled taut, sends the men aloft, and, remaining on deck and forward, he gives his orders to them while on the yards, as to the manner of furling, and has the ropes hauled taut, or let go on deck, as may be necessary.

These instances may serve to show the distinctions between the duties of master and mate in the principal evolutions of a vessel. While in port, the chief mate has much more the control of the vessel than when at sea. As there is no navigating or working of the vessel to be done, the master has little to engage him, except transactions with merchants and others on shore, and the necessary general directions to the mate, as to the care of the ship. Beside the work upon the ship and rigging while in port, the chief mate has the charge of receiving, discharging, stowing and breaking out the cargo. In this he has the entire control, under the general directions of the master. It is his duty to keep an account of all the cargo, as it goes in and comes out of the vessel, and, as he generally gives receipts, he is bound to great care and accuracy. When cargo is coming in and going out, the chief mate will stand in the gangway, to keep an account, and the second mate will be down in the hold with some of the crew, breaking out or stowing. The stowage, however, should still be somewhat under the chief mate's directions. While the master is on shore, the chief mate is necessarily commander of the ship, for the time, and though the law will extend his power proportionably for cases of necessity, yet, except in instances which will not admit of delay, he must not attempt to exercise any unusual powers, but should refer everything to the master's decision. It will be seen, by the laws, that the mate has no right to punish a man during the master's absence, unless it be a case in which delay would lead to serious consequences.

While in port, the chief mate stands no watch at night, but he should always be the first to be called in the morning, and should be up early and order the calling of all hands. In cleaning the ship, as washing down decks, &c., which is done the first thing in the morning, each mate, while at sea, takes charge of it in his watch, in turn, as one or the other has the morning watch; but in port, the second mate oversees the washing down of the decks, under the chief mate's general orders.

While at sea, in tacking, wearing, reefing topsails, &c., and in every kind of "all hands' work," when the master is on deck, the chief mate's place, as I have said, is forward. To give a further notion of the manner of dividing the command, I will describe the evolution of tacking-ship. The master finds that the ship will not lay her course, and tells the chief mate to " see all clear for stays," or " ready about." Upon this, the chief mate goes forward, sends all hands to their stations, and sees everything clear and ready on the forecastle. The master asks, " All ready forward ?" and being answered, " Ay, ay, sir !" motions to the man at the helm to put the wheel down, and calls out, " Helm's a-lee !" The mate answering immediately, " Helm's a-lee,", to let the master know he is heard and understood, sees that the head sheets are let go. At " Raise tacks and sheets !" from the master, the mate, and the men with him, let go the fore tack, while he looks after the overhauling of the other tack and sheet. He also sees to letting go the bowlines for " Let go and haul," and to getting down the head sheets when the ship is about, and trims the head yards, calling out to the men at the braces the usual orders, " Well the main yard !" " Topsail yard, a small pull !" " Topgallant yard, well !" &c. The master usually trims the after yards.

In reefing topsails, the chief mate should not go aloft, but should keep his place forward, and look out for the men on the yards. I am aware that it has been the custom in some classes of vessels, as, in the New York liners, for the chief mate to take the weather earing of a course, especially if a topsail or the other course were reefing at the same time; yet this practice has never generally prevailed, and is now going out of date. I think I may say it is the opinion of all, masters, officers, and men, that it is better for the chief mate to remain on deck. There is always a good deal to be looked after, ropes to be let go or hauled, rigging to be cleared, and the like, beside the importance of having some one to oversee the men on the different yards; which the mate, standing at a little distance, can easily do. He is also the organ of communication between the yards and the deck, and can look after the reefing to more advantage than the master can upon the quarter-deck, where he must stay to watch the helm and sails.

The chief mate is not required to work with his hands, like the second mate and the seamen. He will, of course, let go and belay ropes, and occasionally pull and haul with the men when working ship; but if there is much work to be done, his time and attention are sufficiently taken up with superintending and giving orders.

As to his duties as a watch-officer, it will be necessary to repeat the explanations partly given in the chapter upon the master's duties. The crew are divided equally into two watches, the larboard and starboard; the larboard commanded by the chief mate, and the starboard by the second mate. These watches divide the day between them, being on and off duty every other four hours. This is the theory of the time, but in fact, in nearly all merchant vessels, all hands are kept on deck and at work throughout the afternoon, from one o'clock until sundown; and sometimes, if there is a great deal to be done, as immediately before making port, or after an accident, all hands may be kept throughout the day. This is, however, justly considered hard usage, if long continued, since it gives the men but little time for sleep, and none for reading, or taking care of their clothes. Although all hands may be on deck and at work during a day or a half day, yet the division of time is still kept up. For instance, if it is the mate's watch from 8 A. M. to 12; although all hands should be up from 12 to 5 or 6, yet from 12 to 4 the starboard watch would be considered as "the watch on deck," and the larboard again after 4; and so on; and during those hours the wheel will always be taken by men belonging to the watch on deck, and if any particular duty is ordered to be done by "the watch," that watch which has a man at the helm, and which would have been the only one on deck had not all hands been kept, would do the duty. But though this division is kept up as to the crew and the helmsman, it is not so as to the officers; for when all hands are on deck, the chief mate is always the officer in command, to whichever watch the hour may properly belong. He accordingly looks out for the ship, takes in and makes sail, and trims the yards, and when all hands are on deck at work, as much in the hours of one watch as in those of the other, and he generally calls upon the men of either watch indifferently to pull and haul. But if only the starboard watch is on deck, though the chief mate should be on deck also, yet he will not interfere with the duties of that watch, but would leave the command of the vessel, and the weather side of the quarter-deck, to the second mate. Of course, whenever the master comes on deck, as I have said, in whosever watch it may be, or if all hands are up, he takes the weather side of the quarter-deck, and is considered as having charge of the ship; and the officer of the watch would then give no order with reference to the helm, trimming the yards, making sail, or the like, without a direction from the master.

It will be necessary to make some explanations as to the stations of the chief and second mate. I have said that when all hands are called, the chief mate's place is the forecastle, and the second mate's amidships, or at the braces on the quarter-deck. This is only in working ship with all hands; that is, in tacking, wearing, reefing, coming to anchor, getting under way, &c. Whenever the work is done, and the necessity for the officers' presence at these parts of the vessel ceases, they return to their proper places on the quarter-deck. In a man-of-war there is always a lieutenant of the watch on the weather side of the quarter-deck, whatever work may be going forward, except in the single case of all hands being called to work ship; but it is not so in the merchant service. When the ordinary day's work is going forward, the mates must be about the decks or aloft, like the petty officers of a man-of-war; and it is only while no work is going forward, as in bad weather, on

Sundays, or at night, that the officer of the watch keeps the quarter-deck. At these times he does so, and, if the master is not on deck, does not leave it, except for a short time, and for some necessary duty forward.

It will be seen in the third Part of this book, that the law looks upon the chief mate as standing in a different relation to the master from that of the second mate or the men. He is considered a confidential person, to whom the owners, shippers and insurers look, in some measure, for special duties and qualifications. The master, therefore, cannot remove him from office, except under very peculiar circumstances, and then must be able to prove a justifiable cause. One of these duties which the law throws upon him, is keeping the log-book. This is a very important trust, as the log-book is the depository of the evidence of everything that may occur during the voyage; and the position of the ship, the sail she was under, the wind, &c., at any one moment, may become matters of great consequence to all concerned. So it is with reference to anything that may occur between the master or officers and the crew. As to the manner of keeping the log, it is the custom for each officer at the end of his watch to enter upon the log-slate, which usually lies on the cabin table, the courses, distances, wind and weather during his watch, and anything worthy of note that may have occurred. Once in twenty-four hours the mate copies from this slate into the log-book; the master, however, first seeing the slate, examining it, and making any corrections or observations he may choose. This practice of copying from the slate, which is first submitted to the master, has led, in too many instances, to the mate's becoming the mere clerk of the master, to enter on the log-book whatever the latter may dictate. This is wrong. It is very proper that the master should examine the slate, and suggest alterations as to the ship's reckoning, &c., if necessary; but it is important to all concerned, both to the owners, shippers and insurers, on shore, and the crew of the vessel, that the independence of the mate, as the journalist of the voyage, should be preserved. The master, from the power of his office, can at all times make the situation of a mate who has displeased him extremely disagreeable, and from this cause has great indirect influence over him; the law and the custom should therefore be strictly adhered to which rightly make the chief officer, in this respect, in a manner the umpire between the master and the crew, as well as between all on board and the parties interested on shore.

The law also makes the chief mate the successor to the master, in case the latter should die, or be unable to perform the duties of his office; and this without any action on the part of the crew. It is always important, therefore, that, to the practical seamanship and activity necessary for the discharge of the proper duties of his office, the mate should add a sufficient knowledge of navigation to be able to carry the ship on her voyage in case anything should happen to the master. Indeed, it has been doubted whether a vessel of the largest class, upon a long voyage, would be seaworthy with no navigator on board but the master.

Both the chief and second mates are always addressed by their surnames, with *Mr.* prefixed, and are answered with the addition of *Sir.* This is a requirement of ship's duty, and an intentional omission of it is an offence against the rules and understanding of the service.

CHAPTER III.

SECOND AND THIRD MATES.

SECOND MATE.—Navigation. Station. Watch duties. Day's work. Working ship. Reefing. Furling. Duties aloft. Care of Ship's furniture. Stores. Duties in port.

THIRD MATE.—Working ship. Day's work. Duties aloft—in port. Boating. Stores.

THE duties of the second mate are, to command the starboard watch when the master is not on deck, and to lead the crew in their work. It is not necessary that he should be a navigator, or even be able to keep a journal, though he should know enough of navigation to keep the courses and distances during his watch, and to report them correctly on the slate. There are also many advantages in his being acquainted with navigation and able to keep the log, as, in case of the chief mate's meeting with any accident, or being removed from office. The second mate, however, does not, by law, necessarily succeed to the office of chief mate, as the chief mate does to that of master; but it lies with the master for the time being to appoint whom he chooses to the office of chief mate : yet, if the second mate is capable of performing the duties of the office, he would ordinarily be appointed, as a matter of course.

When the starboard watch alone is on deck, and the master is below, the second mate has charge of the ship. When both watches are on deck, the chief mate is officer of the deck, to whichever watch the time may belong, according to the division of the hours. When the master is on deck, he commands, in one watch as well as in the other. But the second mate does not give up the charge of the vessel to the chief mate, if he should happen to be on deck during the starboard watch, unless all hands are up. While he has charge of the vessel in his watch, his duties are the common ones of a watch officer; that is, to have an eye to the helm, watch the weather, keep a general look-out round the horizon, see to the trimming of the yards and making and taking in of the light sails, give the master notice of anything important that occurs, heave the log and keep an account of the winds, courses, rate of sailing, &c., and enter the same on the slate at the end of the watch. In these things the chief mate has no right to interfere, when it is not his watch on deck. But in all matters connected with the day's work and jobs, the second mate acts under the chief mate in his own watch, as that department belongs peculiarly to the chief mate. In working days, when the crew are employed about the ship and rigging, it is usual for the chief mate to tell the second mate what to do in his watch, and sometimes he remains on deck a few minutes to see to the commencement of the work. And while day's work is going forward, during the time that the chief mate has a watch below, as the second mate is expected to do jobs like a common seaman, it is the custom for the master to be on deck a good deal in the starboard watch and look after the vessel. While work is going forward, the second mate is about decks and aloft; but at other times, as at night, or on Sunday, or during bad weather, when day's work cannot be kept up, his place is on the quarter-deck; though still, he leaves it whenever anything is to be done forward or aloft which requires the presence of a whole watch, as, setting or taking in a lower or topmast studding-sail, or any of the heavy sails.

When all hands are called to work ship, as in reefing, tacking, wearing, getting under way, coming to anchor, &c., the second mate's place is aft, at the fore and main braces and main and mizen rigging; and generally, in all ship's duty, the chief mate and larboard watch belong forward, and the second mate and starboard watch aft. In tacking ship, the second mate looks out for the lee fore and main braces, sees them belayed to one pin and clear for letting go, lets go the main braces at "Mainsail haul!" and the fore at "Let go and haul!" He also steadies the weather braces as the yards come up. He then sees to getting down the main tack, hauling out the main and mizen bowlines, hauling aft the main sheet, and, in short, has charge of all the duty to be done upon the quarter-deck and in the waist.

In getting under way, the second mate takes a handspike at the windlass with the men, the place which custom has assigned him being the windlass-end. If anything is to be done with the braces while the men are heaving at the windlass, it is his duty to attend to it, as the chief mate must be looking out for the ground tackle.

In reefing, the second mate goes aloft with the men, and takes his place at the weather earing. This is his proper duty, and he will never give it up, unless he is a youngster, and not strong enough or sufficiently experienced to lead the men on the yard. As soon as the order is given to clew down for reefing, and the halyards are let go, if there are hands enough to haul out the reef-tackles, he should go aloft, see that the yard is well down by the lifts, and then lay out to the weather yard-arm, and get his earing rove by the time the men are upon the yard. He then hauls it out and makes fast. If both topsails are reefed at once, he goes to the main; but if one sail is reefed at a time, he goes with the men from one to the other, taking the weather earing of each. He also goes aloft to reef a course, and takes the weather earing of that, in the same manner. He is not expected to go upon the mizen topsail yard, as the mizen topsail is a small sail, and can be reefed by a few men, or by the light hands.

In furling sails, the second mate goes aloft to the topsails and courses, and takes the bunt, as that is the most important place in that duty. He is not expected to go upon the mizen topsail yard for any service, and though in bad weather, and in case of necessity, he would do so, yet it would be out of the usual course. He might also, in heavy weather, assist in furling a large jib, or in taking the bonnet off; but he never furls a topgallant sail, royal or flying jib. In short, the fore or main topsail and the courses are the only sails which the second mate is expected to handle, either in reefing or furling. And, as I said before, if the sails are reefed or furled by the watch, he leads the starboard watch on the main and maintopsail yards, and the best man in the larboard watch leads them at the fore.

Although the proper place for the second mate on a

yard, is the bunt in furling, and the weather earing in reefing, and it is the custom to give him a chance at them at first, yet he cannot retain them by virtue of his office; and if he has not the necessary strength or skill for the stations, it is no breach of duty in a seaman to take them from him; on the contrary, he must always expect, in such a case, to give them up to a smarter man. If the second mate is a youngster, as is sometimes the case, being put forward early for the sake of promotion, or if he is not active and ambitious, he will not attempt to take the bunt or weather earing.

In the ordinary day's work done on shipboard, the second mate works with his hands like a common seaman. Indeed, he ought to be the best workman on board, and to be able to take upon himself the nicest and most difficult jobs, or to show the men how to do them. Among the various pieces of work constantly going forward on the vessel and rigging, there are some that require more skill and are less disagreeable than others. The assignment of all the work belongs to the chief mate, and if the second mate is a good seaman (by which sailors generally understand a good workman upon rigging,) he will have the best and most important of these allotted to him; as, for instance, fitting, turning in and setting up rigging, rattling down, and making the neater straps, coverings, graftings, pointings, &c.; but if he is not a good workman, he will have to employ himself upon the inferior jobs, such as are usually assigned to ordinary seamen and boys. Whatever may be his capacity, however, he "carries on the work," when his watch alone is on deck, under directions previously received from the chief mate.

It is a common saying among seamen that a man does not get his hands out of the tar bucket by becoming second mate. The meaning of this is, that as a great deal of tar is used in working upon rigging, and it is always put on by hand, the second mate is expected to put his hands to it as the others do. If the chief mate were to take hold upon a piece of work, and it should be necessary to put any tar on it, he might call some one to tar it for him, as all labour by hand is voluntary with him; but the second mate would be expected to do it for himself, as a part of his work. These matters, small in themselves, serve to show the different lights in which the duties of the officers are regarded by all sea-faring men. There are, however, some inferior services, such as slushing down masts, sweeping decks, &c., which the second mate takes no part in; and if he were ordered to do so, it would be considered as punishment, and might lead to a difficulty.

In working ship, making and taking in sail, &c., the second mate pulls and hauls about decks with the rest of the men. Indeed, in all the work he is expected to join in, he should be the first man to take hold, both leading the men and working himself. In one thing, however, he differs from the seamen; that is, he never takes the helm. Neither master nor mates ever take the wheel, but it is left to the men, who steer the vessel under the direction of the master or officer of the deck. He is also not expected to go aloft to reeve and unreeve rigging, or rig in and out booms, when making or taking in sail, if there are men enough; but, as I have said, under ordinary circumstances, only goes aloft to reef or furl a topsail or course. In case, however, of any accident, as carrying away a mast or yard, or if any unusual work is going on aloft, as the sending up or down of topmasts or topsail yards, or getting rigging over the mast-head, sending down or bending a heavy sail in a gale of wind, or the like, then the second mate should be aloft to take charge of the work there, and to be the organ of communication between the men aloft and the chief mate, who should remain on deck, since he must superintend everything fore and aft, as well as a-low and aloft. Sending up or down royal and top-gallant yards, being light work and done by one or two hands, does not call the second mate aloft; but if the topgallant masts are to be sent down, or a jib-boom rigged in in bad weather, or any other work going on aloft of unusual importance or difficulty, the second mate should be there with the men, leading them in the work, and communicating with, and receiving the orders from the deck.

During his own watch, if the master is not on deck, the second mate commands the ship, gives his orders and sees to their execution, precisely as the chief mate does in his; but, at the same time, he is expected to lend a hand at every " all hands rope."

There is another important part of the duties of a second mate; which is, the care of the spare rigging, blocks, sails, and small stuffs, and of the instruments for working upon rigging, as, marlinspikes, heavers, serving-boards, &c. It is the duty of the chief mate, as superintendant of the work, to see that these are on board, and to provide a constant supply of such as are made at sea; but when provided, it is the second mate's duty to look after them, to see them properly stowed away, and to have them at hand whenever they are called for. If, for instance, the chief mate orders a man to do a piece of work with certain instruments and certain kinds of stuff, the man will go to the second mate for them, and he must supply him. If there is no sail-maker on board, the second mate must also attend to the stowing away of the spare sails, and whenever one is called for, it is his duty to go below and find it. So with blocks, spare rigging, strands of yarns, and any part of a vessel's furniture, which an accident or emergency, as well as the ordinary course of duty, may bring into play.

So, also, with the stores. It is his duty to see to the stowing away of the water, bread, beef, pork, and all the provisions of the vessel; and whenever a new cask or barrel of water or provisions is to be opened, the second mate must do it. Indeed, the crew should never be sent into the hold or steerage, or to any part where there is cargo or stores, without an officer. He also measures out the allowance to the men, at the rate ordered by the master. These latter duties, of getting out the stores and weighing or measuring the allowance, fall upon the third mate, if there is one, which is seldom the case in merchant vessels.

While in port, when cargo is taking in or discharging, the second mate's place is in the hold; the chief mate standing at the gangway, to keep account, and to have a general supervision. If the vessel is lying at anchor, so that the cargo has to be brought on or off in boats, then the boating duty falls upon the second mate, who goes and comes in the boats, and looks after the landing and taking off of the goods. The chief mate seldom leaves the vessel when in port. The master is necessarily on shore a good deal, and the second mate must come and go in the boats, so that the chief mate is considered as the ship-keeper. So, if a warp or kedge is to be carried out, or a boat is lowered at sea, as in boarding another vessel, or when a man has fallen overboard, in all such cases the second mate should take charge of the boat.

When in port, the second mate stands no anchor watch, but is expected to be on deck until eight o'clock, which is the hour at which the watch is usually set. If, however, the ship is short-handed, he would stand his watch; in which case it would probably be either the first or the morning watch.

The second mate lives aft, sleeping in the cabin, if there are no passengers, or else in a state-room in the steerage. He also eats in the cabin, but at a second table, taking charge of the vessel while the master and chief mate are at their meals. In packet ships the two mates generally eat together, by themselves, at an earlier hour than the master and passengers.

THIRD MATE.—Merchant vessels bound on long voyages, upon which there are many vicissitudes to be anticipated, sometimes carry a third mate; but this is unusual; so much so, that his duties have hardly become settled by custom. He does not command a watch, but belongs to the larboard watch, and assists the chief mate in his duties. He goes aloft with the larboard watch to reef and furl, as the second mate does with the starboard, and performs very nearly the same duties aloft and about decks. If he is a good seaman, he will take the earing, and bunt on the head yards, as the second mate does on the after yards; and in the allotment of work he will be favoured with the most important jobs, if a good workman, otherwise he will be put upon the work of an ordinary seaman. He is not expected to handle the light sails. He stands no helm, lives aft, and will look out for the vessel at meal-times, if the second mate dines with the master and chief mate. While in port, he will be in the hold or in the boats, as he may be needed, thus dividing the labour with the second mate. Perhaps his place would more properly be in the boats, as that is considered more in the light of fatigue duty. He also relieves the second mate of the charge of the stores, and sees to the weighing and measuring of the allowances; and in his watch on deck, he relieves the chief mate of the inferior parts of his duty, such as washing decks in the morning, and looking after the boys in clearing up the decks at night.

CHAPTER IV.

CARPENTER, COOK, STEWARD, &c.

CARPENTER.—Working ship. Seaman's work. Helm. Duty aloft. Work at his trade. Station. Berth and mess. Standing watch.

SAILMAKER.—Seaman's work. Work at trade. Duty aloft. Standing watch. Berth and mess. Station.

STEWARD.—Duty in passenger-ships. Care of cabin-table—passengers. In other vessels—Master—mate. Aloft. About decks. Working ship.

COOK.—Berth. Standing watch. Care of galley and furniture. Working ship. Duty aloft.

CARPENTER.—Almost every merchant vessel of a large class, or bound upon a long voyage, carries a carpenter.

His duty is to work at his trade under the direction of the master, and to assist in all-hands work according to his ability. He is stationed with the larboard or starboard watch, as he may be needed, though, if there is no third mate, usually with the larboard. In working ship, if he is an able seaman, (as well as carpenter,) he will be put in some more important place, as looking after the main tack and bowlines, or working the forecastle with the mate; and if capable of leading his watch aloft, he would naturally take the bunt or an earing. He is not expected to handle the light sails, nor to go above the topsail yards, except upon the work of his trade. If he ships for an able seaman as well as carpenter, he must be capable of doing seaman's work upon the rigging and taking his turn at the wheel, if called upon; though he would not be required to do it except in bad weather, or in case the vessel should be short-handed. If he does not expressly ship for seaman as well as carpenter, no nautical skill can be required of him; but he must still, when all hands are called, or if ordered by the master, pull and haul about decks, and go aloft in the work usual on such occasions, as reefing and furling. But the inferior duties of the crew, as sweeping decks, slushing, tarring, &c., would not be put upon him, nor would he be required to do any strictly seaman's work, except taking a helm in case of necessity, or such work as all hands join in.

The carpenter is not an officer, has no command, and cannot give an order even to the smallest boy; yet he is a privileged person. He lives in the steerage, with the steward, has charge of the ship's chest of tools, and in all things connected with his trade is under the sole direction of the master. The chief mate has no authority over him, in his trade, unless it be in case of the master's absence or disability. In all things pertaining to the working of the vessel, however, and as far as he acts in the capacity of a seaman, he must obey the orders of the officers as implicitly as any of the crew would;

though, perhaps, an order from the second mate would come somewhat in the form of a request. Yet there is no doubt that he must obey the second mate in his proper place, as much as he would the master in his. Although he lives in the steerage, he gets his food from the galley, from the same mess with the men in the forecastle, having no better or different fare in any respect; and he has no right on the quarter-deck, but must take his place on the forecastle with the common seamen.

In many vessels, during fine weather, upon long voyages, the carpenter stands no watch, but "sleeps in" at night, is called at daylight, and works all day at his trade. But in this case, whenever all hands are called, he must come up with the rest. In bad weather, when he cannot well work at his trade, or if the vessel becomes short-handed, he is put in a watch, and does duty on deck, turning in and out with the rest. In many vessels, especially those bound on short voyages, the carpenter stands his watch, and, while on deck, works at his trade in the day-time, if the weather will permit, and at night, or in bad weather, does watch duty according to his ability.

SAILMAKER.—Some ships of the largest class carry a sailmaker, though usually the older seamen are sufficiently skilled in the trade to make and mend sails, and the master or chief mate should know how to cut them out. As to the sailmaker's duty on board, the same remarks will apply to him that were made upon the carpenter. If he ships for seaman as well as sailmaker, he must do an able seaman's duty, if called upon; and if he does not so ship, he will still be required to assist in all-hands work, such as working ship, taking in and making sail, &c., according to his ability; and in bad weather, or a case of necessity, he may be put with a watch, and required to do ship's duty with the rest. In all-hands work he is mustered with either watch, according to circumstances, and the station allotted to him will depend upon his qualities as a seaman; and, as with the carpenter, if he is a good seaman, he would naturally have some more important post assigned to him. He is not expected to handle the light sails, nor to go above the topsail yards. Nor would the inferior duties of the crew, such as tarring, slushing, and sweeping decks, be put upon him. In bad weather, or in case of necessity, he may be mustered in a watch, and must do duty as one of the crew, according to his ability. Sometimes he stands no watch, and works at his trade all day, and at others he stands his watch, and when on deck in the daytime, and during good weather, works at his trade, and at night, or in bad weather, does duty with the watch. He usually lives in the steerage with the carpenter, and always takes his food from the galley. He has no command, and when on deck belongs on the forecastle with the rest of the crew. In the work of his trade he is under the sole direction of the master, or of the chief mate in the master's absence; but in ship's work he is as strictly under the command of the mates as a common seaman is.

STEWARD.—The duties of the steward are very different in packet ships, carrying a large number of passengers, from those which are required of him in other vessels. In the New York *liners*, for instance, he has waiters or under-stewards, who do most of the labour, he himself having the general superintendence of the department. It is his duty to see that the cabin and state-rooms are kept in order; to see to the laying and clearing of the tables; to take care of the dishes, and other furniture belonging to them; to provide the meals, under the master's direction, preparing the nicer dishes himself; to keep the general charge of the pantry and stores for the cabin; to look after the cook in his department; and lastly, which is as important a part of his duty as any other, to attend to the comfort and convenience of the passengers. These duties, where there are many passengers, require all his time and attention, and he is not called upon for any ship's duty.

In vessels which are not passenger-ships, he does the work which falls to the under-stewards of the large packets: cleans the cabin and state-rooms; sets, tends, and clears away the table; provides everything for the cook; and has charge of the pantry, where all the table furniture and the small stores are kept. He is also the body servant of the master. His relation to the chief mate is somewhat doubtful; but the general understanding is, that, although he waits upon him when at table, and must obey him in all matters relating to the ship's work, yet he is not in any respect his servant. If the mate wishes any personal service done, he would ask it, or make some compensation.

In these vessels the steward must come on deck whenever all hands are called, and in working ship pulls and hauls about decks with the men. The main sheet is called the steward's rope, and this he lets go and hauls aft in tacking and wearing. In reefing and furling he is expected to go upon the lower and topsail yards, and especially the mizen topsail yard of a ship. No seamanship is expected of him, and he stands no watch, sleeping in at night and turning out at daylight; yet he must do ship's duty according to his ability when all hands are called for working ship, or for taking in or making sail. In these things he must obey the mates in the same way that a common seaman would, and is punishable for disobedience. The amount of ship's duty required of him depends, as I have said, upon the number of passengers.

Cook.—The cook almost always lives in the forecastle, though sometimes in the steerage with the steward. He stands no watch, sleeping in at night, and working at his business throughout the day. He spends his time mostly in the cook-house, which is called the "galley," where he cooks both for the cabin and forecastle. This, with keeping the galley, boilers, pans, kids, &c., clean and in order, occupies him during the day. He is called with all hands, and in tacking and wearing, works the fore-sheet. He is also expected to pull and haul about decks in all-hands work, and is occasionally called from his galley to give a pull at a tackle or halyards. No seamanship can be required of him, but he is usually expected to go upon a lower or topsail yard in reefing or furling, and to assist according to his ability in working ship. In regular passenger-ships, however, as he is more exclusively employed in cooking, he is not required to do any duty about decks, except in a case of necessity or of common danger. In some other vessels, too, if strongly manned, neither the cook nor steward is sent upon the yards. Yet it can, without doubt, be required of them, by the custom and understanding of the service, to go upon a lower or topsail yard to reef or furl.

If there are on board armourers, coopers, or persons following any other trades, they take the same place and follow the same rules as to duty that govern the carpenter and sailmaker. In the merchant service, when "all hands" are called, it literally calls every one on board but the passengers, excepting, as I have said, in the case of the cook and steward of strictly passenger-ships. Those persons of whom any duty can be required who do not stand a watch, but sleep in at night and work during the day, are called *idlers*. Beside turning out with "all hands," the idlers are sometimes called up at night to help the watch on deck in any heavy or difficult duty when it is not desirable to call the other watch, who may have had severe service. This is allowable, if practised only in cases of necessity, and not carried to an extreme.

CHAPTER V.

ABLE SEAMEN.

Grades of seafaring persons. Able seaman. Ordinary seaman. Boys. Shipping and rating. Over-rating. Requisites of an able seaman. Hand, reef and steer. Work upon rigging. Sailmaking. Day's work. Working ship. Reefing and furling. Watch duty. Coasters and small vessels.

SEAFARING persons before the mast are divided into three classes,—able seamen, ordinary seamen, and boys or green hands. And it may be remarked here that all green hands in the merchant service are termed *boys*, and rated as such, whatever may be their age or size. In the United States navy, an able seaman receives twelve dollars per month, an ordinary seaman ten, and the boys, or green hands, from four to eight, according to their strength and experience*. In the merchant service, wages are about the same on long voyages; but on voyages to Europe, the West Indies, and the southern ports, they are considerably higher, and very fluctuating. Still, the same proportion between the classes is preserved, an ordinary seaman getting about two dollars less than an able seaman, and the boys, from nothing up to two dollars less than ordinary seamen, according to

---

* The wages of seamen in the Royal Navy are, for able seamen 36s., ordinary 26s., and landmen 23s. per month. Boys of the first class—stout lads of eighteen and upwards, who have been two or three years at sea, have 14s. 3d., and boys of the second class 12s. 9d. per month; but the month being calculated by lunar not calendar time, gives thirteen months' wages in the year. In the merchant service the wages of seamen differs in the various trades, but the *average* of able seamen's wages in merchant ships, may be taken at present at 50s. per *calendar* month, *or* 30l., while the wages of the able seaman in the Queen's fleet is 23l. 8s. per annum. In the latter, however, the term is not broken into intervals, caused by the duration of voyages, and all things considered, the seaman earns as much in the year in the navy as in the merchant service.

circumstances. A full-grown man must ship for boy's wages upon his first voyage. It is not unusual to see a man receiving boy's wages and rated as a boy, who is older and larger than many of the able seamen.

The crews are not rated by the officers after they get to sea, but, both in the merchant service and in the navy, each man rates himself when he ships. The shipping articles, in the merchant service, are prepared for so many of each class, and a man puts his name down and contracts for the wages and duty of a seaman, ordinary seaman, or boy, at his pleasure. Notwithstanding this license, there are very few instances of its being abused; for every man knows that if he is found incompetent to perform the duty he contracts for, his wages can not only be reduced to the grade for which he is fitted, but that something additional will be deducted for the deception practised upon all concerned, and for the loss of service and the numerous difficulties incurred, in case the fraud is not discovered until the vessel has got to sea. But, still more than this, the rest of the crew consider it a fraud upon themselves; as they are thus deprived of a man of the class the vessel required, which makes her short-handed for the voyage, and increases the duty put upon themselves. If, for instance, the articles provide for six able seamen, the men expect as many, and if one of the six turns out not to be a seaman, and is put upon inferior work, the duties which would commonly be done by seamen will fall upon the five. The difficulty is felt still more in the watches; as, in the case I have supposed, there would be in one watch only two able seamen instead of three, and if the delinquent was not a capable helmsman, the increased duty at the wheel alone would be, of itself, a serious evil. The officers also feel at liberty to punish a man who has so imposed upon all hands, and accordingly every kind of inferior and disagreeable duty is put upon him; and, as he finds no sympathy from the crew, his situation on board is made very unpleasant. Indeed, there is nothing a man can be guilty of, short of a felony, to which so little mercy is shown on board ship; for it is a deliberate act of deception, and one to which there is no temptation, except the gain of a few dollars.

The common saying that to hand reef and steer makes a sailor, is a mistake. It is true that no man is a sailor until he can do these things; yet to ship for an able seaman he must, in addition to these, be a good workman upon rigging. The rigging of a ship requires constant mending, covering and working upon in a multitude of ways; and whenever any of the ropes or yards are chafing or wearing upon it, it must be protected by "chafing gear." This chafing gear consists of worming, parcelling, serving, rounding, &c.; which requires a constant supply of small stuffs, such as foxes, sennit, spunyarn, marline, and the like, all which is made on board from condemned rigging and old junk. There is also a great deal of new rigging to be cut and fitted, on board, which requires neat knots, splices, seizings, coverings, and turnings in. It is also frequently necessary to set up the rigging in one part of the vessel or another; in which case it must be seized or turned in afresh. It is upon labour of this kind that the crew is employed in the "day's work," and jobs which are constantly carried forward on board. A man's skill in this work is the chief test of his seamanship; a competent knowledge of steering, reefing, furling, and the like, being taken for granted, and being no more than is expected of an ordinary seaman. To put a marlinspike in a man's hand and set him to work upon a piece of rigging, is considered a fair trial of his qualities as an able seaman.

There is, of course, a great deal of difference in the skill and neatness of the work of different men; but I believe I am safe in saying that no man will pass for an able seaman in a square-rigged vessel, who cannot make a long and short splice in a large rope, fit a block-strap, pass seizings to lower rigging, and make the ordinary knots, in a fair, workmanlike manner. This working upon rigging is the last thing to which a lad training up to the sea is put, and always supposes a competent acquaintance with all those kinds of work that are required of an ordinary seaman or boy. A seaman is generally expected to be able to sew upon a sail, and few men ship for seamen who cannot do it; yet, if he is competent in other respects, no fault can be found with an able seaman for want of skill in sailmaking.

In allotting the jobs among the crew, reference is always had to a man's rate and capacity; and it is considered a decided imputation upon a man to put him upon inferior work. The most difficult jobs, and those requiring the neatest work, will be given to the older and more experienced among the seamen; and of this none will complain; but to single out an able seaman and keep him at turning the spunyarn winch, knotting yarns or picking oakum, while there are boys on board, and other properly seaman's work going forward at the same time, would be looked upon as punishment, unless it were temporarily, or from necessity, or while other seamen were employed in the same manner. Also, in consideration of the superior grade of an able seaman, he is not required to sweep down the decks at night, slush the masts, &c., if there are boys on board and at hand. Not that a seaman is not obliged to do these things. There is no question but that he is, just as much as to do any other ship's work; and if there are no boys on board or at hand at the time, or from any other cause it is reasonably required of him, no good seaman would object, and it would be a refusal of duty to do so: yet if an officer were deliberately, and without necessity for it, when there were boys about decks at the time, who could do the work as well, to order an able seaman to leave his work and sweep down the decks, or slush a mast, it would be considered as punishment.

In working ship, the able seamen are stationed variously; though, for the most part, upon the forecastle, at the main tack or fore and main lower and topsail braces; the light hands being placed at the cross-jack and fore and main topgallant and royal braces. In taking in and making sail, and in all things connected with the working of a ship, there is no duty which may not be required of an able seaman; yet there are certain things requiring more skill or strength, to which he is always put, and others which are as invariably assigned to ordinary seamen and boys. In reefing, the men go out to the yard-arms, and the light hands stand in toward the slings; while in furling, the bunt and quarters belong to the able seamen, and the yard-arms to the boys. The light hands are expected to loose and furl the light sails, as royals, flying jib and mizen topgallant sail, and the men seldom go above the cross-trees, except to work upon the rigging, or to send a mast or yard up or down. The fore and main topgallant sails, and sometimes the flying jib of large vessels, require one or more able seamen for furling, but are loosed by light hands. In short, as to everything connected with working ship, making and taking in sail, &c., one general rule may be laid down. A seaman is obliged to obey the order of the master or officer, asking no questions and making no objection, whether the duty to which he is ordered be that which properly belongs to an able seaman or not; yet as able seamen alone can do the more nice and difficult work, the light hands, in their turn, are expected to do that which requires less skill and strength. In the watch on deck at night, for instance, the able and ordinary seamen steer the ship, and are depended upon in case of any accident, or if heavy sails are to be taken in or set, or ropes to be knotted or spliced; and in consideration of this, if there is light work to be done, as coiling up rigging about decks, holding the log-reel, loosing or furling a light sail, or the like, the boys are expected to do it, and should properly be called upon by the officer, unless from some circumstance it should be necessary to call upon a man. Yet, as I have said before, if ordered, the seaman must do the thing, under any circumstances, and a refusal would be a refusal of his duty.

No man is entitled to the rate or wages of an able seaman who is not a good helmsman. There is always a difference in a ship's company as to this duty, some men being more steady, careful, and expert helmsmen than others; and the best quality cannot be required of every able seaman; yet, if, upon fair trial, in bad weather, a man is found incapable of steering the ship, under circumstances not extraordinary, he would be considered by all on board to have failed of his duty. It should be remembered, however, that there are times when the very best helmsman is hardly able to steer a ship, and if a vessel is out of trim or slow in her motions, no skill can keep her close to her course.

An able seaman is also expected to do all the work necessary for reefing, furling, and setting sail, to be able to take a bunt or earing, to send yards and masts up and down, to rig in and out booms, to know how to reeve all the running rigging of a ship, and to steer, or pull an oar in a boat.

The standard of seamanship, however, is not so high in coasting vessels and those of a smaller class bound upon short voyages, in which all the work that is necessary upon the vessel or rigging is usually done when in port by people hired from on shore. In such vessels many men ship for able seamen, and are considered upon the whole competent, if they are able-bodied, and can hand, reef, and steer, who perhaps would only have shipped for ordinary seamen in vessels bound upon long voyages. In all large-class vessels, and in vessels of almost any class bound upon long voyages, the standard of seamanship is very nearly what I have before described.

CHAPTER VI.

ORDINARY SEAMEN.

Requisites. Hand, reef, and steer. Loose, furl, and set sails. Reeve rigging. Work upon rigging. Watch—duty.

An ordinary seaman is one who, from not being of sufficient age and strength, or from want of sufficient experience, is not quite competent to perform all the duties of an able seaman, and accordingly receives a little less than full wages, and does not contract for the complete qualities of an able seaman. There is a large proportion of ordinary seamen in the navy. This is probably because the power of the officers is so great upon their long cruises to detect and punish any deficiency, and because, if a man can by any means be made to appear wanting in capacity for the duty he has shipped to perform, it will justify a great deal of hard usage. Men, therefore, prefer rather to underrate than to run any risk of overrating themselves.

An ordinary seaman is expected to hand, reef, and steer, under common circumstances, (which includes "boxing the compass;") to be well acquainted with all the running and standing rigging of a ship; to be able to reeve all the studdingsail gear, and set a topgallant or royal studdingsail out of the top; to loose and furl a royal, and a small topgallant sail or flying jib; and perhaps, also, to send down or cross a royal yard. An ordinary seaman need not be a complete helmsman, and if an able seaman should be put in his place at the wheel in very bad weather, or when the ship steered with difficulty, it would be no imputation upon him provided he could steer his trick creditably under ordinary circumstances. In reefing or furling the courses and topsails, an ordinary seaman would not take the bunt or an earing, if there were able seamen on the yard; and perhaps, in the largest-sized vessels, it would not be expected of him to pass an earing, or make up the bunt of a fore or main topsail or course in bad weather, yet he should know how to do both, and should be able to take a bunt or earing on the mizen topsail yard, and on any topsail or lower yard of a small vessel.

It is commonly understood that an ordinary seaman need not be a workman upon rigging. Yet there are probably few men capable of performing the duties of an ordinary seaman, as above detailed, who would not be somewhat acquainted with work upon rigging, and who could not do the simpler parts of it, such as, serving and splicing small ropes, passing a common seizing, or the like; and it is always expected that an ordinary seaman shall be able to make all the hitches, bends, and knots in common use: such as, two half-hitches, a rolling hitch, timber hitch, clove hitch, common bend, and bowline knot. He would also be thought deficient if he could not draw, knot, and ball up yarns, and make spunyarn, foxes, and common sennit. Yet it is said that if he can steer his trick, and do his duty creditably in working ship and taking in and making sail, he is entitled to the rate and wages of an ordinary seaman, though he cannot handle a marlinspike or serving-board.

The duty upon which an ordinary seaman is put, depends a good deal upon whether there are boys or green hands on board or not. If there are, he has a preference over them, as an able seaman has over him, in the light work; and since he stands his helm regularly and is occasionally set to work upon rigging with the men, he will be favoured accordingly in the watch and in common duty about decks. Yet the distinction between ordinary seamen and boys is not very carefully observed in the merchant service, and an ordinary seaman is frequently called upon for boy's duty, though there are boys on board and at hand. If an officer wished for some one to loose a royal, take a broom and sweep the decks, hold the log-reel, coil up a rope, or the like, he would probably first call upon a boy, if at hand; if not, upon an ordinary seaman; but upon either of them indifferently, before an able seaman.

If there are no boys on board, the ordinary seamen do boy's duty; the only difference being, that if they take their trick at the wheel, and do other ordinary seamen's work, the able seamen are not so much preferred over them, as over mere boys and green hands.

CHAPTER VII.

BOYS.

Requisites. Wages. Watch. Day's work. Working ship. Helm. Duties aloft and about decks.

Boy is the term, as I have said before, for all green hands, whatever may be their size or age; and also for boys, who, though they have been at sea before, are not large and strong enough for ordinary seamen. It is the common saying, that a boy does not ship to know anything. Accordingly, if any person ships as a boy, and upon boy's wages, no fault can be found with him, though he should not know the name of a rope in the ship, or even the stem from the stern. In the navy, the boys are divided into three classes, according to their size and experience, and different duties are put upon them. In the merchant service, all except able and ordinary seamen are generally upon the same wages, though boys' wages vary in different voyages. Sometimes they get nothing, being considered as apprentices; and from that they rise to three, five, and sometimes eight dollars per month. Whatever boy's wages may be, a person who ships for them for that voyage, whether more or less, is rated as boy, and his duty is according to his rate.

In the ordinary day's work, the boys are taught to draw and knot yarns, make spunyarn, foxes, sennit, &c., and are employed in passing a ball or otherwise assisting the able seamen in their jobs. Slushing masts, sweeping and clearing up decks, holding the log-reel, coiling up rigging, and loosing and furling the light sails, are duties that are invariably put upon the boys or green hands. They stand their watches like the rest, are called with all hands, go aloft to reef and furl, and work whenever and wherever the men do, the only difference being in the kind of work upon which they are put. In reefing, the boys lay in toward the slings of the yard, and in furling they go out to the yard-arms. They are sent aloft immediately, as soon as they get to sea, to accustom them to the motion of a vessel, and to moving about in the rigging and on the yards. Loosing and furling the royals, setting topgallant studdingsails and reeving the gear, shaking out reefs, learning the names and uses of all the ropes, and to make the common hitches, bends, and knots, reeving all the studdingsail gear, and rigging in and out booms, and the like, is the knowledge first instilled into beginners. There is a good deal of difference in the manner in which boys are put forward in different vessels. Sometimes, in large vessels, where there are plenty of men, the boys never take the wheel at all, and are seldom put upon any but the most simple and inferior duties. In others, they are allowed to take the wheel in light winds, and gradually, if they are of sufficient age and strength, become regular helmsmen. So, also, in their duties aloft; if they are favoured, they may be kept at the royals and topgallant sails, and gradually come to the earing of a mizen topsail. In work upon rigging, however, a green hand makes but little progress beyond ropeyarns and spunyarn, during his first voyage; since there are men enough to do the jobs, and he can be employed to more advantage in the inferior work, and in making and taking in light sails, steering in light winds, &c.; a competent knowledge of which duty is sufficient to enable him to ship for an ordinary seaman upon the next voyage. It is generally while in the grade of ordinary seaman that the use of the marlinspike is learned. Whatever knowledge a boy may have acquired, or whatever may be his age or strength, so long as he is rated as a boy, (and the rates are not changed during a voyage unless a person changes his ship,) he must do the inferior duties of a boy. If decks are to be cleared up or swept, rigging to be coiled up, a man is to be helped in his job, or any duty to be done aloft or about decks which does not require the strength or skill of a seaman, a boy is always expected to start first and do it, though not called upon by name.

CHAPTER VIII.

MISCELLANEOUS.

Watches. Calling the watch. Bells. Helm. Answering. Stations. Food. Sleep.

WATCHES.—A watch is a term both for a division of the crew, and for the period of time allotted to such division. The crew are divided into two watches, larboard and starboard; the larboard commanded by the chief mate, and the starboard by the second mate. These watches divide the time between them, being on and off duty, or, as it is termed, on deck and below, every other four hours. If, for instance, the chief mate with the larboard watch have the first night watch, from eight to twelve, at the end of the four hours the starboard watch is called, and the second mate takes the deck, while the larboard watch and the chief mate go below until four in the morning. At four they come on deck again, and remain until eight; having what is called the "morning watch." As they will have been on deck eight hours out of the twelve, while the starboard watch, who had the middle watch, from twelve to four, will only have been up four hours, they are entitled to the watch below from eight till twelve, which is called the "forenoon watch below." Where this alternation of watches is kept up throughout the twenty-four hours, four hours up and four below, it is called having "watch and watch." This is always given in bad weather, and when day's work cannot be carried on; but in most merchant vessels, it is the custom to keep all hands from one P. M. until sundown, or until four o'clock. In extreme cases, also, all hands are kept throughout the day; but the watch which has had eight hours on deck at night should always be allowed a forenoon watch below, if possible.

The watch from four to eight P. M. is divided into two half-watches of two hours each, called *dog-watches.* The object of this is to make an uneven number of watches, seven instead of six; otherwise the same watch would stand during the same hours for the whole voyage, and those who had two watches on deck the first night would have the same throughout the trip. But the uneven number shifts the watches. The dog-watches coming about sundown, or twilight, and between the end of a day's work and the setting of the night watch, are usually the time given for recreation,—for smoking, telling yarns, &c., on the forecastle; things which are not allowed during the day.

CALLING THE WATCH.—As soon as eight bells are struck, the officer of the watch gives orders to call the watch, and one of the crew goes to the scuttle, knocks three times, and calls out in a loud voice, "All the starboard (or larboard) watch, ahoy!!" or, "All star-bowlines, ahoy!" or something of the kind, and adds, "Eight bells," or the hour; usually, also, a question, to know whether he is heard, as, "Do you hear the news there, sleepers?" Some one of the watch below must answer, "Ay, ay!" to show that the call has been heard. The watch below is entitled to be called in a loud and audible voice, and in the usual manner; and unless called, they cannot be expected to come up. They must also turn out at once and come on deck as soon as they are called, in order that the other watch may go below, especially as they are never called until the hour has expired, and since some minutes are allowed for turning out, dressing, and getting on deck. The man whose turn it is to take the helm goes immediately aft, and ought to be the first on deck, as the two hours' duty at the helm at night is tedious, and entitles a man to be speedily relieved. It is considered a bad trait in a man to be slack in relieving the helm. The relieving the helm is also the sign that the watch is changed, and no man is permitted to go below until that has been done. It is a man's watch on deck so long as one of his watch is at the wheel.

BELLS.—The time at sea is marked by bells. At noon, eight bells are struck, that is, eight strokes are made upon the bell; and from that time it is struck every half-hour throughout the twenty-four, beginning at one stroke and going as high as eight, adding one at each half-hour. For instance, twelve o'clock is eight bells, half past twelve is one bell, one o'clock is two bells, half past one three bells, and so on until four o'clock, which will be eight bells. The watch is then out, and for half past four you strike one bell again. A watch of four hours therefore runs out the bells. It will be observed, also, that even bells come at the full hours, and the odd bells at the half-hours. For instance, eight bells is always twelve, four, or eight o'clock; and seven bells always half past three, half past seven, or half past eleven.

The bells are sounded by two strokes following one another quickly, and then a short interval; after which, two more; and so on. If it is an odd number, the odd one is struck alone, after the interval. This is to make the counting more sure and easy; and, by this means, you can, at least, tell whether it is an hour or a half-hour.

HELM.—Neither the master nor mates of a merchant vessel ever take the helm. The proper helmsmen are the able and ordinary seamen. Sometimes the carpenter, sailmaker, &c., if they are seamen, are put at the helm; also the boys, in light winds, for practice. Each watch steers the ship in its turn, and the watch on deck must supply the helmsman, even when all hands are called. Each man stands at the helm two hours, which is called his *trick*. Thus, there are two tricks in a watch. Sometimes, in very cold weather, the tricks are reduced to one hour; and if the ship steers badly, in a gale of wind, two men are sent to the wheel at once. In this case, the man who stands on the weather side of the wheel is the responsible helmsman, the man at the lee wheel merely assisting him by heaving the wheel when necessary.

The men in the watch usually arrange their tricks among themselves, the officers being satisfied if there is always a man ready to take the wheel at the proper time. In steering, the helmsman stands on the weather side of a wheel and on the lee side of a tiller. But when steering by tiller-ropes with no hitch round the tiller-head, or with a tackle, as in a heavy gale and bad sea, when it is necessary to ease the helm a good deal, it is better to stand up to windward and steer by the parts of the tackle or tiller-ropes.

In relieving the wheel, the man should come aft on the lee side of the quarter-deck, (as indeed he always should unless his duty lies to windward,) go to the wheel behind the helmsman and take hold of the spokes, so as to have the wheel in command when the other lets go. Before letting go, the helmsman should give the course to the man that relieves him in an audible voice, and the new man should repeat it aloud just as it was given, so as to make it sure that he has heard correctly. This is especially necessary, since the points and half-points are so much alike that a mistake might easily be made. It is the duty of the officer of the watch to be present when the wheel is relieved, in order to see that the course is correctly reported and understood; which is another reason why the course should be spoken by both in a loud tone. It is unseamanlike and reprehensible to answer, "Ay, ay!" or, "I understand," or the like, instead of repeating the course.

If a vessel is sailing close-hauled and does not lay her course, the order is, "Full and by!" which means, by the wind, yet all full. If a vessel lays her course, the order then is her course, as N. W. by W., E. by S., and the like.

When a man is at the wheel, he has nothing else to attend to but steering the ship, and no conversation should be allowed with him. If he wishes to be relieved during his trick, it should not be done without the permission of the officer, and the same form of giving and repeating the course should be gone through, though he is to be absent from the helm but a minute or two.

If an order is given to the man at the wheel as to his steering, he should always repeat the order, distinctly, that the officer may be sure he is understood. For instance, if the order is a new course, or "Keep her off a point!" "Luff a little!" "Ease her!" "Meet her!" or the like, the man should answer by repeating the course or the order, as "Luff a little, sir," "Meet her, sir," &c., and should not answer, "Ay, ay, sir!" or simply execute the order as he understands it. This practice of repeating every, even the most minute order at the wheel, is well understood among seamen, and a failure or refusal to do so is an offence sometimes leading to disagreeable results.

If, when the watch is out and the other watch has been called, all hands are detained for any purpose, as, to reef a topsail, to set studding sails, or the like, the helm should not be relieved until the work is done and the watch ready to go below.

ANSWERING.—The rule has just been stated which requires a man at the wheel to answer by repeating distinctly the order given him. The same rule applies to some other parts of a seaman's duty, though to none so strictly, perhaps, as to that. In tacking, where the moment of letting go a rope or swinging a yard is very important, the order of the master is always repeated by the officer on the forecastle. This enables the master to know whether he is heard and understood, to repeat his order if it is not answered at once, and to correct any mistake, or obviate some of its consequences. The same may be said generally of every order to the proper or instant execution of which unusual importance is attached. If, for instance, a man is stationed by a rope to let it go upon an order given, if an order is addressed to him which he supposes to be for that purpose, he should answer, " Let go, sir ! " and usually adds, " All gone ! " as soon as it is done. Green hands should bear in mind that whenever an order is of a kind which ought to be repeated, it must be so, without reference to a man's distance from the officer who gives the order, but just as much if standing a few feet from him as if at the masthead, since, upon the whole, the chance of misapprehension is not much less in one case than in the other.

The common run of orders, however, are sufficiently answered by the usual reply of " Ay, ay, sir ! " which is the proper seaman's answer, where the repetition of the order is not necessary. But *some answer or other should always be made to an order*. This is a rule difficult to impress upon beginners, but the reasonableness of it is obvious, and it is well understood among all seafaring persons ; and even though an officer should see that the man was executing his order, he still would require, and has a right to demand, a reply. The rule is as strictly observed by the master and officers between themselves, as it is required by them of the men ; for the reason is the same. It is almost unnecessary to say that the addition " Sir " is always to be used in speaking to the master or to either of the mates. The mates in their turn use it to the master. " Mr." is always to be prefixed to the name of an officer, whether chief or second mate.

In well-disciplined vessels, no conversation is allowed among the men when they are employed at their work ;

that is to say, it is not allowed in the presence of an officer or of the master; and although, when two or more men are together aloft, or by themselves on deck, a little low conversation might not be noticed, yet if it seemed to take off their attention, or to attract the attention of others, it would be considered a misdemeanour. In this respect the practice is different in different vessels. Coasters, fishermen, or small vessels on short voyages, do not preserve the same rule; but no seaman who has been accustomed to first-class ships will object to a strictness as to conversations and laughing, while at day's work, very nearly as great as is observed in a school. While the crew are below in the forecastle, great license is given them; and the severest officer will never interfere with the noise and sport of the forecastle, unless it is a serious inconvenience to those who are on deck. In working ship, when the men are at their stations, the same silence and decorum are observed. But during the dog-watches, and when the men are together on the forecastle at night, and no work is going forward, smoking, singing, telling yarns, &c., are allowed; and, in fact, a considerable degree of noise and *skylarking* is permitted, unless it amounts to positive disorder and disturbance.

It is a good rule to enforce, that whenever a man aloft wishes anything to be done on deck, he shall hail the officer of the deck, and not call out, as is often done, to any one whom he may see about decks, or generally to have a thing done by whoever may happen to hear him. By enforcing this rule the officer knows what is requested, and may order it and see that it is done as he thinks fit; whereas, otherwise, any one about decks, perhaps a green hand, may execute the order upon his own judgment and after his own manner.

STATIONS.—The proper place for the seamen when they are on deck and there is no work going forward, is on the forecastle. By this is understood so much of the upper deck as is forward of the after fore-shroud. The men do not leave this to go aft or aloft unless ship's duty requires it of them. In working ship they are stationed variously, and go wherever there is work to be done. The same is the case in working upon rigging. But if a man goes aft to take the wheel, or for any other purpose which does not require him to go to windward, he will go on the lee side of the quarter-deck.

Food, Sleep, &c. — The crew eat together in the forecastle, or on deck, if they choose, in fine weather. Their food is cooked at the galley, and they are expected to go to the galley for it and take it below or upon the forecastle. The cook puts the eatables into wooden tubs called " kids," and of these there are more or less, according to the number of men. The tea or coffee is served out to each man in his tin pot, which he brings to the galley. There is no table, and no knives or forks, to the forecastle ; but each man helps himself, and furnishes his own eating utensils. These are usually a tin pot and pan, with an iron spoon.

The usual time for breakfast is seven bells, that is, half-past seven o'clock in the morning. Consequently, the watch below is called at seven bells, that they may get breakfast and be ready to take the deck at eight o'clock. Sometimes all hands get breakfast together at seven bells ; but in bad weather, or if watch and watch is given, it is usual for the watch below to breakfast at seven bells, and the watch on deck at eight bells, after they are relieved. The dinner-hour is twelve o'clock, if all hands get dinner together. If dinner is got " by the watch," the watch below is called for dinner at seven bells (half-past eleven), and the other watch dine when they go below, at twelve.

If all hands are kept in the afternoon, or if both watches get supper together, the usual hour is three bells, or half-past five ; but if supper is got by the watch, three bells is the time for one watch, and four for the other.

In bad weather, each watch takes its meals during the

watch below, as, otherwise, the men would be liable to be called up from their meals at any moment.

As to the time allowed for SLEEP; it may be said, generally, that a sailor's watch below is at his own disposal to do what he chooses in, except, of course, when all hands are called. The meal-times, and time for washing, mending, reading, writing, &c., must all come out of the watch below; since, whether there is work going forward or not, a man is considered as belonging to the ship in his watch on deck. At night, however, especially if watch and watch is not given, it is the custom in most merchant vessels, in good weather, to allow the watch to take naps about the decks, provided one of them keeps a look-out, and the rest are so placed that they can be called instantly. This privilege is rather a thing winked at than expressly allowed; and if the man who has the look-out falls asleep, or if the rest are slow in mustering at a call, they are all obliged to keep awake. In bad weather, also, or if near land, or in the track of other vessels, this privilege should not be granted. The men in each watch usually arrange the helms and look-outs among themselves, so that a man need not have a helm and a look-out during the same watch. A man should never go below during his watch on deck, without permission; and if he merely steps down into the forecastle for an instant, as, to get his jacket, he should tell some one, who may speak to him at once, if the watch is called upon.

PART III.

LAWS RELATING TO THE PRACTICAL DUTIES OF MASTER AND MARINERS.

CHAPTER I.
THE VESSEL.

Title. Bill of sale. Registry. Enrolment. Licence. Documents. Certificates. Passport. Sea-letter. List of crew. Bill of health. General clearance. Clearing manifest. Invoice. Bill of lading. Charter-party. Log-book. Manifest. List of passengers and crew. Remaining sea-stores. Medicine-chest. Provisions.

TITLE.*—The bill of sale is the proper evidence of title to all vessels. It is the instrument of transfer which is used in all maritime countries, which courts of law look to for proof of title, and which is in most cases absolutely required.[1]

---

[1] 5 Rob. Ad. 155. 1 Mason, 139; 2 do. 435; 4 do. 390. 16 Mass. 336. 7 Johns. 308. But see 3 Pick. 89. 16 Mass. 663.

---

* IN ENGLAND.] *Title.*—The bill of sale would not of itself be considered satisfactory evidence of the title to a ship or vessel, exercising the privileges of a British ship; it should, in all cases, be accompanied by a proper certificate of registry, (see the Register Act 3 & 4 W. 4, c. 55, s. 34); and it should be ascertained that the parties in the actual possession of the ship or vessel, or who would be entitled to such possession on her arrival in port, are the same as are named as owners in the registry. When the ship is here, in the country of its owners, and a delivery of actual possession is possible, such delivery is necessary to give a perfect title to the buyer in case of a sale of the whole ship; and if the buyer suffers the seller to remain in possession and act as owner, and the seller should have an execution issued against him, or should become bankrupt before the buyer takes possession, the property may be considered as remaining in the seller, and seized and disposed of

Possession of the vessel should also accompany the bill of sale, whenever it is practicable. If the bill of sale is transferred while the vessel is at sea, possession should be taken immediately upon her arrival in port. The fact of the bill of sale being with one person and the actual possession of the vessel with another, after there has been an opportunity to transfer it, will raise a presumption of fraud, and make the parties liable to losses and difficulties in dealing with creditors, and such as purchase in good faith.[1]

REGISTRY, ENROLMENT, AND LICENCE*.—The laws of

---

[1] 4 Mass. 663.   4 Mason, 183.   9 Pick. 4.   6 Mass. 422; 15 do. 477; 18 do. 389.

---

accordingly.—See 6 Geo. 4, c. 16, s. 70; Abbott on Shipping, 6th Edition, by Serjt. Shee, 14, and the authorities there cited.

Title of Mortgagee, &c.—The claim of a mortgagee of a ship or vessel, or any share or shares thereof, is not preferred to that of the general creditors, unless he has taken care on lending his money, that his debt and security shall appear in the book of registry, and on the back of the certificate.—See 3 & 4 W. 4, c. 55, s. 42, 43; Abbott on Shipping, 6th Edition, 16. And a mortgagee or trustee for sale of a ship or vessel for payment of debts, whose mortgage or assignment shall have been duly registered, is not to be deemed an owner, nor his interest to be affected by the subsequent bankruptcy of the mortgagor or assignor, on the ground of reputed ownership.—3 & 4 W. 4, c. 55, s. 42, 43.

* IN ENGLAND.] *Registry.*—The laws of England have given similar privileges to ships or vessels entitled to be registered as *British* vessels. For an enumeration of these privileges, and for the particular provisions and directions as to the registry of ships, see the Register Act, 3 & 4 W. 4, c. 55.

According to this act, if a ship or vessel not being duly registered, and not having obtained a proper certificate of registry, shall exercise the privileges of a *British* ship, the same is subject to forfeiture and may be seized by any officer of the customs, s. 4.

And by the Navigation Act, 3 & 4 W. 4, c. 54, it is enacted, that no ship shall be admitted to be a *British* ship unless duly registered and navigated as such, s. 12.

But British-built boats or vessels under fifteen tons burthen, wholly owned and navigated by British subjects, although not registered as British ships, shall be admitted to be British vessels in all navigation in the rivers, and upon the coasts of the United

the United States have given many privileges to vessels built, owned, and commanded by our own citizens. Such vessels are entitled to be registered, enrolled or licensed, according to circumstances, and are thereupon considered

---

Kingdom, or of the British possessions abroad, not proceeding over sea, except within the limits of the respective colonial governments within which the managing owners of such vessels respectively reside; and all British-built boats or vessels wholly owned and navigated by *British* subjects, not exceeding the burthen of thirty tons, and not having a whole or a fixed deck, and being employed solely in fishing on the banks and shores of Newfoundland, and of the parts adjacent, or on the banks and shores of the provinces of Canada, Nova Scotia, or New Brunswick, adjacent to the Gulf of St. Lawrence, or on the north of Cape Canso, or of the islands within the same, or in trading coastwise within the said limits, shall be admitted to be British boats or vessels, although not registered, so long as such boats or vessels shall be solely so employed, s. 13. And all ships built in the *British* settlements at Honduras, and owned and navigated as *British* ships, shall be entitled to the privileges of *British* registered ships, in all direct trade between the United Kingdom or the *British* possessions in America and the said settlements; provided the master shall produce a certificate under the hand of the superintendant of those settlements, that satisfactory proof has been made before him that such ship (describing the same) was built in the said settlements, and is wholly owned by *British* subjects; provided also that the time of the clearance of such ship from the said settlements for every voyage shall be indorsed upon such certificate by such superintendant, s. 14.

The ships or vessels entitled to be registered are such only as are wholly of the built of the United Kingdom, or of the Isle of Man, or of Guernsey or Jersey, or of some of the colonies, plantations, islands or territories, in Asia, Africa or America, or of Malta, Gibraltar or Heligoland, which belong to her Majesty at the time of the building of such ships or vessels; or such ships or vessels as shall have been condemned in any Court of Admiralty as prize of war, or condemned in any competent court as forfeited for the breach of the laws made for the prevention of the slave-trade, and which belong to her Majesty's subjects duly entitled to be owners of registered ships or vessels.—See *Register Act*, 3 & 4 W. 4, c. 55, s. 5.

The name of a registered ship or vessel cannot be changed; and the owner or owners, before taking in any cargo, must cause to be painted in white or yellow letters, of a length of not less than four inches upon a black ground, on some conspicuous part of the stern, the name by which such ship or vessel shall have been registered,

"vessels of the United States, entitled to the benefits and privileges appertaining to such ships." The only vessels entitled to a register are those built in the United States and owned wholly by citizens thereof; vessels captured in war by our citizens, and condemned as prizes; and vessels adjudged to be forfeited for breach of the laws of the United States, being wholly owned by such citizens. No owner is compelled to register his vessel, but unless registered (with the exception of those enrolled and licensed in the coasting and fishing trades) she is not

---

and the port to which she belongs, in a distinct and legible manner, and must so preserve the same; penalty for omission, &c., 100*l.*—*Register Act*, 3 & 4 W. 4, c. 55, s. 24.

No registry can be made or certificate obtained until the owner or owners shall, in the manner directed by the act, make a declaration as to the name of the ship, her port and master, the description of the ship, the name, occupation, and residence of every part owner, with other particulars tending to prove them to be subjects of her Majesty, 3 & 4 W. 4, c. 55, s. 13.

A bond is required to be given at the time of registry by the master and owner or owners, in a penalty varying in proportion to the burthen of a ship, but never exceeding 1000*l.*; and such bond is to be as a security that the certificate shall not be lent, sold, or disposed of, but solely used for the service of the ship for which it is granted, and shall be given up within a month in certain cases specified in the act.

If the master cannot attend at the time of registry, by reason of the absence of himself and the ship at some other port, a separate bond may be given by him at the port where the ship may then be, s. 20.

No greater number than thirty-two persons are entitled to be legal owners at one and the same time as tenants in common, or to be registered as such. This, however, is not to affect the equitable title of minors, heirs, legatees, creditors, or others exceeding that number, duly represented by or holding from any of the persons within the said number registered as legal owners by any shares, s. 33.

Partners in trade are to be considered as one person only in estimating such number, s. 32.

When the master of a registered ship shall be changed, a memorandum of such change must be indorsed upon the certificate of registry, and the new master must give a bond in the like penalties and under the same conditions as are contained in the bond required to be given at the time of registry, s. 21.

entitled to the privileges and benefits of a "vessel of the United States," although she be built, owned, and commanded by citizens thereof.[1]

Vessels employed wholly in the whale-fishery, owned by an incorporated company, may be registered, so long as they shall be wholly employed therein.[2] If not so owned and registered, they must be enrolled and licensed.[3]

The name of every registered vessel, and the port to which she belongs, must be painted on her stern, on a black ground, in white letters, of not less than three inches in length. And if any registered vessel is found without her name and the name of her port so painted, the owners thereof forfeit fifty dollars.[4]

In order to the obtaining of a register, oath must be made that the master is a citizen of the United States.[5] If the master of a registered vessel is changed, or if the vessel's name is altered, such fact must be endorsed upon the register at the custom-house, otherwise she will cease to be considered a vessel of the United States.[6]

If any certificate of registry is fraudulently or knowingly used for any ship or vessel not at the time entitled to it, such ship or vessel, with her tackle, apparel and furniture, shall be forfeited to the United States.[7] If an enrolled or licensed vessel is about to proceed on a foreign voyage, she must surrender her enrolment and licence, and take out a register, or she, together with her cargo, will be liable to forfeiture.[8] In case of the loss of a register, the master may make oath to the fact, and obtain a new one.

All vessels engaged in the coasting and fishing trades, above twenty tons burden, in order to be entitled to the privileges of vessels of the United States in those trades,

---

[1] Act 1792, ch. 45, § 1.   [2] Act 1831, ch. 350, § 1.
[3] 3 Summer, 342.   2 Law Rep. 146 contra.
[4] Act 1792, ch. 45, § 3.   [5] Do. § 4, § 12.
[6] Act 1792, ch. 45, § 23.   [7] Do. § 27.
[8] Act 1793, ch. 52, § 8.

must be enrolled and licensed; and if less than twenty tons, must be licensed.[1] The same qualifications and requisites in all respects are demanded in order to the enrolling and licensing of a vessel, which are required for registering.[2] The name must be painted on the stern in the same manner, under penalty of 20 dollars.[3]

If any vessel licensed for the fisheries engages in any other business not expressly allowed by the licence, she is forfeited.[4] Vessels, however, licensed for the mackerel trade are not forfeited in consequence of having been engaged in catching cod, or other fish; but they are not entitled to the bounty allowed to vessels in the cod fisheries.[5] The officers and at least three-fourths of the crew of every fishing vessel must be American citizens, or they can recover none of the bounties.[6]

DOCUMENTS.*—Every registered vessel should have a

---

[1] Act 1793, ch. 52, § 1. [2] Do. § 2. [3] Do. § 11.
[4] Act 1793, ch. 52, § 32.
[5] Acts 1828, ch. 119, § 1, and 1836, ch. 55, § 1.
[6] Act 1817, ch. 204, § 3.

---

* IN ENGLAND.] *Documents.*—The certificate of registry specifies the name, occupation, and residence of every owner, in the proportions mentioned on the back of it; the name of the ship, the place to which she belongs, her tonnage, the name of the master, the time and place of the built, or of condemnation; the name of the surveying officer, the number of decks and masts; the length, breadth, height between decks, if more than one—or depth of the hold, if only one deck; whether rigged with a standing or running bowsprit; the description of her stern, whether carvel or clinker built; and gallery, and kind of head, if there be any. And on the back are indorsed the names of the several owners, with the number of 64th shares held by each, 3 & 4 W. 4, c. 55, s. 2.—*Abbott on Shipping,* 6th Edition, 61.

The master must procure and keep on board all the papers and documents required for the manifestation and protection of the ship and cargo, by the law of the countries from and to which the ship is bound, and by the law of nations in general, and treaties between particular states.—*Abbott on Shipping,* 6th Edition, 302. The documents and papers expected to be found on board a neutral ship are—1. The *passport, sea brief,* or *sea letter.* 2. The *proofs of property, bill of sale, &c.* 3. The *muster-roll.* 4. The *certificate of registry.*[1] This is an abstract of the record of registry, showing the names and residences of the owners, the place where the vessel was built, with a particular description of the vessel. This document shows the national character of the vessel, and is important to prove neutrality in time of war between other powers. For the same reasons, an enrolled vessel should have a *certificate of enrolment*[2]. Vessels bound to Europe should have *passports*. A passport is a permission from the government for the vessel to go upon her voyage, and contains a description of the vessel, crew, &c., and the name of the master. Vessels bound round Cape Horn or the Cape of Good Hope should have *sea-letters*. These contain a description of the cargo, &c., and are written in four languages—English, French, Dutch and Spanish. The two latter documents are rendered necessary or expedient by reason of treaties with foreign powers. Every vessel should have a *list of crew*. This specifies the name, age, place of birth and residence, &c., of each one of the ship's company; and is, of course, very useful when sailing among belligerents. The other documents are the *bill of health, general clearance, clearing manifest, invoice* and *bill of lading* for the cargo, *charter-party*, if one has been given, and the *log-book*. On entering at the custom-house, the papers required in addition to these are the *manifest, list of passengers,* and *crew*, and of *remaining sea-stores*.

MEDICINE CHEST *.—Every vessel belonging to citizens

---

[1] Act 1792, ch. 45.   [2] Act 1793, ch. 52.

charter-party. 5. The *bills of lading.* 6. The *invoice.* 7. The *log-book.* 8. The *bill of health.*—See *Marshall on Insurance*, Book i. c. 9, s. 6. As to the manifest or written contents required for the importation of goods into Great Britain, see 6 G. 4, c. 107, ss. 3–7. As to the coasting-trade, see same stat., ss. 100–114.—*Abbott on Shipping*, 6th Edition, 302, *n.*

* IN ENGLAND.] *Medicine Chest.*—By the act 5 & 6 W. 4, c. 19, s. 12, every ship bound on a foreign voyage is required to have and keep constantly on board a "sufficient supply of medicines suitable to accidents and diseases arising on sea voyages."

of the United States, of the burden of one hundred and fifty tons or upwards, navigated by ten or more persons in the whole, and bound on a foreign voyage, must be provided with a medicine chest, put up by some apothecary of known reputation, and accompanied by directions for using the same. This chest must be examined and refitted by the same or some other apothecary at least once in a year [1]. The same rule applies to vessels of seventy-five tons and upwards, navigated by six persons in the whole, and bound to the West Indies [2].

NATIONAL CHARACTER OF CREW[*].—In order to be placed upon the most favourable footing as to duties, bounties, &c., it is necessary that the master, officers, and two thirds of the rest of the crew of vessels in the foreign trade, and officers and three fourths of the crew of fishing and coasting vessels, should be citizens, or " persons not the subjects of any foreign prince or state[3]." Nevertheless, while foreigners are employed in our vessels, they are under the protection of our laws as " mariners and seamen of the United States[4]."

---

[1] Act 1790, ch. 56, § 8.   [2] Act 1805, ch. 88, §1.
[3] Act 1817, ch. 204, § 3, 5, 6.   [4] Sumner, 115.

---

[*] IN ENGLAND.] *National Character of Crew.*—Every British registered ship is required to be navigated in every part of the world, by a master who is a British subject, and by a crew whereof three-fourths, at least, are British seamen; and if such ship be employed in a coasting voyage from one part of the United Kingdom to another, or in a voyage between the United Kingdom and the islands of Guernsey, Jersey, Alderney, Sark, or Man, or from one of the said islands to another of them, or from one part of either of them to another of the same, or be employed in fishing on the coasts of the United Kingdom, or of any of the said islands, then the *whole* of the crew shall be *British* seamen.—See *Navigation Act*, 3 & 4 W. 4, c. 54, s. 13.

It is provided, however, that a ship not required to be wholly navigated by *British* seamen, shall be deemed duly navigated by one *British* seaman for every twenty tons of her burthen, although the number of other seamen shall exceed one-fourth of the whole crew, s. 16.

As to the persons qualified to be master of a *British* ship, or to be, or considered, as *British* seamen within the act, see ss. 16, 17.

PROVISIONS *.—Every vessel of the United States bound on a voyage across the Atlantic, shall, at the time of leaving the last port from which she sails, have on board, well secured under deck, at least sixty gallons of water, one hundred pounds of salted beef, and one hundred pounds of wholesome ship bread, for every person on board, (over and above any stores that the master or passengers may have put on board;) and in like proportions for shorter or longer voyages. If any vessel is not so provided, and the crew are put upon short allowance of bread, flesh, or water, they can recover an additional day's wages for every day they are so allowanced[1].

PASSENGERS †.—The same provision, with the addi-

---

[1] Act 1790, ch. 56, § 9.

* IN ENGLAND.] *Provisions.*—The master of every outward-bound ship shall, upon application to an officer called the *searcher,* receive a *victualling bill,* for the shipment of such stores as he may require, and as shall be allowed by the collector and controller for the use of the ship, according to the voyage upon which she is about to depart; and no articles taken on board shall be deemed to be stores, except such as shall be borne on such *victualling bill,* 3 & 4 W. 4, c. 52, s. 63.

† IN ENGLAND.] *Passengers.*—Every ship carrying passengers from any port or place in the United Kingdom, or in the islands of Guernsey, Jersey, Alderney, Sark, or Man, or any voyage to or for any port or place out of Europe, and not being within the Mediterranean Sea, must have on board good and wholesome provisions for the use and consumption of the passengers, over and above the victualling of the crew, to the amount or in the proportion following, viz., a supply of pure water to the amount of five gallons to every week of the computed voyage for every passenger, such water being carried in tanks or sweet casks, and a supply of bread, biscuit, oatmeal, or bread stuffs, to the amount of seven pounds weight to every week of the computed voyage for every such passenger. But to the extent of one-third of such supply, seven pounds weight of potatoes may be deemed equivalent to one pound weight of bread, biscuit, oatmeal, or bread stuffs, in the supply of any ship bound to some place in North America.

And when any ship shall be destined to call at a port or place in the course of her voyage, for the purpose of filling up her water, a supply of water at the rate before mentioned for every week of the computed voyage to such port or place of calling, will be sufficient.

tion of one gallon of vinegar, must be made for every passenger; and if, in default of these, the passengers are put on short allowance, each passenger can recover three dollars for every day he is so allowanced [1].

If any vessel takes on board a greater number of passengers than two for every five tons, custom-house measurement, the master forfeits 150 dollars for every such passenger; and if the number by which they exceed two for every five tons shall amount to twenty, the vessel becomes forfeited [2].

---

[1] Act 1819, ch. 170, § 3.   [2] Do. § 1, § 2.

The number of weeks deemed necessary for the voyage of any such ship, according to her destination, shall be determined by the following rule of computation.

For a voyage to North America ten weeks; South America, on the Atlantic Ocean, or to the West Coast of Africa, twelve weeks; the Cape of Good Hope fifteen weeks; the Mauritius eighteen weeks; and for any other voyage, twenty-four weeks.—See the act 5 & 6 W. 4, c. 53, "for regulating the carriage of passengers from the United Kingdom," sect. 3 and 4; and 1 & 2 Vict., c. 113, s. 26, as to foreign vessels.

And no such ship is allowed to proceed on her voyage with more persons than in the proportion of three persons for every five tons of the registered burthen of such ship, the master and crew being included in such number.

The ship carrying such passengers, is required to have a height of five feet and a half between decks; and when only two tiers of berths, there shall be an interval of six inches, at the least, between the deck or platform, and the floor of the lower tier, throughout the whole extent thereof, 5 & 6 W. 4, c. 53, s. 2.

For the other regulations now in force on this important subject, the reader is referred to the act itself.

But from this act is expressly excepted all ships in which the number of passengers shall not exceed one for every five tons of their registered burthens, s. 20.

Penalties from 5*l.* to 20*l.*, are imposed upon the master for non-compliance with the regulations, without prejudice to any right of action the passenger may have in respect of the breach, or non-performance of any contract between him and the master and owners, s. 17.

For the regulations as to the carriage of passengers between Great Britain and Ireland, see the act 4 G. 4, c. 88.

CHAPTER II.

THE MASTER'S RELATION TO VESSEL AND CARGO.

Revenue duties and obligations. List of crew. Certificate. Sea letter. Passport. List of Passengers. Manifest. Sea Stores. Unloading. Post-office. Report. Citizenship. Coasting licence. Power to sell and hypothecate. Keeping and delivering cargo. Deviation. Collision. Pilot. Wages and advances.

REVENUE DUTIES AND OBLIGATIONS *.—The master of every vessel bound on a foreign voyage, before

---

* IN ENGLAND.] *Revenue duties and obligations.*—By the 3 & 4 Wm. 4, c. 52, entitled " An Act for the general regulation of the customs," it is enacted—

That no goods shall be shipped or water-borne, to be shipped on board any ship, in any port or place in the United Kingdom, or in the Isle of Man, to be carried beyond seas, before due entry outwards of such ship, and due entry of such goods shall be made and *cocket* granted, nor before such goods shall be duly cleared for shipment in manner thereinafter directed, and that no stores shall be shipped for the use of such ship, except such as are borne on the victualling bill of such ship, under pain of forfeiture. s. 61.

That no ship on board of which any goods or stores shall have been shipped for parts beyond the seas, shall depart from such port until such ship shall have been *duly cleared* outwards for her intended voyage, under pain of forfeiture by the master of 100*l.*, s. 62.

It may be useful to state in this place in what this " duly clearing " of a ship consists.

The master of every outward-bound ship shall upon application to an officer, called the *searcher*, receive a *victualling bill* for the shipment of such stores as he may require, and as shall be allowed by the collector and controller for the use of the ship according to the voyage upon which she is about to depart, and no articles taken on board shall be deemed to be stores, except such as shall be borne on such *victualling bill*, s. 63. He shall also, before any goods be taken on board, deliver to the collector or controller a certificate from the proper officer, of the clearance inwards or coastwise of such ship of her last voyage, specifying what goods, if any, have been reported inwards for exportation, and also deliver to the collector or controller an account, signed by the master or his agent, of the entry outwards of such ship for her intended voyage setting forth clearance, must give to the collector of the customs a list of the crew, specifying their names, places of birth and the name and tonnage of the ship, the name of the place to which she belongs if *British*, or of her country if foreign, the name of the master, of the place for which she is bound, and of the place in such port at which she is to take in her lading for the voyage. The particulars of such account shall be written and arranged in such form and manner as the collector and controller shall require; and such account shall be the entry outwards of such ship, and shall be entered in a book to be kept by the collector for the information of all persons interested; and if any goods be taken on board any ship before she shall have been entered outwards, the master shall forfeit 100*l*. If, however, it become necessary to lade any heavy goods before the whole of the inward cargo is discharged, it shall be lawful for the collector and controller to issue what is called a *stiffening order* for that purpose, s. 64.

Every person entering outward goods for export beyond the seas shall deliver to the collector or controller a bill of the entry thereof (fairly written, or fairly written in part, and fairly printed in part, 1 & 2 Vict. c. 113) in words at length, expressing the name of the ship and of the master, and of the place to which the goods are to be exported, and of the person in whose name the goods are to be entered, and the quantities and proper denomination or descriptions of the several sorts of goods, and shall pay down any duties which may be due upon the exportation of any such goods, and such person shall also deliver at the same time one or more duplicates of such bill in which all sums and numbers may be expressed in figures, and the particulars contained in such bill shall be written and arranged in such form and manner as the collector and controller shall require, and thereupon the collector and controller shall cause a *cocket* to be written for such goods, making it known that such goods have been entered, and shall sign such *cocket* and deliver it to the person who shall have made such entry, and who shall keep and be responsible for the proper use of the same, s. 65.

Before any part of the goods, for which any *cocket* shall have been granted, shall be shipped or water-borne, to be shipped, the same shall be duly cleared for shipment with the *searcher*; and before any goods be cleared for shipment, the particulars of the goods for each clearance shall be indorsed on such *cocket*, together with the number and denomination or description of the respective packages containing the same; and on the margin of such indorsement shall be delineated the respective marks and numbers of such packages, and to each such indorsement shall be subjoined in words at length an account of the total quantities of each sort of goods intended in such indorsement, and the total of each sort of package

residence, and containing a description of their persons; whereupon he is entitled to a certified copy of the same

---

in which such goods are contained, distinguishing, &c.; and all goods shipped or water-borne, to be shipped, not being duly cleared as aforesaid, shall be forfeited, s. 70.

The person clearing such goods for shipment shall upon each occasion produce the *cocket* so indorsed to the searcher, and shall also deliver a *shipping bill*, or copy of such indorsement, referring by names and date to the *cocket* upon which such *indorsement* is made, and shall obtain the order of the searcher for the shipment of such goods, which indorsement and shipping bill shall be written and arranged as the collector and controller shall require, s. 71.

Before any ship shall be cleared outwards with goods on board, the master shall deliver a *content* of such ship to the *searcher*, setting forth the name and tonnage of such ship, and the place and places of her destination, and the name of the master, and also an account of the goods shipped on board, and of the packages containing such goods, and of the marks and numbers upon such packages, and also before the clearance of such ship, the *cockets*, with the indorsements and clearances thereon, for the goods shipped, shall be finally delivered by the respective shippers of such goods to the *searcher*, who shall file the same together, and shall attach with a seal a label to the file, showing the number of *cockets* in the file, and shall compare the particulars of the goods in the *cockets* with the particulars of the goods in such *content*, and shall attest the correctness thereof by his signature on the *label*, and on the *content;* and the master of the ship shall make and sign a declaration before the collector or controller to the truth of such *content*, and shall answer to the collector or controller such questions concerning the ship, the cargo, and the intended voyage, as shall be demanded of him; and thereupon the collector or controller shall clear such ship for her intended voyage, and shall notify such clearance, and the date thereof upon the *content*, and upon the label to the file of cockets, and upon the victualling bill, and also in the book of ships' entries outwards, for the information of all parties interested, and shall transmit the *content* and the *cockets*, and the *victualling bill*, to the searcher, s. 78. The *file of cockets* and the *victualling bill*, shall thereupon be delivered by the searcher to the master of such ship; and such *file of cockets* and *victualling bill* so delivered, shall be kept by the master of such ship, as the authority for departing from the port with the several parcels and packages of goods, and of stores on board, so far as they shall agree with the particulars in the indorsements on such *cockets*, or with such *victualling bill*, s. 79. When the ship has arrived at the place of her destination, the master must

from the collector. This copy he must deliver, under a penalty of 400 dollars, to the first boarding officer upon

---

take care that she be safely moored or anchored, and report his ship and crew, and deliver his manifest and other papers, according to the law and custom of the place.

By the same act 3 & 4 W. 4, c. 52, it is also enacted, " That no goods shall be unladen from any ship arriving from ports beyond the seas, at any port or place in the *United Kingdom*, or the *Isle of Man*, nor shall bulk be broken after the arrival of such ship within four leagues of the coast, before due *report* of such ship, and due *entry* of such goods, shall have been made, and *warrant* granted in manner thereinafter directed; that no goods shall be unladen, except at such times and places, and in such manner and by such persons, and under the care of such officers as is thereinafter directed; and that all goods not duly reported, or which shall be unladen contrary thereto, shall be forfeited; and if bulk be broken contrary thereto, the master of such ship shall forfeit 100*l.*; and if any alteration in the stowage be made to facilitate the unlading, or any part of the cargo be staved or destroyed, or any package opened within four leagues of the coast, the ship shall be deemed to have broken bulk, s. 2.

That no goods shall be imported from parts beyond the seas in any *British* ship, nor any tobacco in any ship, unless the master shall have on board a *manifest* of such goods, or of such tobacco, made out and dated, and signed by him at the place where the same, or the different parts of the same, were taken on board; and every such *manifest* shall set forth the name and the tonnage of the ship, the name of the master, and of the place to which the ship belongs, and of the place or places for which they are destined respectively; and shall contain a particular account and description of all the packages with the marks, &c.; and of such goods as are stowed loose, and the names of the respective shippers and consignees, as far as the same can be known to the master. A general account must be subjoined, s. 3.

That before any ship shall be cleared out, or depart from any place in any of the *British* possessions, abroad, or from any place in *China*, with any goods for the *United Kingdom*, or the *Isle of Man*, the master of such ship shall produce the *manifest* to the collector or controller of the customs, or other proper officer, who shall certify upon the same the date of the production thereof to him, s. 4.

That if any goods shall be imported into the *United Kingdom*, or into the *Isle of Man*, without such *manifest*, or if any goods contained in such *manifest*, be not on board, the master shall forfeit 100*l.*; and if he refuse to produce such *manifest*, and deliver

his arrival in the United States, and produce the persons named therein, unless the same have been discharged in

a copy thereof to any officer of the customs, who within four leagues of the coast, shall demand the same, he shall also forfeit 100*l*., ss. 6 and 7.

That the master of every ship arriving from any such ports beyond the seas, shall within twenty-four hours of such arrival, and before bulk broken, make due *report* of such ship, and make and subscribe a declaration of the truth of the same before the collector or controller of such port; and such *report* shall contain an account of the particular marks, numbers, and contents, of all the different packages or parcels of goods on board, and the particulars of such goods as are stowed loose, to the best of his knowledge; and of the place and places where such goods were respectively taken on board, and of the burthen of such ship, and of the country where such ship was built; or if *British*, of the port of registry, and of the country of the people to whom such ship belongs; and of the name and country of the person who was master during the voyage; and of the number of people by whom such ship was navigated, stating how many are subjects of the country to which such ship belongs, and how many are of some other country; and in such *report*, it shall be further declared, whether and in what cases such ship has broken bulk in the course of her voyage; and what part of the cargo, if any, is intended for importation at another port in the *United Kingdom*; and what part, if any, is prohibited to be imported, except to be warehoused for exportation only; and what part, if any, is intended for exportation in any such ship, to ports beyond the seas; and what surplus stores or stock remain on board such ship; and if a *British* ship, what foreign-made sails or cordage, not being standing or running rigging, are in use on board such ship; and the master of any ship who shall fail to make such report, shall forfeit 100*l*., s. 8.

That the master of every ship shall, at the time of making such report, deliver to the collector or controller, the *manifest* of the cargo, where a *manifest* is required; and if required, shall produce to him any bill or bills of lading, or a true copy thereof, for any and every part of the cargo, and shall truly answer all such questions relating to the ship and cargo, and crew, and voyage, as shall be put to him by such collector or controller; and in case of failure or refusal, or if such *manifest*, or bill of lading, or copy, shall be false; or if any bill of lading be uttered by any master, and the goods expressed therein shall not have been *bonâ fide* shipped on board; or if any bill of lading, uttered or produced by any master, shall not have been signed by him, or any such copy shall not have been received or made by him, previously to his leaving the place

a foreign country, with the consent of the consul or other commercial agent thereto certified in writing under his hand and official seal; or by showing that they have died or absconded, or been impressed into foreign service[1]. The duplicate list of the crew shall be a fair copy, in one uniform handwriting, without erasure or interlineation[2].

The owners must also obtain from the collector of the customs a certified copy of the shipping articles. This must be produced by the master before any consul or commercial agent who may demand it, and all erasures in it or writings in a different hand shall be deemed fraudulent, unless satisfactorily explained[3].

The master of every vessel of the United States, on arriving at a foreign port, must deposit with the consul, or other commercial agent, his certificate of registry, sea letter, and passport (if he have one,) under a penalty of 500 dollars. The consul returns them to him, upon his obtaining a clearance[4].

Upon arriving in the United States, the master must report to the collector a list of passengers, specifying their names, age, sex, occupation, the country of which they are citizens, and that in which they intend to reside. This is under a penalty of 500 dollars[5].

Vessels arriving from foreign ports must unlade and

---

[1] Act 1803, ch. 62, § 1.   [2] Act 1840, ch. 28, §1.   [3] Do.
[4] Act 1803, ch. 62, § 2.   [5] Act 1819, ch. 170, § 4.

---

where the goods expressed in such bill of lading, or copy, were shipped, such master shall forfeit 100*l.*, s. 11.

That every ship shall come as quickly up to the proper place of mooring or unlading, as the nature of the port will admit, and without touching at any other place; and in proceeding to such place, shall bring to, at stations appointed by the commissioners of his Majesty's Customs, for the boarding of ships by the officers of the customs; and after arrival at such place of mooring, or unlading, such ship shall not remove from such place, except directly to some other proper place, and with the knowledge of the proper officer of the customs, on penalty of 100*l.*, to be paid by the master of such ship, s. 13.

deliver their cargoes between sunrise and sunset, unless by special permission of the collector of the port.

In making out manifests of cargoes, the master must specify what articles are to be deemed *sea stores*, and declare the same upon oath. If the collector deems the amount excessive, he may charge them with a duty. If the cargo is found to exceed the manifest, the excess is forfeited to the government, and the master is liable to pay treble the amount[1].

If the master land any of the *sea stores*, without first obtaining a permit, such stores are forfeited, and the master becomes liable to pay treble the value of them[2].

The master subjects himself to a fine of 200 dollars if the vessel departs on a foreign voyage without a *passport*.

It is the duty of the master, coming from a foreign port, to have a *manifest* of cargo, and a copy of the same made out and ready for delivery to any officer of the customs who may board the vessel within four leagues of the coast[3]. Unless this manifest is produced, no merchandise can be unloaded from the vessel. The manifest shall specify the port where the merchandise was received, the port to which it is consigned, the name, built, and description of the vessel, with the name of the master and owner, the marks and numbers of each package of goods, with the name of the consignee; and also the names of the passengers with their baggage, and the account of all remaining sea stores[4].

If any goods are unladed within four leagues of the coast, or within the limits of any district, without authority from the proper officer, except in case of accident or necessity—which must be strictly proved—such goods are forfeited, and the master and mate incur, respectively, a penalty of 1000 dollars for each offence[5].

If the master refuses to exhibit his manifest and deliver a copy of the same to the boarding officer, or to

---

[1] Act 1799, ch. 128, § 45.   [2] Do.   [3] Do. 23.
[4] Act 1819, ch. 170, § 4.   [5] Act 1799, ch. 128, § 27.

inform him of the true destination of the vessel, he incurs a penalty of 500 dollars for each offence[1].

The master must deposit all his letters in the post-office before entering his cargo; and if he shall break bulk before depositing his letters, he forfeits 100 dollars for each offence[2].

If any merchandise is imported into the United States not contained in the manifest, the master of the vessel forfeits a sum equal to the value of such merchandise; and if any of it belongs or is consigned to the master, or to any officer or seaman on board, it becomes forfeited; unless it shall be made to appear that the omission occurred by accident or mistake[3].

The master of a vessel arriving from a foreign port must report himself to the collector within twenty-four hours, and within forty-eight hours he must make a further and more particular report in writing, under penalty of 100 dollars; and if he shall attempt to leave the port without entry he forfeits 400 dollars[4].

If any articles reported in the manifest are not found on board, the master forfeits 500 dollars, unless it shall be made to appear that the same was caused by accident or mistake.

The master of every vessel bound on a foreign voyage must deliver a manifest of cargo to the collector, and obtain a clearance, under penalty of 500 dollars[5].

The master of every vessel enrolled and licensed in the coasting trade must be a citizen of the United States; and if the vessel trades to any other than an adjoining state, three-fourths of the crew must be citizens. If the master of a coasting vessel is changed, such change must be reported to the collector of the port where the change is made[6].

The master of every coasting vessel must deliver up his licence within three days after it expired, or if the

---

[1] Act 1799, ch. 128, § 26. [2] Act 1825, ch. 275, § 17.
[3] Act 1799, ch. 128, § 24. [4] Do. § 30.
[5] Do. § 3. [6] Act 1793, ch. 52, § 12.

vessel was then at sea, within three days after her first arrival thereafter, under a penalty of 50 dollars.

The master of a coasting vessel departing from one great district to another, must deliver to the collector duplicate manifests of all the cargo on board, under penalty of 50 dollars; and within forty-eight hours after his arrival at the port of delivery, and before breaking bulk, he must deliver to the collector the manifest certified to by the collector of the former port, under penalty of 100 dollars[1]. If the vessel shall at any time be found without a manifest on board, the master forfeits 20 dollars, and if he refuses to inform the officer of his last port of departure, he forfeits 100 dollars[2].

POWER TO SELL AND HYPOTHECATE*.—The master has, in certain cases, power to hypothecate the ship and cargo, and also to sell a part of the cargo; and in certain extreme cases a sale of the ship and cargo made from necessity, and in the utmost good faith, will be upheld. His right to do any of these acts is confined to cases of necessity, in distant ports, where he cannot get the advice of the owner. The safest rule for the master is, to bear in mind that his duty is to *prosecute the voyage*, and that all his acts must be done for this purpose, and in good faith. If a necessity arises in a foreign port for the repairing or supplying of the ship, he must, in the first instance, make use of any property of the owner he may

---

[1] Act 1793, ch. 52, § 17.   [2] Do. § 18.

---

* IN ENGLAND.] *Power to sell and hypothecate.*—The law, as respects the authority of the master to sell or hypothecate the ship and cargo, is the same in England as in the United States.

The master of a ship has not, unless in a case of extreme necessity, authority to sell the ship, and he is bound seriously and deliberately to try every other expedient before disposing of the ship or any part of the cargo.—See *Abbott on Shipp.*, 6th edit., s. 597; 4 *Campb.*, 138. See also, 1 *Bing.*, 243; 3 *Brod. & Bing.*, 151; 8 *Taunt.*, 755; 3 *Brod. & Bing.*, 147; 1 *Bing.*, 445.

The observations as to the keeping, transportation, and delivery of the cargo are equally applicable to the masters of British vessels.

have under his control other than cargo[1]. If, however, he has money of the owner in his hands, put on board for the purpose of procuring a cargo, he is not bound to apply this first; but must use his discretion, bearing in mind that all repairs have for their sole object the prosecution of the voyage, which might be defeated by making use of these funds[2]. His next recourse should be to the personal credit of the owner, by drawing bills or otherwise[3].

If these means fail, he is next to hypothecate (that is, pledge) the ship (bottomry), or cargo (respondentia), or freight, or sell part of the cargo, according to circumstances. If the owner of the ship is also owner of the cargo, the better opinion seems to be, that the master may take whichever of these means can be adopted with the least sacrifice of the owner's interest; though probably selling part of the cargo would almost in all cases be the least favourable course for all the purposes of the voyage[4]. If the owner of the ship is not owner of the cargo, the master should bear in mind that he is agent of the former, and has generally no further control over the cargo than for safe keeping and transportation[5]. He should therefore first exhaust the credit of the ship and freight by hypothecation; and if these means fail, he then becomes, by necessity, agent for the owners of the cargo for the purposes of the voyage, and may hypothecate the whole, or sell a part, according to circumstances. As to selling part, he should remember that his duty is to carry forward the objects of the voyage, and that selling a large part would probably impair these objects more than hypothecating the whole[6].

In no case can any of the cargo be sold or hypothecated to repair or supply the ship, unless these repairs and supplies are to be for the benefit of the cargo. The strictest proof is always required that the repairs were in

---

[1] 3 Mason, 255. [2] Do. [3] 2 Wash. C. C. 226.
[4] 2 Wash. C. C. 226. [5] Do.
[6] 3 Mason, 255. 1 Wash. C. C. 49; 2 Do. 226. 3 Rob. 240.

the first place necessary, and, in the next place, that they were for the benefit of the cargo, and not merely for the good of the ship-owner[2].

A further question arises, whether the master has ever, and when, the right to sell the whole cargo and the ship itself. If it should be impossible to repair the ship and send her on the voyage by any of the means before mentioned, it then becomes the master's duty to forward the cargo to the port of destination by some other conveyance. If neither of these things can be done, then he becomes, from necessity, agent of the owner of the cargo, and must make the best disposition of it in his power. If the goods are perishable, the owner cannot be consulted within a reasonable time, and has no agent in the port, and something must be done with the cargo, and there is no one else to act—then the master must dispose of it in such a way as best to subserve the interest of its owner. He should take the advice of the commercial agent or other suitable persons, should also use his own judgment and act with good faith, and take care to preserve evidence that he has so done. If all these requisites are not complied with, he will incur the danger of having his acts set aside[2].

The rule as to the sale of the ship is very nearly the same, except that it is, perhaps, still more strict. If all means for repairing the vessel and sending her on her voyage have failed, and a case of absolute necessity arises, the master may make sale of her. As a prudent man, he should have the sale made, if possible, under the authority of the judicial tribunals of the place. Even this will not, of itself, render the sale valid, but will go far toward sustaining it. He should consult the consul, or other suitable persons; should have a survey made; should take care to have the sale conducted publicly and with the best faith in all parties, and to preserve evidence of the same. Although a person should

---

[1] 2 Wash. 226; 3 Rob. 240.   [2] 2 Wash. C. C. 150. 3 Rob. 240.

buy in good faith, yet the sale will be set aside unless it can be shown that there was the strictest necessity for it. The master must not become a purchaser himself, and even if he afterwards buy of one who purchased at the sale, this transaction will be very narrowly watched, and he will be bound to show the very highest good faith in all parties [1].

The strictness of these rules should not deter the master from acting, where the interest of all requires it, but will show him the risk that is run by acting otherwise than with prudence and entire honesty. He should remember, too, that in taking command of a vessel, he not only covenants that he will act honestly and with the best of his judgment, but also holds himself out as having a reasonable degree of skill and prudence [2].

As to the safe keeping, transportation, and delivery of the cargo, the master's duties and obligations are those of a common carrier upon land. He is bound to the strictest diligence in commencing and prosecuting the voyage, a high degree of care both of vessel and goods, and is held liable for all losses and injuries not occasioned by inevitable accident, or by the acts of public enemies. He is answerable also for unnecessary delays and deviations, and for the wrongful or negligent acts of all persons under his command. At the termination of the voyage, he must deliver the goods to the consignee or his agents. A landing upon the wharf is a sufficient delivery, if due notice be given to the parties who are to receive them. He is not, however, bound to deliver until the freight due is paid or secured to his satisfaction, as he has a lien upon the goods for his freight; but the consignee can require the goods to be taken from the hold, in order that he may examine them, before paying freight. In such case they should not go out of the possession of the master or his agents.

---

[1] 5 Mason, 465.   2 Sumner, 206.   Edwards, 117.
[2] 1 Dallas, 184.

DEVIATION.*—The master must not deviate from the course of the voyage. By a *deviation* is meant, technically, any alteration of the risk insured against, without necessity or reasonable cause. It may be by departing from the regular and usual course of the voyage, or by any unusual and unnecessary delay. A deviation renders the insurance void, whether the loss of the vessel is caused by the deviation or not. It is not a deviation to make a port for repairs or supplies, if there be no unnecessary delay, nor to depart from the course of the voyage in order to succour persons in distress, to avoid an enemy, or the like.

It is the master's duty, within twenty-four hours after arriving at his first port, to make a *protest* in case of any accident or loss happening to vessel or cargo. The log-book also should be carefully kept, without interlineations or erasures. The master must also enter a protest in case any American seaman is impressed, and transmit

---

* IN ENGLAND.] *Deviation.*—The first part of the observations under this head will apply to British ships. While a vessel is detained at a port of necessity, it seems to be no deviation to take in an additional cargo, if no additional delay or risk is occasioned thereby.—*Abbott on Shipp.*, 6th edit., 319; 9 *East*, 195; 11 *East*, 347; 12 *East*, 131.

On the arrival of the vessel at her homeward port, and when compelled by accidents or injury to put back or into a port other than that of her destination, it is usual for the master to present himself before a notary, and cause a *protest* to be noted, and afterwards drawn up or *extended*. British consuls at foreign ports are empowered by statute (5 and 6 Wm. 4, c. 62, s. 15,) to perform notarial acts; but, inasmuch as their attestation would probably not be deemed abroad of equal authenticity with that of the regular public notary, the master would do well to address himself to that functionary.

With whatever formalities drawn up, this protest cannot be received in our courts as evidence for the master or his owners; but it may be evidence against him and them; and he should take care to supply from the log-book, his own recollection, and that of the mate, or trustworthy mariners, true and faithful instructions for its preparation.—See *Abbott on Shipp.*, 6th edit., 335, and cases there cited.

a copy of the same to the secretary of state, under a penalty of 100 dollars¹.

COLLISION*.—A vessel having the wind free must

---

¹ Act 1796, ch. 36, § 5.

---

* IN ENGLAND.] *Collision.*—The master is bound to his owners for the exercise of reasonable skill and care in the management of the vessel, and he and they are bound in like manner to every one who is affected by his acts, within the scope of his employment; he must, therefore, during the whole course of the voyage at sea, at anchor, and in port,—perhaps even when a licensed pilot is on board,—be vigilant, to avoid the peril of collision.—*Abbott on Shipp.*, 6th edit., 200 ; 3 *Hagg. Ad. Rep.*, 176.

It is said that there are four possibilities under which collision may occur. "In the first place, it may happen without blame being imputable to either party, as where the loss is occasioned by a storm, or any other *vis major.* In that case the misfortune must be borne by the party on whom it happens to light ; the other not being responsible to him in any degree. Secondly, a misfortune of this kind may arise where both parties are to blame ; where there has been want of due diligence, or of skill, on both sides ; in such a case the rule of law is, that the loss must be apportioned between them as having been occasioned by the fault of both of them. Thirdly, it may happen by the misconduct of the suffering party only ; and then the rule is, that the sufferer must bear his own burthen. Lastly, it may have been the fault of the ship which ran the other down, and in this case the innocent party would be entitled to an entire compensation from the other." —2 *Dod. Ad. Rep.*, 83.

The established rules of nautical practice as explained by professional men, the usages and regulations of particular ports and rivers, the state of the wind, the tide, and the light, the degree of vigilance of the master and crew, and all other circumstances bearing upon the conduct and management of both vessels, will be considered in determining this question. But of the sea as of the road, the law recognises no inflexible rule the neglect of which by one party will dispense with the exercise of ordinary care and caution in the other.—See *Abbott on Shipp.*, 6th edit., 207, and cases there cited.

In case of damage done by a foreign ship to any *British* ship, barge, boat, buoy, or beacon, such foreign ship may, by order of a judge, be arrested, until the master, owner, or consignee, undertake to appear and be defendant in any action brought for such loss or damage, and give security for all costs and damages which may be recovered in such action.—1 & 2 Geo. IV., c. 75, s. 32.

By a recent regulation of the Trinity Board, when two *steam-*

make way for a vessel close-hauled. The general practice is, that when two vessels approach each other, both having a free or fair wind, the one with the starboard tacks aboard keeps on her course, or, if any change is made, she luffs, so as to pass to windward of the other; or, in other words, each vessel passes to the right. This rule should also govern vessels sailing on the wind and approaching each other, when it is doubtful which is to windward. But if the vessel on the larboard tack is so far to windward that if both persist in their course the other will strike her on the lee side, abaft the beam, or near the stern; in such case, the vessel on the starboard tack must give way, as she can do so with less loss of time and greater facility than the other. These rules are particularly intended to govern vessels approaching each other under circumstances that prevent their course and movements being readily discerned with accuracy, as at night or in a fog. At other times, circumstances may render it expedient to depart from them. A steamer is considered as always sailing with a fair wind, and is bound to do whatever would be required of a vessel going free [1].

PILOT *.—The master must take a pilot when within the usual limits of the pilot's employment [2]. If he neglects or refuses so to do, he becomes liable to the owners, freighters, and insurers. If no pilot is at hand, he must make signals, and wait a reasonable time. The master is to be justified in entering port without a pilot only by extreme necessity. After the pilot is on board, the master has no more control over the working of the ship until she is at anchor [3].

---

[1] Report of Benjamin Rich and others to District Court of Mass.
[2] 6 Rob. 316. 7 T. R. 160.
[3] 2 B. & Ad. 380. 3 Kent's Com. 175 c.

---

vessels meet and are in danger of collision, both vessels are required to put the helm *a-port*.

* IN ENGLAND.] *Pilot*.—What is here said is applicable to British vessels. For the provisions relating to pilots and pilotage, see the Act 6 Geo. IV., c. 125.

WAGES, ADVANCES, &c.*—The master has no lien upon the ship for his wages [1]. He is supposed to look to the personal responsibility of the owner. He has a lien on freight for wages, and also for his advances and necessary expenses incurred for the benefit of the ship [2]. He can sue in admiralty *in personam*, but not *in rem;*—that is, he can sue the owner personally, but cannot hold the ship. It does not seem to be settled in the United States whether the master has a lien on the ship for advances made abroad for the benefit of the vessel [3]. In case of sickness, the master's right to be cured at the expense of the ship seems to be the same as that of the seamen [4].

CHAPTER III.

THE MASTER'S RELATION TO PASSENGERS AND OFFICERS.

Treatment of passengers. Removal of officers.

PASSENGERS †.—The contract of passengers with the master is not for mere ship-room and personal existence on board, but for reasonable food, comforts, necessaries, and kindness. In respect to females, it extends still

---

[1] 3 Mason, 91. 11 Pet. R. 175.
[2] Ware, 149. But see 5 Wend. 314.
[3] 3 Mason, 255. [4] 1 Sumner, 451.

---

* IN ENGLAND.] *Wages, Advances, &c.*—The master can only sue the owners personally for his wages in a court of common law. But as he generally receives the freight and earnings of the ship, and may pay himself out of the money in his hands, he has not often occasion for the aid of a court of justice to obtain his right.— *Abbott on Shipp.*, 6th edit., 587.

The master has no *lien* on the ship or freight for wages or disbursements.—See 9 *East*, 426; 1 *B. & A.*, 575; *Abbott on Shipp.*, 6th edit., 124, and cases there cited.

† IN ENGLAND.] *Passengers.*—The party must, however, prove that he has really been a sufferer and that there was a real grievance, before he can recover in an action.—See 8 *Car. & P.* 56.

further, and includes an implied stipulation against obscenity, immodesty, and a wanton disregard of the feelings. An improper course of conduct in these particulars will be punished by the court, as much as a personal assault would be[1].

OFFICERS*.—The master may remove either of his officers from duty for fraudulent or unfaithful conduct, for gross negligence and disobedience, or for palpable incapacity. But the causes of removal must be strong and evident[2]; and much more so in the case of the chief mate than of the second mate. Any temporary appointments, made by the master, are held at his pleasure, and stand upon a different footing from those of persons who originally shipped in the character in question[3].

When a man ships in a particular capacity, as carpenter, steward, or the like, he is not to be degraded for slight causes. He stipulates for fair and reasonable knowledge and due diligence, but not for extraordinary qualifications[4].

The right of the master to compel an officer, who has been removed, to do duty as a seaman before the mast, has never been completely established; but the better opinion would seem to be that he may do it in a case of necessity. Merchant vessels have no supernumeraries, and if the master can show that the officer was unfit for the duties he had undertaken, and thus made it necessary to take some one from the forecastle to fill his place, and that, by this means, the ship had become short-handed,

---

[1] 3 Mason, 242.   [2] 4 Wash. 334.   [3] Gilpin, 83.
[4] 4 Mason, 84.   Abbott Shipp. 147 n.   Ware, 109.

---

* IN ENGLAND.] *Officers.*—By the common law of England the master has authority over all the mariners on board the ship.

The observations, therefore, under this head would seem to apply to *British* vessels. The only general rule that can be laid down on the subject is, that the master should on all occasions act according to the common usage, bearing in mind that he may be called upon to justify his acts and conduct in a court of law, and this, too, by the testimony of other persons.

he may turn the officer forward, assuming the responsibility for the act, as well as the risk of justification. He would be required to show a much stronger cause for removing the chief mate than would be insisted upon in the case of a second mate; and probably this necessity for exacting seaman's duty would be held to extend no further than an arrival at the first port where other hands could be shipped.

Nothing but evident unfitness or gross and repeated misconduct will justify the master in turning a person forward who shipped in another capacity, as carpenter, cook, or steward. But in such cases, he undoubtedly may do so. Still, when before the mast, he cannot require of them the duty of able seamen, unless they are such in fact.

CHAPTER IV.

THE MASTER'S RELATION TO THE CREW.

Shipment. Shipping Papers. Discharge. Imprisonment. Punishment.

SHIPMENT.*—The master of every vessel of the United States, bound on a foreign voyage, and of all coasting

---

* IN ENGLAND.] *Shipment.*—By the Act 5 & 6 Wm. 4, c. 19, the master of every ship belonging to an English subject, trading to parts beyond the seas, or of any *British* registered ship of the burden of eighty tons, employed in any of the fisheries of the United Kingdom, or in trading coastwise, or otherwise, must make a similar contract in writing (shipping-articles) with each seaman (apprentices excepted), and in default thereof shall forfeit £10, s. 2.

If after entering into such agreement a mariner neglect or refuse to join the ship, or to proceed to sea in her, or absent himself without leave, any justice of the peace, upon complaint of the fact made upon oath by the master, mate, or owner of the ship, is required by his warrant to cause the seaman to be apprehended and brought before him; and in case he shall not give a reason to the satisfaction of such justice for his neglect, refusal, or absence, as the case may be, such justice may commit him to the House of Correction, there to be kept to hard labour for a period not exceeding

vessels of fifty tons burden, must make a contract in writing (shipping articles) with each seaman, specifying the voyage, terms of time, &c.; and in default thereof shall forfeit 20 dollars for every case of omission, and shall be obliged to pay every such seaman the highest rate of wages that have been paid for such voyages at the port of shipment within three months previous to the commencement of the voyage[1]. And when the master ships a seaman in a foreign port, he must take the list of crew and the duplicate of the shipping-articles to the consul or commercial agent, who shall make the proper entries thereupon; and then the bond originally given for the return of the men shall embrace each person so shipped. All shipments made contrary to this or

---

[1] Act 1790, ch. 56, § 1.

---

thirty days; but if the seaman consent to join the ship, the justice, at the request of the master, instead of committing the seaman, may order him to be conveyed on board the ship, or delivered to the master for the purpose of proceeding upon the voyage, and may award to the master costs not exceeding forty shillings, to be abated from the wages of such seaman, s. 10.

As regards temporary absence—

If such seaman shall wilfully and without leave absent himself from the ship or otherwise from his duty, he shall (in all cases not of absolute desertion, or not treated as such by the master) forfeit out of his wages to the master or owner two days' pay for every twenty-four hours of such absence, and in a like proportion for any less period of time, or at the option of the master, the amount of such expenses as shall have been necessarily incurred in hiring a substitute to perform his work, s. 7.

In cases of absolute desertion, such seaman shall forfeit to the owner or master all his clothes and effects on board, and all wages and emoluments; and in case of desertion abroad, shall be liable to the increased wages which may be paid to a substitute, s. 9.

The forfeitures are not incurred unless due entries shall be made in the log-book, as required by the act.

The entry into the naval service of her Majesty by any seaman in the merchant service, shall not be deemed a desertion, or incur any penalty or forfeiture of wages, clothes, or effects, s. 45.

The master is required to deliver the shipping-articles to the consul or vice-consul on arrival at a foreign port, under the penalty of £25, s. 48.

any other act of Congress shall be void, and the seaman may leave at any time, and claim the highest rate of wages paid for any man who shipped for the voyage, or the sum agreed to be given him at his shipment[1].

At the foot of every such contract there shall be a memorandum in writing of the day and hour on which such seaman shall render himself on board. If this memorandum is made and the seaman neglects to render himself on board at the time specified, he shall forfeit one day's pay for every hour he is so absent, provided the master or mate shall, on the same day, have made an entry of the name of such seaman in the log-book, specifying the time he was so absent. And if the seaman shall wholly neglect to render himself on board, or, after rendering, shall desert before sailing, so that the vessel goes to sea without him, he then forfeits the amount of his advance and a further sum equal thereto, both of which may be recovered from himself or his surety[2].

There is no obligation upon the master to make these memorandums and entries, other than that the forfeitures cannot be inflicted upon the seamen, unless they have been made literally, according to the form of the statute.

If any seaman who has signed the articles shall desert during the voyage, the master may have him arrested and committed to jail until the vessel is ready to proceed, by applying to a justice of the peace, and proving the contract, and the breach thereof by the seaman[3].

Every vessel bound on a foreign voyage shall have on board a duplicate list of the crew, and a true copy of the shipping-articles, certified by the collector of the port, containing the names of the crew, which shall be written in a uniform hand, without erasures or interlineations. This copy the master must produce to any consul or commercial agent of the United States who shall require

---

[1] Act 1840, ch. 23, § 1. [2] Act 1790, ch. 56, § 2. [3] Do. § 7.

it; and it shall be deemed to contain all the conditions of the contract. All erasures and interlineations shall be deemed fraudulent, unless proved to be innocent and *bona fide*. Every master who shall go upon a foreign voyage without these documents, or shall refuse to produce them when required, shall forfeit 100 dollars for each offence, besides being liable in damages to any seaman who may have been injured thereby[1].

DISCHARGE*.—If the master discharges any seaman

---

[1] Act 1840, ch. 23, § 1.

* IN ENGLAND.] *Discharge.*—Whenever any ship belonging to an English subject, except in cases of wreck or condemnation, shall be sold at any port out of her Majesty's dominions, the master [unless the crew in the presence of the British consul or vice-consul, or in case of there not being any such consul or vice-consul, then in the presence of one or more British resident merchants at such port, shall signify their consent in writing to be there discharged] is required, besides paying them their wages under the agreement, either to provide them with adequate employment on board some other British vessel homeward-bound, or to furnish the means of sending them back to the port in her Majesty's dominions at which they were originally shipped, or to some port of the United Kingdom, as shall be agreed upon, by providing them with a passage home, or depositing with the consul or vice-consul such a sum of money as shall be by him deemed reasonably sufficient to defray the expenses of their subsistence passage, 5 & 6 W. 4, c. 19, sect. 17.

And if the master of such ship shall force on shore and leave behind, or shall otherwise wilfully and wrongfully leave behind on shore or at sea, in any place in or out of her Majesty's dominions, any person belonging to his crew before the return to or arrival of such ship in the United Kingdom, or before the completion of the voyage or voyages for which such person shall have been engaged, whether such person shall have formed part of the original crew or not; every person so offending shall be deemed guilty of a misdemeanour, and shall suffer such punishment by fine or imprisonment, or both, as to the court (at home or abroad) before which he shall be convicted shall seem meet, s. 40.

And the master shall not discharge any of his crew, whether foreigner or British subject, at any of her Majesty's colonies or plantations, without the sanction in writing of the governor, secretary, or other officer appointed in that behalf, or in the absence of such authorities near the place where the ship is lying, then of the chief officer of customs, resident at or near such place; nor at any

in a foreign port, with his own consent, he shall pay to the consul three months' wages for every such seaman, in addition to the wages then due to him, two-thirds to go to the seaman upon his taking passage for the United States, and the remainder to be retained by the consul, to make a fund for the relief of destitute seamen[1]. The master of every vessel bound to the United States shall, upon the request of the consul, take on board any seaman, and transport him to the United States, on terms not exceeding ten dollars for each seaman, under penalty of 100 dollars for every refusal. He is not, however, bound to receive more than two men to every hundred tons[2].

The whole policy of the United States discourages the discharge of seamen in foreign ports. If the seaman is

---

[1] Act 1803, ch. 62, § 3. See also Act 1840, ch. 23, § 5.
[2] Act 1803, ch. 62, § 4.

---

other place abroad, without the sanction of her Majesty's minister, consul, or vice-consul, or, in their absence, of two respectable merchants resident there, all which functionaries and merchants are empowered to inquire in a summary way into the grounds of such proposed discharge, by examination on oath, and to grant or refuse such sanction according to their discretion, s. 41.

And no master shall leave behind at any place abroad any person of his crew on the plea of such person not being in a condition to proceed on the voyage, or having deserted from the ship, unless upon a previous certificate in writing from such functionaries or merchants, if there be any such within reasonable distance, and there be time to procure the same, certifying that the person so intended to be left is not in such condition, or has deserted and disappeared, and cannot be brought back; and such functionaries are authorised, on the application of any such master, to inquire by examination on oath into the circumstances, and give or refuse such certificate according to the result of such examination, s. 42.

The master of every ship bound to Great Britain is bound, at the request of the consul, to receive on board seamen not exceeding four persons for every hundred tons of his ship's burthen, and to transport them to Great Britain, on being paid by the commissioners of the navy for such of them as he may not want toward his own complement of men, according to such rate per day as shall be authorised by the commissioners for executing the office of lord high admiral, 11 Geo. 4, and 1 W. 4, c. 20, s. 82.

discharged against his consent, and without justifiable cause, he can recover his wages up to the time of the vessel's return, together with his own expenses. The certificate of the consul will not of itself prove the sufficiency of the cause of discharge. Though the seaman shall have made himself liable to be discharged, yet if he repents and offers to return to duty, the master must receive him, unless he can show a sufficient cause of refusal[1]. If the master alleges, as a cause for discharging a seaman, that he was a dangerous man, it must be shown that the danger was such as would affect a man of ordinary firmness[2].

In addition to the master's liability to the seaman, he is criminally liable to the government for discharging a mariner without cause. The statute enacts that if the master shall, when abroad, force on shore or leave behind any officer or seaman without justifiable cause, he shall be fined not exceeding five hundred dollars, or imprisoned not exceeding six months, according to the aggravation of the offence[3].

Notwithstanding these liabilities, the master may discharge a seaman for gross misconduct; yet the right is very strictly construed[4].

IMPRISONMENT*.—The master has the right to im-

---

[1] Ware, 65. 4 Mason, 541, 84.   [2] Ware, 9.
[3] Act 1825, ch. 276, § 10.   [4] Abbott on Shipp., 147, note.

---

* IN ENGLAND.] *Imprisonment* and *Punishment.*—By the law of England, the master of a ship has a right to correct and punish a disorderly or delinquent mariner in a reasonable manner. This punishment may be by the actual infliction of corporal punishment if absolutely necessary; but before the master proceeds to punish in this manner he should take the advice of the persons next below him in authority, as well to prevent the operation of passion in his own breast, as to secure witnesses to the propriety of his conduct.

The master may be called upon by action at law to answer to a mariner, who has been beaten or imprisoned by him or by his order in the course of a voyage; and for the justification of his conduct, he should be able to show not only that there was a sufficient cause for chastisement, but also that the chastisement itself was reasonable

prison a seaman in a foreign port, in a case of urgent necessity, but the power has always been very closely watched by courts of law. " The practice of imprisoning seamen in foreign jails is one of doubtful legality, and is to be justified only by a strong case of necessity[1]." "The master is not authorised to punish a seaman by imprisonment in a foreign jail, unless in cases of aggravated misconduct and insubordination[2]." If he does so punish him, he is not permitted to deduct his wages during the time of imprisonment, nor charge him with the expense of it[3]. If the imprisonment is without justifiable cause, the master is not excused by showing that it was ordered by the consul[4]. And, generally, the advice of a consul is no justification of an illegal act[5].

PUNISHMENT. — The master may inflict moderate correction on a seaman for sufficient cause; but he must take care that it is not disproportionate to the offence. If he exceeds the bounds of moderation, he is treated as a trespasser, and is liable in damages[6]. In respect to the mode of correction, it may be by personal chastisement, or by confinement on board ship, in irons, or otherwise[7]. But there must not be any cruelty or unnecessary severity exercised. The mode, instruments, or extent of the punishment, are not laid down by law. These must depend upon circumstances. In cases of urgent necessity, as of mutiny, weapons may be used which would be unlawful at other times; but even in these cases they must be used with the caution which the law requires in other cases of self-defence and vindication of rightful authority[8].

---

[1] Gilpin, 31.   Ware, 19.   [2] Ware, 503.
[3] Ware, 9, 503.   [4] Ware, 367.   [5] Gilpin, 31.
[6] 1 Peters' Ad. 186, 172.   2 Do. 420.   1 Wash. 316.
[7] 1 Peters' Ad. 186, 168.   15 Mass 365.   [8] Same cases.

---

and moderate; otherwise the mariner may recover damages proportionate to the injury received.—*Abbott on Shipp.*, 6th edit., 156; 2 *Bos. & Pull.* 224.—See also, on this subject, 1 *Hag.* 161, 271, 384, 395; 6 *C. & P.* 471; 5 & 6 W. 4, c. 19, s. 38.

It is not necessary that the punishment should be inflicted to suppress the offence at the time of its commission. It may be inflicted for past offences, and to promote good discipline on board. But the reference to by-gone acts should be very clear and distinct, or they will be presumed to have been forgiven[1]. In many cases prudence may require a postponement of the proper punishment. The authority of the master, being in its nature parental, must be exercised with a due regard to the rights and interests of all parties. He has a large discretion, but is held to answer strictly for every abuse of it[2]. The law enjoins upon him a temperate demeanour and decent conduct towards seamen. He risks the consequences, if he commences a dispute with illegal conduct and improper behaviour[3]. In all his acts of correction, he must punish purely for reformation and discipline, and never to gratify personal feelings[4]. If a master generally permits or encourages disorderly behaviour in his ship, he is less excusable for inflicting unusual punishment on account of misconduct arising out of that disorder[5]. If the case admits of delay, and the master does not make proper inquiry before punishing, he takes the consequences upon himself[6].

This power over the liberty and person of a fellow-man, being against common right, and intrusted to the master only from public policy, regarding the necessities of the service, is to be sparingly used, and a strict account will be required of its exercise. The master is responsible for any punishment inflicted on board the vessel, unless in his absence, or when he is prevented by force from interfering[7]. Neither will absence always be an excuse. If he had reason to suppose that such a thing might be done, and did not take pains to be present and interfere, he will be liable. Neither (as is often sup-

---

[1] 1 Hagg. 271.
[2] 15 Mass. 365. 3 Day, 294.
[3] 4 Wash. 340.
[4] 1 Pet. Ad. 168, 173, note.
[5] Bee, 239.
[6] 1 Hagg. 271.
[7] 2 Sumner, 1. Ware, 219.

posed) will the advice, or even the personal superintendence or orders of a consul, or any foreign authority, relieve the master of his personal responsibility [1]. He may ask advice, but he must act upon his own account, and is equally answerable for what he does himself, and what he permits to be done on board his vessel by others. The seaman is entitled to be dealt with by his own captain, under whom he shipped, and whom he may hold responsible at the end of the voyage; and this responsibility is not to be shaken off by calling in the aid of others. In case of an open mutiny, or of imminent danger to life and property, the master may make use of the local authorities; but then he is to remember that he can use them no further than for the purpose of quelling the mutiny, or of apprehending the felon. As soon as his authority is restored, the parental character is again thrown upon him, and all acts of punishment must be upon his own responsibility. He has no right to punish criminally. He has no judicial power. If a seaman has committed an offence further than against the internal order and economy of the ship, and which moderate correction is not sufficient to meet, the master must bring him home, (in confinement, if necessary,) or send him immediately by some other vessel, to be tried by the laws and by a jury of his country [2].

The practice of subjecting American seamen to foreign authority, or to persons whom they cannot well hold answerable,—like that of foreign imprisonment,—is an odious one, and must be justified by an overpowering necessity.

A recent statute [3] makes it the duty of consuls to exert themselves to reclaim deserters and discountenance insubordination, and authorizes them to employ the local authorities, where it can usefully be done, for those purposes. But this will unquestionably be restricted to the

---

[1] Ware, 367. Gilpin, 31. Act 1840, ch. 23, § 1.
[2] 1 Pet. Ad. 168.

apprehension of the deserter, and the quelling of the revolt or mutiny; and as soon as these ends are attained, the sole responsibility of the master in dealing with the crew will re-attach.

If the master is present while the mate, or any subordinate officer, inflicts punishment upon any of the crew, or if it is inflicted under such circumstances as would raise a presumption that the master was knowing of it, and he does not interfere, he will be held to have adopted it as his own act, and will be answerable accordingly [1].

In addition to the master's liability to the seamen in damages for abuse of power, he is also liable, as a criminal, to fine and imprisonment. A recent statute enacts, that "if any master, or other officer, of an American vessel, shall, from malice, hatred or revenge, and without justifiable cause, beat, wound, or imprison any one or more of the crew of such vessel, or withhold from them suitable food or nourishment, or inflict on them any cruel or unusual punishment, every such person so offending shall, on conviction thereof, be punished by fine not exceeding one thousand dollars, or by imprisonment not exceeding five years, or by both, according to the nature and aggravation of the offence [2]." It is held that the word "crew," in this statute, includes officers; and accordingly a master was punished for unjustifiably confining and otherwise mal-treating his chief mate [3].

To constitute "malice" in the above statute, it is not necessary to show malignity as it is commonly understood, or brutality; but the term, in law, requires no more than a "wilful intention to do a wrongful act." An offence is punishable under this act, even although no bad passions came into play, (as hatred or revenge,) for the term "malice," in law, covers all cases of intentional wrong, in their mildest form [4].

If a seaman desires to lay any complaint before a

---

[1] 2 Sumner, 1.
[2] Act 1835, ch. 313, § 3.
[3] 3 Sumner, 209.
[4] 2 Sumner, 584.

consul in a foreign port, the master must permit him to land for that purpose, or else inform the consul immediately of the fact, stating his reasons in writing for not allowing the man to land. If he refuses to do this, he forfeits one hundred dollars, and is liable to the seaman in damages [1].

CHAPTER V.

PASSENGERS[*].

Provisions. Treatment. Passage-money. Deportment. Services.

In Chapter I. of the Third Part, under the title "Provisions," it will be seen that the vessel must have on board, well secured under deck, at least sixty gallons

---

[1] Act 1840, ch. 23, § 1.

[*] IN ENGLAND.] *Passengers.*—See note to chap. i., under this title. The time when the passage-money becomes due will depend upon the contract made, or the established usage.

It appears that in *West India* voyages, the passage-money is paid before the commencement of the voyage, and is not to be returned, although the voyage is defeated, 4 *Campb.*, 241; and see 8 *Car. & P.*, 392.

The rule of the *East India* trade requires a passenger who refuses to go in consequence of a delay in the sailing of a vessel, to forfeit half the amount of the passage-money agreed for; and which, it would seem, may be recovered in cases where the time of sailing is not made an essential part of the contract, and the ship sails within a reasonable time. 5 *Car. & P.*, 569.

A passenger who is on board in time of danger, is bound, at the master's call, to do works of necessity, in defence of the ship if attacked, and for the preservation of the lives on board, 3 *Bos. & Pull.*, 612. Yet as he may lawfully, except under peculiar circumstances, depart the ship, should he voluntarily remain, at the risk of his personal safety, to assist her in her distress, he may be entitled to remuneration for his services, 1 *Rob. Ad. Rep.*, 285, 306; 3 *Rob. Ad. Rep.*, 292; *Abbott on Shipping*, 6th edition, 189.

As to the right to *confine* a passenger, see 1 *Campb.*, 58.

of water, one hundred pounds of salted beef, one hundred pounds of wholesome ship bread, and one gallon of vinegar for each passenger, on a voyage across the Atlantic, and in like proportion for shorter or longer voyages. This, too, must be in addition to the private stores of the master or passengers [1].

The master is also forbidden to take on board more than two passengers for every five tons [2].

The contract of passengers with the master is not for mere ship-room and personal existence on board, but for reasonable food, comforts, necessaries, and kindness. In respect to females it extends yet farther, and includes an implied stipulation against obscenity, immodesty, and a wanton disregard of the feelings. A course of conduct oppressive and malicious in these respects will be punished by the court, as well as a personal assault [3].

No passage-money is due to a ship upon an engagement to transport a passenger, before the arrival of the vessel at the port of destination. Where the passenger has paid in advance, he can reclaim his money if the voyage is not performed. If a voyage is partially performed, no passage-money is due, unless the expenses of the passenger, or the means of proceeding to the place of destination, are paid or tendered to him; in which case passage-money in proportion to the progress in the voyage is payable [4].

A passenger must submit to the reasonable rules and usages of the ship. He has no right to interfere with its discipline and internal regulations. Indeed, in a case of necessity, and for the order and safety of the ship, the master may restrain a passenger by force; but the cause must be urgent, and the manner reasonable and moderate.

In case of danger and distress, it is the duty as well as the interest of the passenger to contribute his aid, accord-

---

[1] Act 1819, ch. 170, § 3. [2] Do. § 1.
[3] 3 Mason, 342. [4] 1 Pet. Ad. 126.

ing to his ability, and he is entitled to no compensation therefor. He is not, however, bound to remain on board in time of danger, but may leave the vessel if he can; much less is he required to take upon himself any responsibility as to the conduct of the ship. If, therefore, he performs any extraordinary services, he becomes entitled to salvage [1].

CHAPTER VI.

MATES AND SUBORDINATES.

Mates included in the " crew." Removal. Succession. Log-book. Wages. Sickness. Punishment. Subordinates. Pilots.

IN all the statutes which entitle the " crew," or the " seamen," of a vessel to certain privileges as against the master or owner, these words, " crew" and "seamen," are construed to include the mates; as, for instance, the statute requiring a certain amount of provisions to be on board; the statute requiring a medicine-chest, and that which punishes the master for illegal and cruel treatment of any of the crew. In all these cases the mates are entitled to the same privileges and protection with the seamen [2].

The *chief mate* * is usually put on board by the owner, and is a person who is looked to for extraordinary services and responsibility. Accordingly, he cannot be removed by the master, unless for repeated and aggravated misconduct, or for palpable incapacity [3]. He acts in the stead of the master in case the latter dies, and whenever

---

[1] 2 B. and P. 612. 1 Pet. Ad. 70. 2 Hagg. 3.
[2] 1 Sumner, 151; 3 do. 209. 4 Mason, 104.
[3] 1 Pet. Ad. 244. 4 Wash. 338.

---

* IN ENGLAND.] The observations as to the chief mate and other officers, would seem to apply to such officers of British vessels.

he is absent[1]. He is then entrusted with the care of the ship, and the government of the crew. If he is appointed to act as mate by the master during the voyage, he holds his office at the master's pleasure [2]; but if he originally shipped in that capacity, he cannot be removed without proof of gross and flagrant misconduct, or of evident unfitness. Nor will one or two single instances of intemperance, disobedience, or negligence, be sufficient; the misconduct must be repeated, and the habit apparently incorrigible [3].

The second mate and other inferior officers do not stand upon so firm a footing as the chief mate; yet they cannot be removed by the master, unless for gross and repeated acts of disobedience, intemperance, dishonesty or negligence, or for palpable incapacity.

In case of the death or absence of the master, the chief mate becomes master by operation of law, but the second mate does not necessarily become chief mate. It lies with the new master to appoint whom he pleases to act as chief mate; though, in most cases, it should be the second mate, unless good reason exists for the contrary course. The second mate cannot, however, be degraded by the new master for any other cause than would have justified the former in so doing.

LOG-BOOK.—It is the duty of the chief mate to keep the log-book of the ship. This should be neatly and carefully kept, and all interlineations and erasures should be avoided, as they always raise suspicion. The entries should be made as soon as possible after each event takes place, and nothing should be entered which the mate would not be willing to adhere to in a court of justice. (See page 153.)

In Chapter III. of the Third Part, under the title "Master's relation to Officers," page 213, will be found a discussion of the question, whether the master can compel an officer to do duty before the mast.

---

[1] 4 Mason, 541. 1 Sumner, 151.   [2] Gilpin, 83.
[3] 1 Pet. Ad. 244. 4 Wash. 338.

In Chapters VIII., X., XI. and XII. of Part III., under the titles "Revolt," "Forfeiture," "Desertion," &c., will be found the laws upon those subjects relating to seamen. And it may be generally remarked, that all those laws apply as well to the officers as to the foremast men. An officer forfeits his wages by desertion, and is criminally liable for mutiny, revolt, &c., like a common seaman. As to the questions what constitutes a revolt, mutiny, &c., and when absence or leaving a vessel is excusable, and when it works a forfeiture, and as to when wages are due, I would refer the reader to those titles in Chapters VIII., X., XI. and XII. of Part III., above referred to.

WAGES. — Officers may sue in admiralty for their wages, and may arrest the ship, into whosoever hands it may have passed [1]; which is not the case with the master, who is supposed to look solely to the personal responsibility of the owners.

SICKNESS. — The right of an officer to be cured at the ship's expense is the same as that of a seaman [2]. The law upon that subject will be found in Chapter IX., title "Sickness," page 240.

PUNISHMENT. — The laws of the United States provide that if any master or officer shall unjustifiably beat, wound, or imprison any of the crew, or withhold from them suitable food and nourishment, or inflict upon them any cruel or unusual punishment, he shall be impri-

---

[1] 1 Pet. Ad. 246.   [2] 1 Sumner, 151.

---

* IN ENGLAND.] *Wages.*—If the hiring be on the usual terms, and made by word or by writing only, and not by deed, the seamen, or any one or more of them, and every officer, except the master, may sue in the Court of Admiralty; and may, by the process of that court, arrest the ship as a security for their demand, or cite the master or owners, personally to answer them.—*Abbott on Shipping*, 6th edition, 588 ; 1 Edw., 235.

If the wages do not exceed £20 they may be received in a summary way under the act 5 & 6 W. 4, c. 19, as hereafter stated.—See cap. 12.

soned not exceeding five years, and fined not exceeding 1000 dollars for each offence[1]. The officers, as part of the "crew," are entitled to the protection of this statute, against the master's acts; and, on the other hand, they are liable under it for any abuse of a seaman[2].

The law as to the officer's right to punish a seaman has been clearly settled, and is very simple. The sole authority to punish, for correction and discipline, resides with the master[3]. An officer has no right to use force with a seaman, either by chastising or confining him, except in a single class of cases; that is, upon an emergency which admits of no delay, and where the use of force is necessary for the safety of life and property. If a seaman is about to do an act which may endanger life or property, and instant action is required, the officer may confine him, or use force necessary to prevent him. So, if the immediate execution of an order is important, and a seaman, by obstinacy or wilful negligence, prevents or impedes the act, the officer may use force necessary to secure the performance of the duty. In these cases there must be a pressing necessity which will not admit of delay; for if delay is practicable, the officer must report to the master, and leave the duty of correction with him. A mate can in no case punish a seaman for the general purposes of correction and discipline, and still less for personal disrespect to himself[4]. If the master is not on board, and cannot be called upon, the authority of the officer is somewhat enlarged; but, even in this case, so far as a delay is practicable, he must leave the seaman to be dealt with by the master when he returns. Except in the cases and in the manner before mentioned, the officer is liable as a trespasser for any force used with a seaman.

If the officer acts under the authority, express or implied, of the master, he will not be held liable, even though the punishment should be excessive and unjusti-

---

[1] Act 1835, ch. 313, § 3.   [2] 4 Mason, 104. 3 Sumner, 209.
[3] 2 Sumner, 584.   [4] Do. 1. 584.

fiable; for he is, in such cases, only the agent of the master, who is responsible for the act[1]. Yet, if the punishment be so excessive as to show malice or wantonness on the part of the officer, or there be anything in his conduct to imply the same, he will be liable in some measure himself.

SUBORDINATES. — There are a number of men, usually, in merchant vessels, who are in not any respect officers, but who differ from the common seamen in that they ship in particular capacities, and to perform certain duties. These are the carpenter, steward, cook, &c. Such persons are not to be degraded for slight causes, though the master unquestionably has the power to do so upon sufficient grounds[2]. He may also require them to do duty, if necessary, before the mast. He may require them to take the place of persons who have been obliged to do their work[3]; but he cannot exact from them the duty of able seamen, unless they are such in fact. Repeated acts of disobedience, intemperance, and gross negligence, and evident incapacity for the duties undertaken, are justifying causes of removal[4]. In all other respects this class of persons stands upon the same footing with common seamen. They have the same privileges, and are under the same obligations and penalties[5].

PILOTS*.—When a pilot, who is regularly appointed, is on board, he has the absolute control of the navigation of the vessel[6]. He is master for the time being, and is alone answerable for any damage occasioned by his own negligence or default[7].

A pilot may sue in admiralty for his wages[8].

A pilot cannot claim *salvage* for any acts done within the limits of his duty, however useful and meritorious

---

[1] Ware, 219. [2] 4 Mason, 84. Ware, 109. [3] Ware, 109.
[4] Ware, 109. [5] 2 Pet. Ad. 268. [6] 1 Johns. 305.
[7] 1 Pet. Ad. 223. 1 Mason, 508. [8] 1 Mason, 508.

---

* IN ENGLAND.] *Pilots.*—See the act 6 G. 4, c. 125, as to pilots, and the rates and recovery of pilotage.

they may have been [1]. If towing is necessary, pilots are bound to perform it, having a claim for compensation for damages done to their boats, or for extra labour [2]. If extraordinary pilot service is performed, additional pilotage is the proper reward, and not salvage [3]. If, however, the acts done by the pilot are clearly without and beyond his duty as pilot, he may claim salvage [4].

CHAPTER VII.

SEAMEN. SHIPPING CONTRACT.

Shipping contract—how formed—how signed. Erasures and interlineations. Unusual stipulations.

By the law of the United States *, in all foreign voyages, and in all coasting voyages to other than an adjoining state, there must be an agreement in writing, or in

---

[1] Gilpin, 60. 10 Peters R. 108. [2] 2 Hagg. 176.
[3] 2 Hagg. 176.   [4] 1 Rob. 106. Gilpin, 60.

---

* IN ENGLAND.] The shipping contract required to be made by the law of England, is similar to the one prescribed by the law of the United States.

The form of it is given by the act 5 & 6 W. 4, c. 19; see the schedule to the act. This agreement, called the "Ship's Articles," must specify what monthly or other wages each seaman is to be paid, the capacity in which he is to act, and the nature of the voyage in which the ship is intended to be employed, so that the seaman may have some means of judging of the probable period for which he is likely to be engaged. The agreement must also contain the day of the month and year in which it is made; must be signed by the master in the first instance, and by the seamen respectively, at the port or place where such seamen shall be respectively shipped; and the master must cause the same to be, by or in the presence of the party who is to attest their respective signatures thereto, truly and distinctly read over to every such seaman before he is required to sign, in order that he may be able to understand the purport and meaning of the engagement he enters into, and the terms to which he is bound, 5 & 6 W. 4, c. 19, s. 2.

Any agreement contrary to or inconsistent with the provisions of

print, with every seaman on board the ship, (excepting only apprentices and servants of the master or owner,) declaring the voyage, and term or terms of time, for the last-mentioned statute, and with the right to wages given to a seaman by the maritime law, in case of freight earned by ships subsequently lost, is declared not to be binding upon him, s. 5.

By signing the agreement, a seaman does not forfeit his lien upon the ship, nor is he deprived of his remedy for the recovery of wages against the ship, the master, or the owners, s. 5.

The master and owners are bound, on reporting a ship's arrival from "parts beyond the seas," at her port of destination in the United Kingdom, to deposit a true copy of this agreement with the collector or controller of the customs there, that the means of ascertaining the terms and conditions of it may be accessible to all who are interested in it.

The masters of ships employed in the fisheries on the *British* coasts, or trading from port to port of the *United Kingdom,* or making regular voyages to the *Channel Islands,* or to ports on the continent of *Europe,* between the river *Elbe,* inclusive, and *Brest,* must twice in every year deposit copies of all such agreements entered into by them during the preceding six months, s. 3.

If any master carry out to sea a seaman without having first entered into such an agreement with him, he forfeits 10*l.* in respect of every seaman so carried out. If he neglect to cause the agreement to be read over to the seaman, he forfeits 5*l.*; and if he neglect to deposit a true copy of it with the collector or controller of the customs, 50*l.*, s. 5.

The master must deposit the ship's articles on his arrival at any foreign port, with the British consul, or vice-consul, for preservation during the ship's stay there; penalty for omission 25*l.*, s. 48.

No seaman shall be shipped by the master at any such foreign port, except with the privity of such consul, or vice-consul, to be indorsed upon the agreement, under a penalty of 25*l.*, s. 49.

The master must produce the muster-roll of the ship, and the agreement with the crew, to the captain, commander, or other commissioned officer of any of her Majesty's ships requiring a production and sight thereof, under the penalty of 25*l.*, s. 50.

The master must also, upon demand, produce such muster-roll and agreement to the registrar and officers of customs in the British possessions abroad, under the penalty of 50*l.*, s. 51.

When a written contract is made, it becomes the only evidence between the parties; and a mariner cannot recover anything agreed to be given in reward for his service, which is not specified in the articles.—*Abbott on Shipping,* 6th edition, 550; 2 *Bos. & Pull.,* 116; 2 *Rob. Ad. Rep.,* 241.

which such seaman is hired [1]. This contract is called the *shipping-articles*, and all the crew, including the master and officers, usually sign the same paper; it not being requisite that there should be a separate paper for each man. If there is not such a contract signed, each seaman could, by the old law, recover the highest rate of wages that had been given on similar voyages, at the port where he shipped, within three months next before the time of shipment [2]. By the law of 1840, he may, in such case, leave the vessel at any time, and demand the highest rate of wages given to any seaman during the voyage, or the rate agreed upon at the time of his shipment [3]. A seaman not signing the articles, is not bound by any of the regulations, nor subject to the penalties of the statutes [4]; but he is, notwithstanding, bound by the rules and liable to the forfeitures imposed by the general maritime law [5].

These shipping-articles are legal evidence, and bind all parties whose names are annexed to them, both as to wages, the nature and length of the voyage, and the duties to be performed [6]. Accordingly, seamen have certain rights secured to them with reference to these papers. In the first place, the master must obtain a copy of the articles, certified to by the collector of the port from which the vessel sails, to take with him upon the voyage. This must be a fair and true copy, without erasures or interlineations. If there are any such erasures or interlineations, they will be presumed to be fraudulent, and will be set aside, unless they are satisfactorily explained in a manner consistent with innocent purposes, and with the provisions of laws which guard the rights of mariners. These articles must be produced by the master before any consul or commercial agent to whom a seaman may have submitted a complaint [7].

---

[1] Act 1790, ch. 56, § 1.   [2] Do. § 1.   [3] Do. 23, § 10.
[4] Act 1790, ch. 56, § 1.   [5] 1 Pet. Ad. 212.
[6] 3 Mason, 161. Act 1840, ch. 23, § 3.
[7] Act 1840, ch. 23, § 2, 19.

Every unusual clause introduced into the shipping-articles, or anything which tends to deprive a seaman of what he would be entitled to by the general law, will be suspiciously regarded by the courts; and if there is reason to suppose that any advantage has been taken of him, or if the contract bears unequally upon him, it will be set aside. In order to sustain such a clause, the master or owner must show two things: first, that the seaman's attention was directed toward it, and its operation and effect explained to him; and, secondly, that he received some additional compensation or privilege in consideration of the clause. Unless the court is satisfied upon these two points, an unusual stipulation unfavourable to a seaman will be set aside [1]. For instance, seamen are entitled to have a medicine-chest on board, and in certain cases to be cured at the ship's expense; and the court set aside a clause in the shipping-articles in which it was stipulated that the seamen should bear all the expense, even though there were no medicine-chest on board [2]. Another clause was set aside, in which the voyage was described as from Baltimore to St. Domingo and *elsewhere*, on the ground that seamen are entitled to have their voyage accurately described [3].

Some clauses which are not such as to be set aside, will yet be construed in favour of seamen, if their interpretation is at all doubtful [4]. A clause providing that no wages should be paid if the vessel should be taken or lost, or detained more than thirty days, was set aside, seamen being entitled to wages up to the last port of delivery [5]. If the amount of wages merely be omitted in the articles, there seems to be some doubt as to the introduction of other evidence to show the rate agreed upon, and as to the seaman's being entitled by statute to the highest rate

---

[1] 2 Sumner, 443. 2 Mason, 541.   [2] 2 Mason, 541.
[3] 1 Hall's Law Jour. 207. 2 Gall. 477, 526. 2 Dods. 504. Gilpin 219.
[4] 1 Pet. Ad. 186, 215.   [5] 2 Sumner, 443.

of wages current [1]. If a seaman ships for a general coasting and trading voyage to different ports in the United States, and the articles provide for no time or place at which the voyage shall end, the seaman may leave at any time, provided he does not do so under circumstances peculiarly inconvenient to the other party [2].

If, however, the voyage is accurately described, and the wages specified, the seaman cannot be admitted to show that his contract was different from that contained in the articles [3].

It is no violation of the contract if the vessel departs from the voyage described, by accident, necessity, or superior force [4].

CHAPTER VIII.

SEAMEN—CONTINUED.

Rendering on board. Refusal to proceed. Desertion or absence during the voyage. Discharge.

RENDERING ON BOARD [*].—If, after having signed the articles, and after a time has been appointed for the seaman to render himself on board, he neglects to appear, and an entry to that effect is made in the log-book, he forfeits one day's pay for every hour of absence; and if the ship is obliged to proceed without him, he forfeits a sum equal to double his advance [5]. These forfeitures apply to the commencement of the voyage, and cannot be exacted unless a memorandum is made on the articles, and an entry in full in the log-book. A justice of the peace may, upon complaint of the master, issue a war-

---

[1] Gilpin, 452. Abb. on Shipp. 434, note. Act 1840, ch. 23. § 10.
[2] Ware, 437.   [3] Gilpin, 305.   [4] 2 Hagg. 243.
[5] Act 1790, ch. 56, § 2.

---

[*] IN ENGLAND.] *Rendering on board.*—See note to cap. 4, under title "Shipment."

rant to apprehend a deserting seaman, and commit him to jail until the vessel is ready to proceed upon her voyage. The master must, however, first show that the contract has been signed, and that the seaman departed without leave, and in violation of it [1].

REFUSAL TO PROCEED*.— If, after the voyage has begun, and before the vessel has left the land, the first officer and a majority of the crew shall agree that the vessel is unfit to proceed on the voyage, either from fault or deficiency in hull, spars, rigging, outfits, provisions, or crew, they may require the master to make the nearest or most convenient port, and have the matter inquired into by the district judge, or two justices of the peace, taking two or more of the complainants before the judge. Thereupon the judge orders a survey, and decides whether the vessel is to proceed, or stop and be repaired and supplied; and both master and crew are bound by this decision. If the seamen and mate shall have made this complaint without reason, and from improper motives, they are liable to be charged with the expenses attending it [2].

If, when the vessel is in a foreign port, the first or any other officer and a majority of the crew shall make complaint, in writing, to the consul, that the ship is unfit to proceed to sea, for any of the above reasons, the consul shall order an examination, in the same manner; and the decision of the consul shall bind all parties. If the consul shall decide that the vessel was sent to sea in an unsuitable condition, by neglect or design, the crew shall be entitled to their discharge and three months' additional pay; but not if it was done by accident or innocent mistake [3].

It is no justification for refusing to do duty and proceed

---

[1] Act 1790, ch. 56, § 7.   [2] Do. § 3.
[3] Act 1840, ch. 23, § 12—15.

---

* IN ENGLAND.] *Refusal to proceed.*—What is here said would seem to be applicable to British vessels.

upon the voyage, that a new master has been substituted in place of the one under whom the seaman originally shipped [1]; and if a blank is left for the name of the master, the seaman is supposed to ship under any who may be appointed [2]. The same rule applies to the substitution or appointment of any other officer of the ship during the voyage.

DESERTION OR ABSENCE DURING THE VOYAGE *.—If, during the voyage, the seaman absents himself without leave, for less than forty-eight hours, and an entry thereof is made in full in the log-book, he forfeits three days' pay for each day's absence. But if the absence exceeds forty-eight hours, he forfeits all his wages then due, and all his goods and chattels on board the vessel at the time, and is liable to the owner in damages for the expense of hiring another seaman [3]. If he deserts within the limits of the United States, he is liable to be arrested and committed to jail, until the vessel sails [4]. If he deserts or absents himself in a foreign port, the consul is empowered to make use of the authorities of the place to reclaim him. If, however, the consul is satisfied that the desertion was caused by unusual or cruel treatment, the seaman may be discharged, and shall receive three months' additional wages [5]. It is not a desertion for a seaman to leave his vessel for the purpose of procuring necessary food, which has been refused on board; nor is a seaman liable if the conduct of the master has been

---

[1] 1 Mason, 443. Bee, 48. 2 Sumner, 582.
[2] 6 Mass. 300.   [3] Act 1790, ch. 56, § 5.
[4] Act 1790, ch. 56, § 7.   [5] Act 1840, ch. 23, § 9.

---

* IN ENGLAND.] *Desertion or absence during the voyage.*— See note to cap. 4, under title "*Shipment.*"

If the master propose to take the ship on a voyage not designated by the articles, the mariners may leave the ship without being guilty of desertion.—1 *Hag.*, 248; 2 *Hag.*, 243.

Want of provisions will justify the seaman in leaving the ship, and *extreme* misconduct and ill treatment on the part of the master may also justify desertion.—See *Abbott on Shipp.*, 6th edit., 152, 153.

such as to make it dangerous for him to remain on board[1], or if the shipping-articles have been fraudulently altered[2]. Even in a clear case of desertion, if the party repents, and seeks to return to his duty within a reasonable time, he is entitled to be received on board again, unless his previous conduct had been such as would justify his discharge[3].

As to the effect of deserting upon wages, and what is desertion in such cases, see the subject, "Wages affected by Desertion," Chapter XI.

DISCHARGE [*].—By referring to Chapter IV., "Master's Relation to Crew," the seaman will find that, though the master has power to discharge a seaman for gross and repeated misconduct, yet that this right is closely watched, and any abuse of it is severely punished. He will also find there a statement of his own rights and privileges, with reference to a discharge. It has been seen that he may demand his discharge of the consul, if the vessel is not fit to proceed, and is not repaired, or if he has been cruelly and unjustifiably treated[4].

If a vessel has been so much injured that it is doubtful whether she can be repaired, or the repairs cannot be made for a long time, during which it would be a great expense to the owners to support the seamen in a foreign country, it is held that the crew may be discharged, upon the owners' paying their passage home, and their wages up to the time of their arrival at the place of shipment[5].

As to discharge at the end of the voyage, see "Wages affected by Desertion," Chapter XI.

---

[1] Hagg. 63.   [2] Do. 182.   [3] 1 Sumner, 373.
[4] Act 1840, ch. 23, § 9, 14.   [5] 2 Dodson, 403.

---

[*] IN ENGLAND.] *Discharge.*—See note to cap. 4, under this title.

CHAPTER IX.

SEAMEN—CONTINUED.

Provisions. Sickness. Medicine-chest. Hospital money. Relief in foreign ports. Protection.

PROVISIONS *.—For the benefit of seamen it has been enacted that every vessel bound on a voyage across the Atlantic, shall have on board, well secured under deck, at least sixty gallons of water, one hundred pounds of wholesome ship bread, and one hundred pounds of salted flesh meat, over and above the stores of master or passengers, and the live stock. And if the crew of any vessel not so provided shall be put upon short allowance of water, flesh, or bread, such seaman shall recover from the master double wages for every day he was so allowanced [1]. The same rule applies to other voyages than those across the Atlantic, and the amount of provisions stowed below must be in proportion to the length of the voyage, compared with one across the Atlantic [2]. It also applies to seamen shipped in foreign ports, as well as to those shipped in the United States [3]. It has been thought that if the articles enumerated cannot be procured, the master may substitute other wholesome provisions; but it is doubtful whether even this will free him from the penalty; at least it will not unless he can show that it was impossible to procure them at the last port of departure [4].

Besides this special enactment, a seaman may always recover damages of a master who unnecessarily and wantonly deprives him of sufficient food and nourishment [5]. If, however, the short allowance is caused by inevitable

---

[1] Act 1790, ch. 56, § 9.   [2] Do.   [3] 1 Pet. Ad. 223.
[4] 1 Pet. Ad. 229, 223. Bee, 84. Abb. 135, note. Ware, 454.
[5] 2 Pet. Ad. 409.

---

* IN ENGLAND.] *Provisions.*—See note to cap. 1, under title "Provisions."

accident, without any fault of the master or owner, or is a matter of fair discretion in a case of common danger, the master is not liable. Another law of the United States provides, that if any master or other officer shall wilfully and without justifiable cause withhold suitable food and nourishment from a seaman, he shall be fined not exceeding one thousand dollars, and imprisoned not exceeding five years[1]. The master may at any time, at his discretion, put the crew upon an allowance of water and eatables; but if it is a short allowance, he must be able to give a justifying reason.

SICKNESS. MEDICINE-CHEST *.—Every vessel of one hundred and fifty tons or upwards, navigated by ten or more persons in all, and bound on a voyage beyond the United States, and every vessel of seventy-five tons or upwards, navigated by six or more persons in the whole, and bound from the United States to any port in the West Indies, is required to have a chest of medicines, put up by an apothecary of known reputation, and accompanied by directions for administering the same. The chest must also be examined at least once a year, and supplied with fresh medicines[2].

In case of dispute, the owner must prove the suffici-

---

[1] Act 1835, ch. 313, § 3.
[2] Act 1790, ch. 56, § 8; 1805, ch. 88, § 1.

---

* IN ENGLAND.] *Sickness.—Medicine-chest.*—Every ship sailing from the United Kingdom to any place out of the same shall have, and keep constantly on board the same, a sufficient supply of medicines suitable to accidents and diseases arising on sea-voyages; and in case any default shall be made in providing or keeping supplied such medicines as aforesaid, or in case any of the seamen shall receive any hurt or injury in the service of the ship, the expense of providing the necessary surgical and medical advice, and attendance and medicines, which the seaman shall stand in need of until he shall have been cured, or shall have been brought back to some port of the United Kingdom, shall be borne and defrayed by the owner and master of the ship, or one of them, without any deduction whatever on that account from the seaman's wages.—5 & 6 Wm. IV., c. 19, s. 18.

ency of the medicine-chest. It does not lie with the seaman to prove its insufficiency [1].

If a vessel has a suitable medicine-chest on board, it would seem that the ship is not to be charged with the medicines and medical advice which a seaman may need. But the ship is still liable for the expenses of his nursing, care, diet, and lodging [2]. Accordingly, if a seaman is put on shore at an hospital or elsewhere, for his cure, the ship is chargeable with so much of the expense as is incurred for nursing, care, diet, and lodging; and unless the owner can specify the items of the charge, and show how much was for medical advice, and how much for other expenses, he must pay the whole [3]. The seaman is to be cured at the expense of the ship, of a sickness or injury sustained in the ship's service [4]; but if he contracts a disease by his own fault or vices, the ship is not chargeable [5]. A sick seaman is entitled to proper nursing, lodging, and diet. If these cannot be had, or are not furnished on board the vessel, he is entitled to be taken on shore to an hospital, or to some place where these can be obtained. It is often attempted to be shown that the seaman was put on shore at his own request. This is no defence. He is entitled to be put on shore if his disease requires it; and it is seldom that proper care can be taken of a seaman on board ship [6].

If a seaman requires further medicines and medical advice than the chest and directions can give, and is not sent ashore, it would seem that the ship ought to bear the expense; but this point has never been decided [7]. If the medicine-chest can furnish all he needs, the ship is exempted [8].

HOSPITAL MONEY *.—Every seaman must pay twenty

---

[1] 2 Mason, 445.   [2] 1 Mason, 541. 1 Sumner, 151.
[3] 1 Pet. Ad. 256, note.   [4] 1 Sumner, 195.
[5] Gilpin, 434. 1 Pet. Ad. 142, 152.
[6] 1 Pet. Ad. 256, note.
[7] Gilpin, 435. 1 Pet. Ad. 142, 152, 255.   [8] 2 Mason, 541.

---

* IN ENGLAND.]—*Hospital Money.*—All masters of merchant

cents a month, out of his wages, for hospital money. This goes to the establishment and support of hospitals for sick and disabled seamen [1].

RELIEF IN FOREIGN PORTS*.—If a vessel is sold in a foreign port and her crew discharged, or if a seaman is discharged with his own consent, he can receive two months' extra wages of the consul, who must obtain it of the master [2]. This applies only to the voluntary sale of the vessel, and not when the sale is rendered necessary by shipwreck. If, however, after the disaster the vessel might have been repaired at a reasonable expense and in a reasonable time, but the owner chooses to sell, the two months' pay is due. To escape the payment, the owner must show that he was obliged to sell [3].

It is also the duty of the consuls to provide subsistence and a passage to the United States for any Ameri-

---

[1] Act 1798, ch. 94, § 1. [2] Act 1803, ch. 62, § 3.
[3] Ware, 485 ; Gilpin, 198.

---

ships, and owners working their own ships, are to pay 2s. per month, and all seamen or other persons employed in any merchant ship, 1s. per month, for hospital money in England.—4 & 5 Wm. IV., s. 5 and 6.

The master is to deduct this monthly duty from the wages of the seaman, and to pay it, and the amount due from himself, to the receiver appointed under the Act—sec. 7.

* IN ENGLAND.]—*Relief in Foreign Ports.*—See note to cap. 4, under title " Discharge."

If by shipwreck, capture, or any cause whatever, any seafaring men or boys, subjects of Great Britain, are cast away, or left, or be in distress in foreign parts, the governors, minister, and consuls appointed by her Majesty, or where none such are resident, two or more *British* merchants there residing, are required, under a penalty of £100 for each man or boy, to provide them subsistence and a passage home.—11 Geo. IV. and 1 Wm. IV., c. 20, s. 82.

And when any person forced on shore, or left behind, shall be relieved under the provisions of the 11 Geo. IV., and Wm. IV., c. 20, then in addition to the wages due from, and the penalties imposed on, the master, her Majesty shall be entitled to sue such master or owner for all the charges and expenses incurred in the subsistence, necessary clothing, and conveyance home, of such person.—5 & 6 Wm. IV., c. 19., s. 40.

can seaman found destitute within their districts. The seamen must, if able, do duty on board the vessel in which they are sent home, according to their several abilities [1].

The crew of every vessel shall have the fullest liberty to lay their complaints before the consul or commercial agent in any foreign port, and shall in no respect be restrained or hindered therein by the master or any officer, unless sufficient and valid objection exist against their landing. In which case, if any seaman desire to see the consul, the master must inform the consul of it forthwith; stating, in writing, the reason why the seaman is not permitted to land, and that the consul is desired to come on board. Whereupon the consul must proceed on board and inquire into the causes of complaint [2].

PROTECTION. — Every American seaman upon applying to the collector of the port from which he departs, and producing proof of his citizenship, is entitled to a letter of protection. The collector may charge for this twenty-five cents.

CHAPTER X.

SEAMEN—CONTINUED.

Punishment. Revolt and mutiny. Embezzlement. Piracy.

PUNISHMENT [*].—As to the right of the master to punish a seaman by corporal chastisement, imprisonment on shore, confinement on board, &c., and the extent of that right, and the master's liability for exceeding it,—the seaman is referred to Chapter IV., "The Master's relation to the Crew," title "Imprisonment," and "Punishment." He will there see that the master pos-

---

[1] Act 1803, ch. 62, § 4. [2] Act 1840, ch. 23, § 1,
[3] Act 1796, ch. 36, § 4.

[*] IN ENGLAND.]—*Punishment.*—See note to cap. 4, page 219.

sesses this right to a limited extent, and that he is strictly answerable for the abuse of it. Disobedience of orders, combinations to refuse duty, dishonest conduct, personal insolence, and habitual negligence and backwardness, are all causes which justify punishment in a greater or less degree.

The contract which a seaman makes with the master, is not like that of a man who engages in any service on shore. It is somewhat military in its nature [1]. The master has great responsibilities resting upon him, and is entitled to instant and implicit obedience. To ensure this, regular and somewhat strict discipline must be preserved. The master, also, cannot obtain assistance when at sea, as any one can who is in authority upon land. He must depend upon the habits of faithful and respectful discharge of duty which his crew have acquired; and if this fails, he may resort to force. He is answerable for the safety of the ship, and for the safe keeping and delivery of valuable cargoes, and in almost all cases he is the first person to whom the owner of the vessel and cargo will look for indemnity. Considering this, the seamen will feel that it is not unreasonable that the master should have power to protect himself and all for whom he acts, even by force if necessary [2]. A good seaman, who is able and willing to do his duty faithfully and at all times, and treats his officers respectfully, will seldom be abused; and if he is, the master is liable to him personally in damages, and is also subject to be indicted by the government and tried as a criminal. A seaman should be warned against taking the law into his own hands. If the treatment he receives is unjustifiable, he should still submit to it, if possible, until the voyage is up, or until he arrives at some port where he can make complaint. If he is conscious that he is not to blame, and an assault is made upon him unjustifiably and with dangerous severity, he may defend himself;

---

[1] Ware, 86. 3 Wash. 515.   [2] Ware, 219.

but he should not attempt to punish the offender, or to inflict anything in the way of retaliation [1].

In Chapter VI., title "Mates," the reader will see how far any inferior officer of a vessel may use force with a seaman.

REVOLT AND MUTINY*.—If any one or more of the crew of an American vessel shall by fraud or force, or by threats or intimidations, take the command of the vessel from the master or other commanding officer, or resist or prevent him in the free and lawful exercise of his authority, or transfer the command to any other person not lawfully entitled to it; every person so offending, and his aiders and abbettors, shall be deemed guilty of a revolt or mutiny and felony; and shall be punished by fine not exceeding 2000 dollars, and by imprisonment and confinement to hard labour not exceeding ten years, according to the nature and aggravation of the offence [2]. And if any seaman shall endeavour to commit a revolt or mutiny, or shall combine with others on board to make a revolt or mutiny, or shall solicit or incite any of the crew to disobey or resist the lawful orders of the master or other officer, or to refuse or neglect their proper duty on board, or shall assemble with others in a riotous or mutinous manner, or shall unlawfully confine the master or other commanding officer,—every person committing one or more of these offences shall be imprisoned not exceeding five years, or fined not exceeding 1000 dollars, or both, according to the nature and aggravation of the offence [3].

It will be seen that the first of these laws applies only

---

[1] Do. 3 Wash, 552. [2] Act 1835, ch. 313, § 1. [3] Do. § 2.

* IN ENGLAND.]—*Revolt and Mutiny—Piracy.*—By 7 Wm. IV., 1 Vic. c. 88, s. 3, persons convicted of these offences shall be liable to be transported for life, or for any term not less than fifteen years, or to be imprisoned for any term not exceeding three years.

As to what offences shall be deemed piracy, see the Act 11 & 12 Wm. III., c. 7, s. 9, made perpetual by 6 Geo. I., c. 19; 18 Geo. II., c. 30.—*Abbott on Shipp.*, 6th edit., 165.

to cases where seamen actually throw off all authority, deprive the master of his command, and assume the control themselves, which is to make a revolt. The last is designed to punish endeavours and combinations to make a revolt, which are not fully carried out.

Every little instance of disobedience, or insolent conduct, or even force used against the master or other officer, will not be held a revolt or an endeavour to make a revolt. There must be something showing an intention to subvert the lawful authority of the master [1]. It does not excuse seamen, however, from this offence, that they confined their refusal to one particular portion of their duty. If that duty was lawfully required of them, it is equally a subversion of authority as if they had refused all duty [2].

If the crew interfere by force or threats to prevent the infliction of punishment for a gross offence, it is an endeavour to commit a revolt [3].

To constitute the offence of confining the master, it is not necessary that he should be forcibly secured in any particular place, or even that his body should be seized and held; any act which deprives him of his personal liberty in going about the ship, or prevents his doing his duty freely, (if done with that intention [4],) is a confinement [5]. So is a threat of immediate bodily injury, if made in such a manner as would reasonably intimidate a man of ordinary firmness [6].

In all these cases of revolt, mutiny, endeavours to commit the same, and confinement of the master, it is to be remembered that the acts are excusable if done from a sufficient justifying cause. The master may so conduct himself as to justify the officers and crew in placing restraints upon him, to prevent his committing acts which might endanger the lives of all the persons on

---

[1] 4 Wash. 528. 1 Pet. Ad. 178. [2] 4 Mason, 105.
[3] 1 Sumner, 448. [4] 4 Wash. 428.
[5] 4 Mason, 105. 4 Wash. 548. 1 Sumner, 448. 3 Wash. 525.
[6] Pet. C. C. 213.

board. But an excuse of this kind is received with great caution, and the crew should be well assured of the necessity of such a step, before taking it, since they run a great risk in so interfering[1].

EMBEZZLEMENT*.—If any of the crew steal, or appropriate, or by gross negligence suffer to be stolen, any part of the cargo, or anything belonging to the ship, they are responsible for the value of everything stolen or appropriated.

It is necessary that the fraud, connivance, or negligence of a seaman should be proved against him, before he can be charged with anything lost or stolen; and in no case is an innocent man bound to contribute towards a loss occasioned by the misconduct of another. If, however, it is clearly proved that the whole crew were concerned, but one offender is not known more than another, and the circumstances are such as to affect all the crew, each man is to contribute to the loss, unless he clears himself from the suspicion[2].

PIRACY†.—If the master or crew of a vessel shall, upon the high seas, seize upon or rob the master or crew of another vessel; or if they shall run away with the vessel committed to their charge, or any goods to the amount of 50 dollars; or voluntarily yield them up to pirates;

---

[1] 4 Mason, 105. 1 Sumner, 448. Pet. C. C. 118.
[2] 1 Mason, 105. Gilpin, 461.

---

* IN ENGLAND.]—*Embezzlement.*—If the cargo be embezzled by the fraud or negligence of the seamen, so that the merchant has a right to claim a satisfaction from the master and owners, they may, by the custom of merchants, deduct the value thereof from the wages of seamen by whose misconduct the injury has taken place; and the last proviso introduced into the usual agreement signed by the seamen is calculated to enforce this rule in the case of embezzlement either of the cargo or of the ship's stores. This proviso is to be construed individually as affecting only the particular persons guilty of the embezzlement, and not the whole crew; nor, as it seems, is any innocent person liable to contribute a portion of his wages to make good the loss occasioned by others.—See *Abbot on Shipp.*, 6th edit., 584, 585, and cases there cited.

† IN ENGLAND.]—*Piracy.*—See note, page 245.

or if the crew shall prevent the master by violence from fighting in the defence of vessel or property; such conduct is piracy, and punishable with death[1].

It is also piracy, and punishable with death, to be engaged in any foreign country and kidnapping any negro or mulatto, or in decoying or receiving them on board a vessel with the intention of making them slaves[2].

CHAPTER XI.

SEAMEN'S WAGES.

Affected by desertion or absence;—by misconduct; by imprisonment;—by capture; by loss of vessel and interruption of voyage. Wages on an illegal voyage. Wages affected by death or disability.

WAGES AFFECTED BY DESERTION OR ABSENCE *.—It has been seen that if a seaman, at the commencement of

---

[1] Act 1790, ch. 36, § 8; 1820, ch. 113, § 3.
[2] Act 1820, ch. 113, § 4, 5.

---

* IN ENGLAND.]—*Wages affected by Desertion or Absence.*—See note to cap. 4, title "Shipment."—If any seaman, after having signed the ship's articles, or after the ship has left her first port of clearance, wilfully and without leave, absent himself from the ship, or his duty, he forfeits (in all cases not of absolute desertion, or not treated as such by the master,) out of his wages to the master or owner, the amount of two days' pay for every 24 hours of absence, and in a like proportion for any less period of time, or at the option of the master, the amount of such expenses as have been necessarily incurred in hiring a substitute to perform his work.

If after the ship's arrival at her port of delivery, and before her cargo is discharged, any seaman quits the ship without a previous discharge or leave from the master, he forfeits to the master or owner one month's pay of his wages; but no such forfeiture is incurred, unless the fact of such seaman's temporary absence, neglect of duty, or quitting the ship, be duly entered or recorded in the ship's log-book; and this entry must specify truly the hour of the day at which it occurred, and the period during which the seaman was absent or neglected his duty, the truth of which entry, it shall be incumbent on the owner or master, in all cases of dispute,

the voyage, neglects to render himself on board at the time appointed, and an entry thereof is made in the

to substantiate by the evidence of the mate, or some other credible witness.—5 & 6 W. 4, c. 19, s. 7.

It has been decided that this section of the act applies to the case of the quitting of a ship after her arrival in her port of delivery, but before the discharge of her cargo.—4 M. & W. 285.

If a seaman absolutely desert the ship, he forfeits to the owner or master all wages and emoluments to which he might otherwise have been entitled, and also the clothes and effects he may have left on board, provided the circumstances attending such desertion be entered in the log-book at the time, and certified by the signature of the master, mate, or other credible witness; and the absence of a seaman from the ship for any time within the space of 24 hours immediately preceding the sailing of the ship, without permission of the master, or for any period, however short, under circumstances plainly showing an intention not to return, is to be deemed an absolute desertion.—5 & 6 W. 4, c. 19, s. 9.

It has also been determined that this section of the act applies to the case of the desertion of a ship whilst in foreign parts.—4 M. & W. 285.

A mode of ascertaining the amount of these forfeitures, where the seaman has contracted for the voyage or the run, is expressly provided by the act, s. 8.

If a mariner quit the ship with leave of the master, and when ordered to return, refuses to do so, his wages are forfeited.—See *Abbot on Shipp.*, 6th Edit. 578., and cases there cited.

It has been already stated that the entry into the service of her Majesty is not deemed a desertion, nor followed by the forfeiture of wages. But where a mariner quitted a vessel in defiance of the master, with opprobrious language, *and without any declaration of such intention* when he quitted the vessel, entered on board a King's ship within 24 hours, it was held to be a desertion, working a forfeiture of wages.—2 *Hagg. Ad. Rep.*, 403; *Abbot on Shipp.*, 6th edit., 581.

A forfeiture may be waived by the party entitled to take advantage of it. 2 Campb. 590, and 5 & 6 W. 4, c. 19, s. 7. But a forfeiture is not waived by the acceptance of a seaman's services whilst the ship is in distress, unless such acceptance be continued when the necessity for them has ceased.—3 C. & P. 3.

As regards the *time* of payment of wages. By the 5 & 6 W. 4, c. 19, it is enacted that the master or owner shall pay to every seaman entering into such contract as aforesaid (*i. e.* the ship's articles), his wages, if the same shall be demanded, within the respective periods following; that is to say, if the ship shall be

log-book, he forfeits one day's pay for every hour's absence; and if he shall wholly absent himself, so that the ship is obliged to go to sea without him, he forfeits his advance and as much more [1]. And if at any time during the voyage he absents himself without leave, and returns within forty-eight hours, he forfeits three days' pay for every day's absence; but if he is absent more than forty-eight hours, he forfeits all the wages then due to him, and all his clothes and goods on board at the time [2].

---

[1] Act 1790, ch. 56, § 2.]   [2] Do. § 4.

---

employed in trading coastwise, the wages shall be paid within two days after the termination of the agreement, or at the time when the seaman shall be discharged, whichever shall first happen; and in every other case the wages shall be paid at the latest within three days after the cargo shall have been delivered, or within ten days after the seaman's discharge, whichever shall first happen; in which two cases of delayed payments, the seaman shall, at the time of his discharge, be entitled to be paid on account, one fourth part of the estimated balance due to him; and if any master or owner shall neglect or refuse to make payment in the manner required, he shall for every such neglect or refusal forfeit to the seaman the amount of two days' pay, for each day, not exceeding ten days; during which, payment shall, without sufficient cause, be delayed beyond the period prescribed, for the recovery of which forfeiture the seaman shall have the same remedies as he is entitled to for the recovery of the wages, s. 11.

The preceding clause is not to extend to the case of ships employed in the southern whale fishery, or on voyages for which seamen, by the terms of their agreement, are compensated by shares in the profit of the adventure.

No assignment of wages, made prior to the earning of them, shall be valid or binding upon the party making it.

If a seaman, after having been discharged three days, shall be desirous of proceeding to sea on another voyage, and in order thereto shall require immediate payment of the wages due to him, it shall be lawful for any justice of the peace, on his application, and on satisfactory proof that he would, by delay, be prevented from obtaining employment, to summon the master or owner before him, and if no satisfactory reason shall be assigned for further delay, such justice shall order payment to be made forthwith; in default of compliance with which order, the master or owner shall forfeit £5.; s. 14.

These forfeitures cannot be exacted against the seaman unless there is an entry made in the log-book on the same day that he left, specifying the name of the seaman, and that he was absent without leave [1].

But independently of these regulations, and without the necessity of any entry, &c., a seaman forfeits his wages for deserting the vessel, or absenting himself wrongfully and without leave, by the general law of all commercial nations [2]. If, however, the seaman is absent without fault of his own [3], or if he is obliged to desert by reason of cruel treatment, want of food, or the like, he does not forfeit his wages. But in such case, the seaman must prove that the treatment was such that he could not remain without imminent danger to his life, limbs, or health [4]. If the voyage for which he shipped has been abandoned, or there has been a gross and unnecessary deviation, he does not forfeit his wages for leaving the vessel; but then the change of voyage must have been actually determined upon and known to the seaman [5].

Even if the seaman shall have clearly deserted without justifiable cause, or absented himself more than forty-eight hours, yet, if he shall offer to return and do his duty, the master must receive him, unless his previous conduct would justify a discharge [6]. And if he is so received back, and does his duty faithfully for the rest of the voyage, the forfeiture is considered as remitted, and he is entitled to his wages for the whole voyage [7]. If, however, the owner has suffered any special damage from the wrongful absence of the seaman, as, if the vessel has been detained, or a man hired in his place, all

---

[1] Gilpin, 83, 140, 207. Ware, 309. [2] Ware, 309.
[3] 1 Mason, 45. Bee, 134, 48. Gilpin, 225.
[4] 1 Pet. Ad. 186. Gilpin, 225. 2 Pet. Ad. 420, 428. Ware, 83, 91, 109.
[5] Gilpin, 150. 2 Pet. Ad. 415.   [6] 1 Sumner, 373.
[7] 2 Wash. 272. Gilpin, 145. 1 Sumner, 373. 1 Pet. Ad. 160.

such necessary expenses may be deducted from the wages [1].

A mere leaving of the vessel, though a wrongful absence, is not a desertion, unless it is done with the intention to desert [2]. A seaman is bound to load and unload cargo in the course of the voyage if required of him, and a refusal to do so is a refusal of duty [3]. If the voyage is at an end, according to the articles, and the vessel is safely moored at the port of discharge, the seamen are still bound to discharge the cargo if it is required of them. If they do not, their refusal or neglect does not, however, work a forfeiture of all their wages, but only makes them liable to a deduction, as compensation to the owner for any damage he may have suffered [4]. The custom in almost all sea-ports of the United States is, to discharge the crew, and not to require them to unload cargo at the end of the voyage. This custom is so strong, that if the owner or master wishes to retain the crew, he must give them notice to that effect. Unless the crew are distinctly told that they must remain and discharge cargo, they may leave the vessel as soon as she is safely moored, or made fast. If they are required to remain and discharge cargo, they make themselves liable to a deduction from their wages for a neglect or refusal, but do not forfeit them [5]. The seaman must bear in mind, however, that this is only when the voyage is at an end, and the ship is at the final port of discharge. If he refuses to load or unload at any port in the course of the voyage, and before it is up, according to the articles, he does so at the risk of forfeiting all his wages [6].

The master and owners of a vessel are allowed ten days after the voyage is up, before a suit can be brought

---

[1] Gilpin, 145, 298, 98.   [2] 1 Sumner, 373. Ware, 309.
[3] 1 Pet. Ad. 253.
[4] 1 Sumner, 373.   Gilpin, 208.   Ware, 454.   2 Hagg. 40.
[5] 1 Sumner, 373.   Gilpin, 208.   [6] 1 Pet. Ad. 253.

against them for the wages of the crew[1]. This is in order to give them time to settle all accounts and discover delinquencies. If the crew are retained to unload, then the ten days begin to run from the time the vessel is completely unloaded. But if the crew are not retained for this purpose, but are discharged and allowed to leave the vessel, then the ten days begin to run from the day they are discharged[2].

WAGES AFFECTED BY MISCONDUCT[*].—A seaman may forfeit his wages by gross misconduct; and if not forfeited, he may be liable to have a deduction made from them, for any damage caused to the owner by such misconduct. To create a forfeiture, his misbehaviour must be gross and aggravated[3]. A single act of disobedience, or a single neglect of duty, will not deprive him of his wages[4]. A refusal to do duty in a moment of high excitement caused by punishment will not forfeit wages, unless followed by obstinate perseverance in such refusal[5]. Where *drunkenness* is habitual and gross, so as to create a general incapacity to perform duty, it is a ground of forfeiture of wages. But occasional acts of drunkenness, if the seaman in other respects performs his duty, will not deprive him of his wages[6]. In this, as in all cases of neglect, disobedience, or wilful misconduct,

---

[1] Act 1790, ch. 56, § 6.
[2] 1 Pet. Ad. 165, 210. Ware, 458. Darl. Ad. Pr. 99.
[3] 4 Mason, 84. Bee, 148. [4] 4 Mason, 84.
[5] Do. [6] 2 Hagg. 2. 4 Mason 541.

---

[*] IN ENGLAND.]—*Wages affected by Misconduct.*—If any seaman, without sufficient cause, neglects to perform such duty as shall reasonably be required of him by the master or other person in command of the ship, he is subject to a like forfeiture, as in case of absence, in respect of every offence, and of every 24 hours' continuance of it.—5 & 6 W. 4., c. 19, s. 7.

Any cause which will justify the master in discharging a seaman during the voyage, will also deprive the seaman of his wages.— 2 *Rob. Ad. Rep.*, 261.

which do not create a forfeiture, a deduction may be made if the owner has suffered any loss[1].

In one instance a forfeiture of one-half of a seaman's wages was decreed, in consequence of his striking the master. He did not forfeit the whole, because he had been otherwise punished[2].

If the seaman is imprisoned for misconduct, he does not forfeit the wages that accrued during his confinement; nor, what amounts to the same thing, is he bound to pay those of a person hired in his place during his imprisonment[2].

If the crime of a seaman is against the laws of the United States, and too great for the master's authority to punish, he must be confined and brought home to trial. But this does not forfeit his wages, though any loss or damage to the owner may be deducted[4].

In all cases of forfeiture of wages for misconduct, it is only the wages due at the time of the misconduct that are lost. The wages subsequently earned are not affected by any previous misbehaviour[5].

If a seaman or officer is evidently incapable of doing the duty he shipped for, he may be put upon other duty, and a reasonable deduction may be made from his wages[6].

WAGES AFFECTED BY IMPRISONMENT *.—If a seaman

---

[1] 4 Mason, 541. 1 Sumner, 384. Bee, 237. 2 Hagg. 420. Gilpin, 150. 1 Pet. Ad. 168.
[2] Bee, 184.   [3] Gilpin, 83, 140, 33.   Ware, 9.
[4] 1 Pet. Ad. 168.   [5] 4 Mason, 84.   [6] Ware, 109.

---

* IN ENGLAND.]—*Wages affected by Imprisonment.*—It is apprehended that if a seaman should do any act which would justify the master in ordering him to be imprisoned, such seaman could not recover wages for the time of his imprisonment; but, on the contrary, would be answerable to the owners for any loss or damage they might sustain through his misconduct; and it would seem they might set off such loss or damage against a demand of wages. —2 *Hagg. Ad. Rep.*, 243.

is imprisoned by a warrant from a judge or justice of the peace, within the limits of the United States, for desertion or refusal to render himself on board, he is liable to pay the cost of his commitment and support in jail, as well as the wages of any person hired in his place [1]. So, if a seaman is imprisoned in a foreign port by the authorities of the place for a breach of their laws, the costs and loss to the owner may be deducted from his wages; but not so if he is imprisoned at the request of the master [2]. The right of the master to imprison at all is a doubtful one, and dangerous of exercise; and if he does resort to it, he can never charge the expenses to the seamen, nor deduct their wages during imprisonment [3].

WAGES AFFECTED BY CAPTURE.—If a neutral ship is captured, it is the right and duty of the seaman to remain by the vessel until the case is finally settled [4]. If she is liberated, they are then entitled to their wages for the whole voyage; and if freight is decreed, they are entitled to their wages for as much of the voyage as freight is given [5]. And if at any future time the owners

---

[1] Gilpin, 223.   [2] Gilpin, 223.
[3] Ware, 19, 503.   Gilpin, 83, 233.
[4] 2 Sumner, 443.   1 Pet. Ad. 128.
[5] 2 Gall. 178.   2 Sumner, 443.

---

* IN ENGLAND.]—*Wages affected by Capture.*—The payment of wages depends generally upon the successful termination of the voyage. If in the course of the voyage a total loss or capture of the ship takes place, the seamen lose their wages.—*Abbott on Shipp.*, 6th edit., 571.

It has been held that the condemnation of a vessel for illegal trading on the part of the master, to which the mariners were not parties, does not work a forfeiture of wages, or bar the mariner's action against the owners.—2 *Hagg. Ad. Rep.*, 158.

The payment of wages is divisible, and if a ship has delivered its cargo at one place, the wages are so far due, although the ship be afterwards taken or sunk. But if a ship sail to one place, in order to take in a cargo there to be conveyed to another place, and having received the cargo accordingly, be taken before its arrival at the place of delivery, nothing is payable to the seamen for navigating the ship to the first place.—*Abbott*, 572.

recover the vessel, or her value, upon appeal or by treaty, they are liable for wages[1]. In order to secure his wages in these cases, the seamen must remain by the vessel until her sale or condemnation, and the master cannot oblige him to take his discharge[2]. The condemnation or sale of the vessel puts an end to his contract. If he leaves before the condemnation or sale, with the master's consent, he does not lose his chance of recovering his wages[3]. Even if the vessel is condemned, and the owner never recovers the vessel or its value, yet the seaman is entitled to his wages up to the last port of delivery, and for half the time she lay there[4].

WAGES AFFECTED BY LOSS OF VESSEL OR INTERRUPTION OF VOYAGE*.—If a vessel meets with a disaster, it is the duty of the crew to remain by her so long as they can do it with safety, and to exert themselves to the utmost of their ability to save as much as possible of the vessel and cargo[5]. If they abandon the vessel un-

---

[1] 3 Mason, 161.   [2] 1 Mason, 45.
[3] 1 Mason, 45.   [4] 1 Pet. Ad. 203.
[5] Ware, 49. 1 Pet. 204.

---

* IN ENGLAND.]—*Wages affected by Loss of Vessel or Interruption of Voyage.*—See the last note.

If a ship become disabled on the voyage, the seamen lose their wages. But if the ship has earned its freight, the seamen who have served on board the ship have in like manner earned their wages.

And if a ship sails to several places, wages are payable to the time of the delivery of the last cargo.

And where money is advanced to the owners in part of the freight outward, and the ship perishes before her arrival at the port of delivery, the seamen will be entitled to wages in proportion to the money advanced.—*Abbott,* 558.

Wages are not lost by the hypothecation of the ship, nor even by the sale of it, unless the sale be made under the authority of a competent court ; nor by the ship being wrecked, if the seamen assist in saving from the wreck sufficient to pay them.—*Abbott,* 571.

It is the duty of every mariner to exert himself to the utmost to save as much as possible of the vessel and cargo ; and he is not entitled to any remuneration for such exertions beyond the wages stipulated to be paid to him.—1 *Hagg. Ad. Rep.,* 227.

necessarily, they forfeit all their wages; and if their leaving was necessary and justifiable, yet they lose their wages except up to the last port of delivery and for half the time the vessel was lying there, or for so long as she was engaged with the outward cargo[1]. This rule may seem hard, but its object is to secure the services of the crew in case of a disaster. If by their exertions any parts of the vessel or cargo are saved, they are entitled to wages, and an extra sum for salvage[2]. If the vessel is abandoned and nothing is saved, they lose their wages, except up to the last port of delivery and for half the time the vessel was lying there[3].

The general rule is, that a seaman's wages are secure to him whenever the vessel has earned any freight, whatever may afterwards happen. And a vessel earns freight at every port where she delivers any cargo. For the benefit of seamen a vessel is held to earn freight whenever she goes to a port under a contract for freight, though she go in ballast[4]. A seaman also secures his wages wherever the ship might have earned freight but for the agreement or other act of the owner[5]. If a vessel is on a trading voyage from port to port, and is lost on the homeward passage, wages would probably be allowed for the outward passage, and for half the time she was engaged in trading with the old or new cargoes; the trading and going from port to port being considered the same as though she had been lying in port all the time, and discharging and receiving cargo. Or else, wages would be given up to the last port at which she took in any return cargo, and for half the time she was lying there[6].

These rules apply only to cases where the voyage is

---

[1] Pet. C. C. 182. 3 Sumner, 286.
[2] Ware, 49. Gilpin, 79. 2 Mason, 319. 1 Hagg. 227.
[3] 2 Mason, 329. 1 Pet. Ad. 204, 130; 2 do. 391. 11 Mass. 545. [4] 2 Mason, 319. 1 Pet. Ad. 207.
[5] 3 Sumner, 286. 2 Mason, 319. 2 Hagg. 158.
[6] Pet. C. C. 182. 2 Pet. Ad. 390.

broken up by inevitable accidents, as by perils of the seas, capture, war, or superior force. If the voyage is broken up by the fault of the seamen, they lose all their wages. If, on the other hand, the seamen are compelled to leave, or the voyage is broken up by the fault of the master or owner, as by cruel treatment, want of provisions, or the like, the crew would be justly entitled to wages for the whole voyage contracted for. If the vessel is sold, or the voyage altered or abandoned by the master or owner, not from inevitable necessity, but for their own interest and convenience, then the crew are entitled, by statute, to wages for all the time they were on board, and two months' extra pay[1]. And, by the general law, they would always receive some extra wages as a compensation for the loss of the voyage, and as a means of supporting themselves and procuring a passage home; or, perhaps, full wages for the voyage[2].

WAGES ON AN ILLEGAL VOYAGE *.—A seaman has no remedy for his wages upon an illegal voyage; as, for instance, in the slave trade[3]. Wages have, however, been allowed where it was proved that the seaman was innocent of all knowledge of, or participation in, the illegal voyage[4].

WAGES AFFECTED BY DEATH OR DISABILITY *.—If a seaman dies during the voyage, wages are to be paid up to the time of his death[5]. A seaman is entitled to all his wages during sickness, and during any time he was disabled from performing duty. But if his sickness or disability is brought on by his own fault, as by vice or wilful misconduct, a deduction may be made for the

---

[1] Act 1803, ch. 62, § 3.
[2] 2 Pet. Ad. 264. Bee, 48. 2 Gall, 182. 3 Johns. R. 518.
[3] 9 Wheat. 409. 6 Rob. 207. 2 Mason, 58. Edw. 35.
[4] 9 Wheat. 409.   [5] Bee, 254, 441.

---

* IN ENGLAND.]—*Wages on an Illegal Voyage.*—*Wages affected by Death or Disability.*—The observations under these respective heads are applicable to British vessels.

loss of his services[1]. So where the death of a seaman was caused by his own unjustifiable and wrongful acts, his wages were held forfeited[2]. If a seaman, at the time he ships, is labouring under a disease which incapacitates, or is likely to incapacitate, him during the voyage, and he conceals the same, no wages will be allowed him, or a deduction will be made from them, according to the nature of the case[3]. If, in consequence of sickness, a seaman is left at a foreign port, he is still entitled to wages for the whole voyage[4].

CHAPTER XII.

SEAMEN—CONCLUDED.

Recovery of wages. Interest on wages. Salvage.

RECOVERY OF WAGES*.—A seaman has a threefold remedy for his wages—first, against the master; secondly,

---

[1] 1 Pet. Ad. 142, 138. [2] Do. 142.
[3] 2 Pet. Ad. 263. [4] Bee, 414. 2 Gall. 46. 1 Pet. 117.

---

* IN ENGLAND.] *Recovery of Wages.*—As regards wages not exceeding 20*l.*, it is provided by the act 5 & 6 W. 4, c. 19, that it shall be lawful for any justice of the peace residing near to the place where the ship shall have ended her voyage, cleared at the Custom House, or discharged her cargo, or near to the place of residence of the master or owner, upon complaint on oath by the seaman, or on his behalf, to summon the master or owner before him, and to examine *upon the oath of the parties,* and of their witnesses (if any), touching the complaint and the amount of wages due, and to make order for payment as shall appear to him to be reasonable and just; and that in case such order shall not be obeyed within two days after the making, such justice may issue his warrant to levy the amount awarded, and all expenses, by distress and sale of the goods of the party upon whom the order shall have been made; and if sufficient distress cannot be found, may cause the amount to be levied upon the ship and furniture; and if they be not within his jurisdiction, may cause the party upon whom the order shall be made to be apprehended and committed to gaol, un-

against the owners; and thirdly, against the ship itself and the freight earned[1]. He may pursue any one of these, or he may pursue them all at the same time in courts of admiralty. He has what is called a *lien* upon the ship for his wages; that is, he has a right at any time to seize the vessel by a process of law, and retain it until his claim is paid, or otherwise decided upon by the court. This lien does not cease upon the sailing of the ship on another voyage; and the vessel may be taken, notwithstanding there is a new master and different owners[2]. A seaman does not lose his lien upon

---

[1] Bee, 254. 2 Sumner, 443. 2 Gall. 398.
[2] 2 Sumner, 443. 5 Pet. R. 675.

---

til the amount, with all costs, shall be paid; which award and decision is to be final and conclusive on both parties, s. 15.

And in order to enforce the adoption of this remedy, it is by a subsequent clause enacted, that if any suit for wages instituted in an Admiralty Court, or in any Court of Record in the *British* dominions, it shall appear to the judge that the plaintiff might have had an effectual remedy by the mode above prescribed, the judge is to certify accordingly; and thereupon no costs of suit are to be awarded to the plaintiff, s. 16.

The burthen of producing the written contract in cases of dispute with the mariners, is cast on the master and owners, s. 5.

All suits and actions brought in the Court of Admiralty for seamen's wages, must be commenced within *six* years next after the wages become due, unless the party entitled to sue shall at that time be under the age of twenty-one years, a *feme covert, non compos mentis*, or imprisoned, or unless such party, or the party sued, shall be at that time beyond the seas, in which cases the suit may be brought within *six* years after the party suing shall be of full age, discovert, of sane memory, or at large; or either the party suing, or the party sued, shall return from beyond the seas.—4 Anne, c. 16, ss. 17, 18, and 19.

And actions in the courts of common law are also limited to the same period of *six* years with the same provisoes, unless they are founded on a contract under seal; if they are founded on such a contract, the statutable limitation does not apply to them; but after a lapse of *twenty* years, the claims will be presumed to have been satisfied without any proof of payment.—*Abbott*, 595.

As to the time of wages becoming *due*, see the note to chap. xi., page 249.

the ship by lapse of time. He may take the ship whenever he finds her; though he must not allow a long time to elapse, if he has had any opportunity of enforcing his claim, lest it should be considered a stale demand. In common law courts a suit cannot be brought for wages after six years have expired since they became due. This is not the case in courts of admiralty[1].

The lien of the seaman for wages takes precedence of every other lien or claim upon the vessel[2]. The seamen's wages must be first paid, even if they take up the whole value of the ship or freight. The wreck of a ship is bound for the wages; and the rule in admiralty is, that a seaman's claim on the ship is good so long as there is a plank of her left[3]. If, after capture and condemnation, the ship itself is not restored, but the owners are indemnified in money, the seaman's lien attaches to such proceeds[4]. Besides this lien upon the ship, the seaman has also a lien upon the freight earned, and upon the cargo[5]. He may also sue the owner or master, or both, personally. They are, however, answerable *personally* only for the wages earned while the ship was in their own hands[6]. But a suit may be brought against the *ship* after she has changed owners[7].

A seaman does not lose his lien upon the vessel by taking an order upon the owner[8].

After a vessel is abandoned to the underwriters, they become liable for the seamen's wages, from the time of the abandonment[9].

If at the end of the voyage the crew are discharged and not retained to unload, their wages are due immediately[10]; but they cannot sue in admiralty until ten

---

[1] 2 Gall. 477.   Paine C. C. 180.   3 Mason, 91.
[2] Ware, 134, 41.   [3] 3 Sumner, 50.   1 Ware, 41.
[4] 5 Pet. R. 675.   [5] Ware, 134.   5 Pet. R. 675.
[6] 11 Johns. 72.   6 Mass. 300; 8 do. 483.
[7] 5 Pet. R. 675.   2 Sumner, 443.
[8] Ware, 185.   [9] 4 Mason, 196.
[10] Ware, 458.   Dunl. Ad. Pr. 99.   1 Pet. Ad. 165, 210.

days after the day of discharge¹. If they are retained to unload, then the owner is allowed ten days from the time the cargo is fully discharged. If, however, the vessel is about to proceed to sea before the ten days will elapse, or before the cargo will be unloaded, the seaman may attach the vessel immediately². If the owner retains his crew while the cargo is unloading, he must unload it within a reasonable time. Fifteen working days has frequently been held a reasonable time for unloading, and the ten days have been allowed to run from that time³.

The longest time allowed by law for unloading vessels is twenty days if over 300 tons, and ten days if under that tonnage. Probably seamen would not be held bound to the vessel for a longer time than is thus allowed by law for unloading.

INTEREST ON WAGES*.—In suits for seamen's wages, interest is allowed from the time of the demand; and if no demand is proved, then from the time of the commencement of the suit⁴.

SALVAGE†.—If a vessel is picked up at sea aban-

---

¹ Act 1790, ch. 56, § 6.   ² Do.
³ 1 Pet. Ad. 165. Abb. Shipp. 456, n.
⁴ 2 Gall. 45.

---

* IN ENGLAND.] *Interest on Wages.*—It has been already stated, that if the master or owner shall neglect or refuse to pay the seaman his wages when due, he becomes liable to forfeit to such seaman the amount of two days' pay for each day not exceeding ten days during which payment shall without sufficient cause be delayed, c. 11; see note to c. 11, p. 250.

If the seaman wishes to entitle himself to *interest* upon his wages, he should give a written notice to the master or owner, of his intention to claim such interest if his wages be not paid within a given period.

† IN ENGLAND.] *Salvage.*—The crew of a British vessel cannot claim as salvors or joint-salvors in respect of services performed on board their own vessel, not even in the case of shipwreck.—1 Hag. Ad. Rep., 227.

For further information on this subject, the reader is referred to *Abbott on Shipp.*, 6th edit., title "*Salvage.*"

doned, or in distress, and any of the crew of the vessel which falls in with her go on board, and are the means of saving her, or of bringing her into port, they are entitled to salvage[1]. In this case all the crew who are ready and willing to engage in the service are entitled to a share of the reward, although they may not have gone on board the wreck[2]. The reason is, that where all are ready to go, and a selection is made, there would be injustice and favouritism in allowing any one the privilege more than another. Besides, those who remain have an extra duty to perform, in consequence of the others having gone on board the wreck[3].

Crews are not ordinarily entitled to salvage for services performed on board their own vessel, whatever may have been their perils or hardships, or the gallantry of their services in saving ship and cargo[4]; for some degree of extra exertion to meet perils and accidents, is within the scope of a seaman's duty. In case of shipwreck, however, where, by the general law, wages are forfeited, the court will allow salvage, considering it as in the nature of wages due. In one instance salvage was refused to a part of a crew who rescued the ship from the rest who had mutinied; for this was held to be no more than their duty[5].

Yet seamen may entitle themselves to salvage for services performed on board their own vessel, if clearly beyond the line of their regular duty; as, when the crew rise and rescue the vessel from the enemy after she has been taken[6]. So, where a ship was abandoned at sea, and one or two men voluntarily remained behind, and by great exertions brought her into port[7]. If an apprentice is a salvor, he and not his master, is entitled to the salvage[8]. If one set of men go on board a wreck,

---

[1] Ware, 477. 1 Pet. Ad. 306.
[2] Ware, 477. 2 Pet. Ad. 281. [3] 2 Dodson, 132.
[4] 10 Pet. R. 108. 1 Hagg. 227.
[5] 2 Dods. 14. [6] 1 Pet. Ad. 306.
[7] 2 Cr. 240. 1 Pet. Ad. 48. [8] 2 Cr. 240. 2 Pet. Ad. 282.

but fall into distress and are relieved by others, they do not lose their claim for salvage, but each set of salvors shares according to the merit of its services. If the second set take advantage of the necessity and distress of the first salvors to impose terms upon them, as, that they shall give up all claim for salvage, such conditions will not be regarded by the court [1].

---

[1] 1 Sumner, 400.

THE END.

www.ingramcontent.com/pod-product-compliance
Lightning Source LLC
Chambersburg PA
CBHW050859300426
44111CB00010B/1306